POCKETS

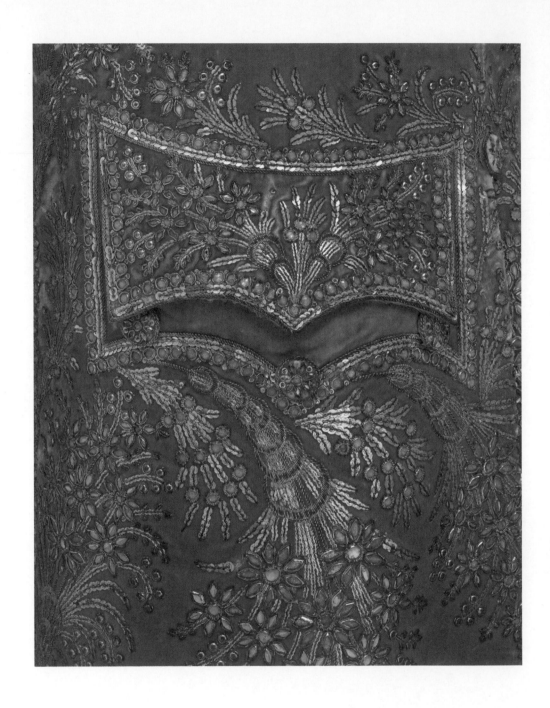

POCKETS

An Intimate History of How
We Keep Things Close

HANNAH CARLSON

ALGONQUIN BOOKS
OF CHAPEL HILL   2023

Published by
ALGONQUIN BOOKS OF CHAPEL HILL
Post Office Box 2225
Chapel Hill, North Carolina 27515-2225

an imprint of Workman Publishing Co., Inc.,
a subsidiary of Hachette Book Group, Inc.
1290 Avenue of the Americas
New York, NY 10104

Printed in China.
Design by Steve Godwin.

The publisher is not responsible for websites (or their content)
that are not owned by the publisher.

Cataloging-in-Publication Data for this title is on file with the
Library of Congress.

ISBN 978-1-64375-154-2 HC
ISBN 978-1-64375-548-9 Ebook

10 9 8 7 6 5 4 3 2 1
First Edition

For my father and first reader,
Robert S. Carlson, and my daughters,
Kieran and Eliza, who listened to these
stories as I collected them.

Throughout *Pockets*, I have endeavored to use terms that designers, makers, and individuals have used to identify themselves or their occupations. Where the book moves into the present day I have endeavored to recognize the advances in our understanding of gender fluidity and expression. The apparel industry still distinguishes men's wear from women's wear, but any history of the pocket cannot help but recognize, as this one does, the material limitations and structural inequities and inconsistencies that follow from enforcing specific gendered and binary ways that people may engage with the world.

Contents

POCKETS

Introduction

After a hasty exit, I patted myself down, checking my pockets to see whether I had stashed anything useful. The scene was Lafayette Street, post-9/11 New York City, and it was impossible to tell whether the midday evacuation underway was just a drill or something more serious. Following the direction to *leave now* meant that most of the women attending the weekly staff meeting had left their handbags, purses, or knapsacks where they had put them, tucked under desks and draped over chairs. As I scanned the thinning crowd, it occurred to me that I was not the only one standing indecisively, at a loss about what to do next.

I was wearing what my limited salary and ambivalent aspirations allowed, which was surprisingly versatile given the constraints of twenty-first-century office attire. I believed I had achieved a certain mood, influenced by the looks of those colleagues I admired (the insouciant, this-is-only-my-day-job folks) while hoping to attain the finish of the ambitious, this-is-my-real-job folks. Yet nothing that I wore was particularly well made: what passes for casual chic these days is most often accomplished via shortcuts in construction. Thanks to global fast fashion, women's clothes, in particular, prioritize trendy new effects over thoughtful design and careful execution. The tiny pockets in my trousers had been included as an afterthought, and my knit top was far too pliant to admit any secure containers.

My office mate (of the climbing-the-ladder camp, clad in an exquisite jacket) no longer bowed his head reverentially as he checked his phone; he must have decided to wait this out someplace more convivial. His digital assistant now tucked over his left breast, a streamlined wallet steadying his back-right flank, an ATM card and subway pass surely sandwiched there, he was off. Before turning away from the crowd on the sidewalk, he raised an eyebrow in my direction, asking if I needed to borrow twenty bucks.

Like this guy, some men have been generous in the lending of their pocket bounty. Some make room for keys and lipstick during a night out. But for the most part the well-pocketed seem unconscious of their built-in good fortune. It is difficult to appreciate what you've always had, and pockets tend to go unnoticed by those who have always enjoyed reliably useful ones. So dependable have they proved that a man might leave his clothes behind on the shore for a quick skinny dip but absentmindedly expect his pockets and their contents to have remained at his disposal.

If not likely, such an oversight was made at least once, and recorded for posterity, by someone who thought quite a lot about hasty exits and insufficient provisions. I encountered Daniel Defoe's *Robinson Crusoe* years after that evacuation drill, having left commercial publishing to teach dress history and material culture (the things that humans make, that we interact with, and that help define us). Defoe's pocket presumption, what his contemporaries called his "notorious blunder," helped crystallize for me why standing on that New York City sidewalk had felt so disconcerting.

Defoe had allowed his famous castaway to wash up on his lonely island with only a knife, a pipe, and some tobacco. Not wanting to doom his character with such a meager inheritance, Defoe engineered a rescue: Crusoe spies his wrecked ship, foundering just offshore. Determined to investigate, he strips his clothes so he can swim to the boat, and once on deck is delighted to find a treasure trove of useful things, including a quantity of sailor's biscuit that has weathered the storm. Stuffing his pockets with the hard rations, Crusoe swims back ashore, planning how he will salvage the remaining supplies of foodstuffs and carpenter's tools. Although mostly unnoticed by readers today, "the famous Passage of his swimming to shore naked, with his Pockets full of Biscuits," was the subject of lively speculation and mirth. According to the *London Journal* in 1725, Defoe's continuity problem was "taken Notice of in Publik" for years after the book's initial publication.

Defoe's blunder likely conjured images ranging from the pleasurably outlandish to the faintly bawdy to receive this level of attention, but it could very well have raised more rudimentary questions (as it did for me) relating to pocket-hood itself. Just what kind of thing is a pocket? And how does having one cause such unreasonable expectations of loyal service?

IN SUBTLE BUT measurable ways, pockets are different from their more renown cousins, the ingenious bags people the world over, and for millennia, have used for specific purposes. Satchels, medicine bags, alms purses, and fashion bags (to name only a very few) can be carried in myriad ways: slung from the shoulder, worn around the neck, balanced on the head, toted by hand, or strapped to a belt. A comparatively late innovation in fitted or tailored apparel, pockets are certainly not the only solution to transporting necessaries. Yet the desire for a pouch integral to clothes—securely stitched into a permanent fold—is one reason pockets have been so widely adopted.

Nineteenth-century essayist and historian Thomas Carlyle believed that pockets were one of the only reasons to wear clothes at all. For humans, the "feeblest of bipeds," clothing does not function, as legions of

Figure 1. *K* page from Sally Sketch's *An Alphabetical Arrangement of Animals for Young Naturalists*, 1821.

theologians would have it, to hide our nakedness, but to compensate for the woeful inadequacies of our very taut skin. Carlyle's 1836 *Sartor Resartus* (Latin for *The Tailor Retailored*) was one of the first books to consider seriously the social role of clothes, and in it he points out the obvious: people are not marsupial mammals. Without pockets (or an unlikely ship close by), they could not carry the tools that, according to Carlyle, make them human—the tools that allow them to act and do.

Carlyle's readers were as tickled by his animal analysis as by the notion that some creatures had innately supplied themselves with secure little containers. Marsupials had been unknown in Europe until reports from Captain James Cook's 1770 voyage to New South Wales described a wonderous animal who leapt great distances on its two hind legs and whose offspring snuggled in an "oblong pouch, of a vast depth." As they welcomed this seemingly amiable creature into the pantheon of wild beasts, authors of everything from political cartoons to alphabet books to philosophical treatises remarked upon the similarities of pocket and pouch. Reading the *K* page from Sally Sketch's 1821 alphabet, children would have learned that a human-made thing could actually be considered an external anatomical part (figure 1). It was not long before wits and pontificators took note of the way pockets had become naturalized. As one exclaimed, "A man without a pocket is a freak of nature!"

More skeptical commentators pointed out the intriguing limits of the marsupial–human comparison. If it was the female of the kangaroo species who sported a "pocket" from which the "young ones" in the alphabet book "are peeping," why was it the male of the human species to whom nature seemed to have granted a near "pockets monopoly"? His suit was honeycombed with pockets, these critics observed pointedly, while his female companion often found herself without a single one. Highlighting this absurdity, the kangaroo mama in Emmy Payne's 1944 children's book *Katy No Pocket* finds herself—against biological law—pouchless, and so she takes a long and arduous journey to "get one" (figure 2). With her son Freddy at her side, struggling to keep up, Katy travels to the city, where she meets someone who seems to be "ALL pockets," a be-tooled workman who kindly gives Katy his apron. His gift will allow Katy to carry her son Freddy about as she should, effortlessly.

Who has pockets and who has had to "get" them is one of the concerns of this book. Although a humble component of dress, pockets reveal much about the organization of daily life, including the way power is unevenly distributed. That the allocation of a fairly straightforward functional element of dress should be gendered is more than just a funny quirk, one of those mysterious traditions akin to placing men's

Figure 2. Illustration of Katy and Freddy in conversation with the aproned workman, by H. A. Rey, published in Emmy Payne's *Katy No Pocket*, 1944.

shirt buttons on the right and women's on the left. However arbitrary, left-facing button placement has not interfered with anyone's dressing in the morning. Differentiated pocket allotment is a more significant matter, and its immediate disadvantages continue to rankle.

Figure 3. *Ritratto di Robinson*, by Tullio Pericoli, 1984. Pericoli's portrait of Robinson Crusoe offers his likeness alongside a visual and textual inventory of the castaway's useful tools. Scissors, saws, compass, and knives float above him like a penumbra, a shadow self, measuring out his very length and width.

How we use those pockets we have at our command (whether a dozen or far fewer) is another concern. What is it that we think we need to bring along, and how has that changed over time? That you might find Freddy ensconced in one of Katy's new pockets—or a mini hacksaw in one of Crusoe's—is no surprise. It is rather the idiosyncratic bits and pieces, the pocket litter, that have proved more intriguing. Questions about the collecting habits of others are responsible for innumerable lists and inventories, tell-alls of the *what's in his pockets* or *what's in her purse* variety that promise insider knowledge regarding people's enthusiasms, aspirations, and anxieties (figure 3). That curiosity can shift to outright affront when what's in the trouser pocket is the human hand. Because trouser pockets, as poet Harold Nemerov observes, provocatively "locate to lust," their use once received inordinate attention from those trying to uphold standards of polite behavior. Under what conditions did some hands-in-pockets poses nonetheless come to signal an attractive sort of elegance and outlaw cool?

WHAT WE MAKE of them is as important as how we make them, and from a design perspective, pockets are operationally unique. They are the only functional part of clothing that does not contribute in some way to the project of dressing the body. Unlike zippers, lacings, buttons, and belt loops, pockets do not help us put on, take off, or adjust the fit of our clothes. One could say that clothing, historically, has been altered to fit the pocket. At the very least, clothing has made room for these wily hitchhikers.

Since the first pockets were incorporated into men's breeches almost five hundred years ago, tailors and dressmakers have stitched them in every conceivable location, most assiduously in the three-piece suit, where they have appeared from the interior breast of the coat to the tip of its tails. In the first Museum of Modern Art exhibition to explore clothing, the architect Bernard Rudofsky charted their distribution across the male body in an installation intended to visualize what he judged to be the excessive pocketing of the mid-twentieth century. In the accompanying catalog Rudofsky employs the conceit of an X-ray to peer under cover, demonstrating that pockets come in pairs and singletons, in different shapes and axial alignments (figure 4). The color-coded schematization makes plain that their placement shifts across the trunk with different articles of clothing. A preponderance congregate around chest and thighs and seem sensitive to right- and left-handedness. A man in trousers, shirt, vest, coat, and

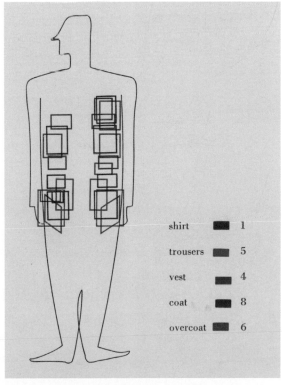

shirt	1
trousers	5
vest	4
coat	8
overcoat	6

Figure 4. 24 Pockets, by Bernard Rudofsky, published in *Are Clothes Modern? An Essay on Contemporary Apparel*, 1947.

overcoat might have at his disposal twenty-four pockets, "layers upon layers" of them.

As pockets proliferated, they acquired highly specialized uses and forms, and it is their diversification as much as their number that manifests our long engagement with them. The bellows pocket expands to accept cargo, for example, while poachers' pockets cleverly disguise illegal spoils at the small of the back. Capacious hand-jammers protect the wearer from both cold and social embarrassment, while the minuscule ticket pocket exchanges flexibility for sure and rapid retrieval. Perhaps only a tailor schooled in the language of bespoke men's wear could tell you why a double besom pocket with flap tucked in is more formal than a gusseted patch pocket with buttoned tab, but any non-expert has enough experience wearing clothes to know that pockets serve as both ornament and functional device. Some make dramatic statements, while others are designed to be unobtrusive. They may lie open, ready for use, or defensively secure themselves with flaps, snaps, or buttons. Designers have crafted pockets in the most whimsical and fantastic shapes, mimicking tennis nets, bureau drawers, and scattered playing cards. In doing so, how have they responded to women's vociferous calls for "pocket equality"?

OUR FONDNESS FOR pockets calls for a revision of what it means to be dressed, to acknowledge that we've achieved our sense of self-sufficiency with an array of concealed compartments. Ease, for most of us, is underwritten by a host of personal possessions—those small articles that allow surreptitious acts of self-care or provide practical or emotional assistance on the go. We count on pockets to protect and defend, a function, however, that can lead to distrust and fear. Hostile encounters between state and citizen are routinely preceded by the expression *Put your hands where I can see them!* We count on pockets even in despair, as when Virginia Woolf, before she waded into the fast-running River Ouse, weighed down her pockets with river stones to ensure her drowning.

Pockets evolved and continue to evolve as clothing and objects do. Will we still require pockets in a future in which conductive thread can be woven into one's sleeve and programmed to open locked doors, obviating the need for keys? People have dreamed of worlds so advanced and enlightened that once necessary equipment could be made superfluous. In the meantime, even when we move through our days generously pocketed, we don't always carry what might be useful. "Got a ship in your pocket?" asks Ralph sardonically in William Golding's *Lord of the Flies*, as the castaway gazes at the horizon, wondering whether salvation will ever arrive. Clearly, some objects cannot be scaled for emergency use (and mobile phones have no make-me-a-ship app). Yet in assiduously accommodating handy implements, makers of clothing recognize a tenacious partnership between garments and objects. When they are included with thoughtfulness, pockets make evident sustained efforts to anticipate human need and augment human capacity. With pockets at our sides, we need never be entirely alone. Even when it feels that we are unaccountably left to our own devices.

Figure 1. Front cover of the Clemens family copy of *The Chronicle of the Cid*, an 1883 edition of a twelfth-century epic poem. Inscribed "Merry Christmas to Clara Clemens / 1884 / from Papa."

CHAPTER 1

Pocket Origins:
"Carried Close, and Secret"

M ark Twain counted pockets among the most useful of inventions. For a man who had witnessed the rise of the steamship, the telegraph, and the cross-continental railroad, pockets would seem a surprising choice. But when he dreamed "of being a knight errant in the middle ages," it was pockets he sorely missed.

Twain's medieval fantasy so disquieted him that he awoke with a start and jotted down the particulars of his bad dream in a notebook he kept at his bedside table for that purpose: "No pockets in the armor. No way to manage certain requirements of nature. Can't scratch. Cold in the head—can't blow—can't get at handkerchief, can't use iron sleeve." Like any good comedian, Twain soon transformed his personal experience into a memorable send up. Upset over the late nineteenth century's cultural rehabilitation of knighthood, which surfaced as fawning praise of unbridled masculinity in figures like cowboys and robber barons, Twain hoped to land an "underhand blow at this nonsense of knight errantry." And he managed to do so while writing what is believed to be one of the first time-travel adventure stories ever written.

When no-nonsense Hank Morgan is transported thirteen centuries back to the Britain of King Arthur in *A Connecticut Yankee in King Arthur's Court*, he reluctantly agrees to do what other knights do, and he suits up to go "holy grailing." In a scene that mirrors his dream, Twain reminds readers that knights were not invincible in their flashing mail and colorful banners, nor could they move with ease as was commonly depicted in popular illustration (figure 1). Trussed up in layers of metal, Morgan sweats like anyone would when encased in a heat-conducting material. Twain's sweaty knight is further incapacitated by his armor's impenetrable surface: as he perspires and wants his handkerchief, he remembers he cannot carry one. "Hang a man that would make a suit of armor without any pockets in it," Morgan swears in the midst of his agony.

The Connecticut Yankee suffers his ordeal in armor so keenly that he proposes a "scandalous" solution: he will henceforth require the knights of the kingdom to carry some kind of purse. Making knights borrow a so-called feminine accessory was yet another way to undermine those "iron dudes" in Twain's estimation. As Twain well knew (he annotated the ample collection of dress-history books in his library), the purse was an almost universal dress feature in the medieval era, carried by men and women alike. In hoping to score a point in his historical contrast between medieval and modern life, though, Twain obscured what is a much more interesting question: why would anyone have agreed to trade in their purses for pockets in the first place?

IDENTIFYING THE CATALYSTS for and mechanisms of such trades is improbably difficult. We tend to gravitate toward origin stories involving a particular personality, especially those where the temperament of the innovator, their ingenuity, and circumstance coincide. Earl Tupper provides one example: the Depression-era tinkerer and independent jobber at Dupont invented resealable containers (Tupperware) after visiting the rural kitchens of his female relatives, who needed to preserve every leftover. Most are less satisfying. Books that promise to reveal the extraordinary origins of common objects, from bubble gum to hula hoops to whistling teakettles, more often than not admit that the exact derivation is unknown. The older and more common the object, the more elusive the individual creators or the precise process of innovation. This is true with any examination of elements of dress. We know buttons with corresponding buttonholes, for example, came into wide use in medieval Europe, because they begin to be referenced in royal wardrobe accounts. Did anyone have that "aha!" moment— *I can engineer a garment that need not be wide enough to slip over my head!* We will never know.

The roots of those objects that seem to have arisen out of common agreement and enjoyed a spontaneous spread, though, are worth attempting to trace. They mark a kind of gulf. We can no longer remember exactly how we got by before the introduction of certain contraptions; we and the world are both a little different since they appeared. That the Connecticut Yankee insists that his armor needs pockets is wonderfully absurd (pockets would seem antithetical to armor's protective function), but it suggests the ways we become entangled with things we have come to take for granted.

THE INDEPENDENT LIFE OF EARLY POCKETS

A SURVEY OF the world history of dress suggests that inset pockets are something of an oddity that arose in the context of European tailoring traditions. Pockets are not traditionally utilized in draped clothing that is folded, wrapped, or tied around the body, such as the Indian dhoti or sari, or in wraparound skirts worn across Southeast Asia, Africa, and the Pacific Islands. They are not placed, in other words, in clothing where social tradition values the integrity of cloth as it is taken from the loom. Wearers either carry a bag or craft temporary pockets made by folding excess cloth over a belt, as, for example, the chuba robe of Tibet, an ankle-length robe that is bound around the waist by a long sash, whose resulting cavity can hold useful items, or the Roman *sinus*, a sling-shaped fold in the toga that late Roman emperor Augustus insisted be searched for weapons.

In most cultures, and for much of the history of the West, people have carried the tools and ephemera of the everyday tucked more or less securely about their clothing, often into a belt, or suspended from a purse or pouch that is itself attached to a belt—and that was the case for the knights to whom Twain consigns a purse in order to feminize or otherwise demean them. Twain's strategy would have failed miserably had he actually traveled back in time: the medieval belt and purse were highly desirable accessories, marks of taste and wealth, an indicator of sex appeal. As the "God of Love" reminded his readers in a popular medieval handbook of 1200, the male suitor who seeks to draw the attention of a prospective lover "is nothing without elegance." Dress as well as you can according to your income, this Love God counseled, but splurge on flashy adornments, like gloves and belt, and be sure to "deck yourself out" with a "silk purse."

And deck themselves out they did. Purses served as a mark of status and bravado essential to the aristocratic warrior ideal. Illustrated manuscripts from the 1300s through the 1400s are full of images depicting stately landowners as well as young, fashion-forward gallants who flaunted luxuriously fabricated purses made of embroidered silk and velvet or fine leather. Some were decoratively embossed or studded with jewels. Purses might be pouchlike in shape or stitched over a metallic frame and might include elaborate clasps and inner compartments. Affixed to a belt slung about the waist or hips, many included a slit through which a dagger could be fastened and displayed. A male figure in an illustrated edition of Boccaccio's *Decameron* wears such a dagger purse (figure 2). The belt and purse combination proved a critical counterpoint to men's dress, cinching in the tunic at the waist or hips and exaggerating the breadth of the shoulders. In 1342, Giovanni Villani, the Florentine historian, complained that these accessories made men look something like tightly girthed horses, as the ornately buckled belts, with their pendulant purses, strained against protruding bellies.

Figure 2. Illustration in a 1414 edition of Giovanni Boccaccio's *The Decameron*.

Women also attached purses to belts, but they wore them low, dangling to about mid-thigh either over or under their gowns. The woman in the Boccaccio illustration suspends her purse under her gown and has hiked up her gown to display it, an apparently evocative gesture (figure 2). According to medieval poets, the placement of belt and purse had enormous erotic appeal. Chaucer's Miller, one of the pilgrims in *The Canterbury Tales*, admires the beautiful Alison's girdle and describes the way it wraps around her lithe figure while her purse swings along and between her legs as she walks. For centuries, how you wore your purse distinguished masculine from feminine dress, but the purse itself did not belong to a single gender.

POCKETS WERE IN use in the medieval era, but they were independent of clothes and apparently humble accessories. *Pocket* is a borrowing of the French word for bag, *poche*, that took on a harsher intonation in medieval Anglo-Norman, as *poke*. When followed by the diminutive, *-ette*, it meant, quite simply, "small bag." Early pockets had a range of uses. Chaucer's *Canterbury Tales* records a pocket lined in wax as among the utensils necessary for the alchemist. In his 1552 book of herbal remedies, William Copland suggested that compounds useful to bind or "staunch the flux" be wrapped in a pocket that could be fastened to the site of the "grievance." For the most part, though, work-a-day pockets were carried about one's person. And, like any bag, they could pass hands or fall into the wrong hands. A henpecked husband in a 1530 broadsheet discovers so much when his domineering wife strips him of his pocket and sword and makes him pull the washing.

Affixing pockets inside clothing—where they were less likely to fall into the wrong hands—was not otherwise an immediately useful idea.

Figure 3. One of a group of garments discovered in a peat bog in Norse Greenland, carbon-dated to between 1180 and 1530.

Through the twelfth century, both sexes were clothed in long, loose robes or tunics. Cloth itself was such an investment in the preindustrial era that European tailors, like many of their global counterparts, made sure to utilize as much of the full length of material as possible. Cloth was far more expensive than labor. By the fourteenth century, tailors began to experiment in earnest with more complex constructions. Tailored dress, in contrast to draped, involves cutting up precious cloth into smaller shapes and then stitching or seaming those shapes together, resulting in a garment that closely follows the contours of trunk and appendages. Sections of those seams could be left unstitched, a strategy evident in rare examples of medieval clothing discovered in a stash of garments recovered from Norse Greenland gravesites. Of the eight intact garments, four include slits positioned in the seams between the front and side panels (figure 3). The slits were carefully finished with overcast stiches to ensure that the opening would not unravel and have been identified in both the men's and women's garments. These small openings at the side seam, positioned at about hip level accessible to the hands, allowed entry to a bag held under the garment. Wearers might have rested their hands in these openings, as does the figure meant to represent Joan, the daughter of King Edward III, in a small sculpture near her father's tomb at Westminster Abbey (figure 4).

Even as European tailors were developing these construction techniques, medieval clothing practice still precluded the pocket's integration. Fine woolen cloth for outerwear, tunics, and overdresses was reused again and again and taken

Figure 4. Sculpture of Joan, the daughter of King Edward III, who mourns by his tomb while reaching through pocket slits in her gown, Westminster Abbey, 1377.

apart and turned inside out for renewal. Because laundering involved beating garments on rocks (before effective soaps), fastenings like buttons were made as removable shanks to avoid damage. Medieval tailors assiduously avoided any element that would have compromised a garment's reuse or care. And these practices of reuse and care were in sync with aesthetics and taste. Tailors drew on closures like buttons and string ties (which laced through small eyelet holes) to make clothing that conformed to and flattered the body, but medieval dress remained relatively free of ornament and still honored uninterrupted cloth surfaces. Inset pockets in such conditions would likely have proved a troublesome appendage.

BREECHES: "NO SAFER A STORE-HOUSE"

IT WAS NOT until tailoring reached a more confident, even exuberant stage that pockets began to make sense. The idea seems to have occurred because of breeches, an article of dress that was understood to be men's special prerogative.

Men's dress noticeably articulated the legs beginning only in the early fourteenth century. (Although trousers have an ancient lineage, originating with horse-riding nomads of the Eurasian steppes and in use by at least 1000 BC, the practice of wearing trousers had vanished in medieval Europe.) Some dress scholars surmise that the development of plate armor instigated a shift to tighter-fitting and bifurcated (or two-legged) garments. Needing to protect the body under the armor, tailors learned to stitch cloth padding that closely hugged each limb (figure 5). Initially, these garments, called hose, looked something like tights; but the top part, from the waist to above the knees, eventually divided and became its own separate covering, called trunk hose or breeches. Women's dress did not follow. While it grew tighter at the bodice, showing off cleavage and waist, women's clothes nevertheless retained the enveloping skirt. This shift in men's garments fueled a

Figure 5. *The Knight and the Lady with Helmet and Lance*, by Master E. S., German, mid-fifteenth century. As firearms developed during the fifteenth century, the tunic-like mail no longer protected the body, and to better deflect projectiles, armorers developed plate armor. Unlike the draped mail, plate armor was fitted to the body and required specially designed padding underneath.

Figure 6. Contemporary international pictograms used to identify gendered public lavatories still highlight the trouser/skirt distinction.

divergence that would eventually give rise to the trousers versus skirt distinction with which we are still familiar (figure 6).

Breeches appeared in a range of styles across Europe and might resemble stiff, rounded pumpkins or droopy, puffy bloomers. So distinctive to the masculine sex were these articles that the power struggle between husband and wife for dominance in one's marriage could be analogized as one between the skirt and the breeches. The "fight for the reeches" (later replaced with the question, Who wears the pants in this family?) was depicted in countless ballads illustrating man and wife literally engaging in a tug-of-war over them (figure 7). As breeches took on this symbolic significance as the seat of patriarchal power, the garment also performed some very real-world duties: not only did they decorously cover the breech, but they also accommodated an astonishingly diverse range of more-or-less useful things.

To achieve full, rounded breeches, tailors stuffed them with hair, tailors' waste, quilted linings, and bombast, a cotton padding. In one of the many instances where material qualities take on figurative meanings, bombast came to stand for an attitude enabled by it. A bombastic man's strut was amplified and enabled through the bombast that swelled his breeches. Critics made lavish sport of fashionable men who swaggered in their "breeches as big as good barrels." Silhouette and size were key to the fashion, and anyone, including serving men and apprentices, could attempt to flaunt it in great breeches, according to critics like the puritan Philip Stubbes. In response, sumptuary

The Married Mans complaint

Who took a Shrow inſtead of a Saint.

Here in this Song is ſet forth to the life
A Hen-peckt Husband and a Head-ſtrong wife
He is as much to blame to let her wear,
     Tune of, *Come off my Mother Sirrah, Sirrah, &c.*

The Breeche s as ſhe is to domi neer
Yet howſoe're 'twil make you ſmile I ſee
But from ſuch Matches Jove deliver me.

Figure 7. *The Married Man's Complaint: Who Took a Shrew Instead of a Saint*, ca. 1550s. A ballad woodcut illustrating the so-called fight for the breeches.

laws, which for centuries had focused almost exclusively on materials (for example, regulating how much gold or silver a knight or a mere gentleman might wear on his doublet) turned to questions of form. By the early 1560s, the English crown passed a series of edicts to limit the "monstrous and outrageous greatness of hosen." A 1562 edict included specific instructions that tailors use no more than one and three-quarters yards of fabric, and allowed them to insert no more than one lining. Well aware of this law, young serving men in a 1564 play disregarded the legislation and stuffed their hose with about seven yards of cloth. They were ridiculed for their willingness to bear such a burden; a character named Grim likens the young men's breeches to duffels of water toted by mules, suggesting such ensembles are "good for none but such as have no buttocks." Grim wonders whether the serving men's motive should be attributed to conceit or whether they were simply doing a service by offering a place where they could lug around "other folk's stuff."

Fashion victims like these serving men faced not only derision but scrutiny by the state when watchers at the city gates checked for compliance with sumptuary law. The nobility tended to be passed over during such dragnets, while those with very little power bore the brunt of the state's attention and supervision. Such was the case of a serving man named Richard Walweyn, who, along with his "monstrous hose," was detained in January 1565. Walweyn's hose were stripped from him, eviscerated, and then strung up on a pike and left to flutter there (disturbingly like severed heads on London Bridge) "where they may aptly be seen and considered by the people as an example of extreme folly." Another working man, a tailor named Thomas Bradshaw, was made to parade home wearing the offending breeches, one leg of his hose torn, its insides trailing, and the other intact. Such public humiliation functioned literally to cut down in size those upstarts who exceeded their station, revealing their vanity to be made up of waste and rags.

Not only waste and rags were tucked into men's breeches. Another anecdote about government oversight of breeches tells the story of an unnamed suspect who was hauled into court—also for wearing "his breeches contrary to the Law"—but who received no punishment. He was spared because his breeches included a newfangled thing called a pocket. As the prisoner approached the judges asking for forgiveness, he reached into the baglike pockets stitched to the inside of his breeches and proceeded to excavate a remarkable trove. In a scene resembling the circus gag where an endless line of clowns exits a tiny car one by one, he drew out a pair of sheets, two tablecloths, ten napkins, four

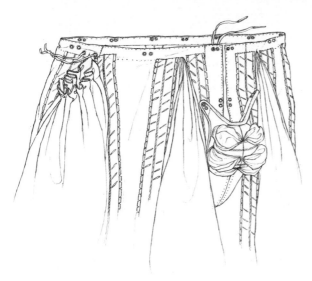

Figure 8. Drawing of the trunk hose worn by Svante Sture in 1567, by Janet Arnold. The single drawstring "pocket bag" lies on the proper right side of hose; the codpiece laces the hose together at the center front, acting like the front fly of trousers. A common contention was that the codpiece also acted as a kind of pocket.

shirts, a brush, a mirror, a comb, a nightcap, and "other things of use." The courtroom was soon "strewn" with his belongings. The suspect then addressed the judges, explaining that he had "no safer a storehouse" in which to secure his possessions. Mightily weighted down, he admitted his breeches felt like "a straight prison." Yet he lauded the effectiveness of his pockets: they served as "a roome to lay up my goods in." Amused by his performance, the judges laughed and dismissed him, telling him not to "alter the furniture of his store-house, but to rid the Hall of his Stuffe, and keep it as it pleased him."

If not quite a storehouse, early pockets like the one in described in this account were sturdier and more capacious than the envelope-shape containers we are familiar with today. In her analysis of the very rare examples of still extant sixteenth-century garments, the dress historian Janet Arnold records what looks like a simple drawstring bag stitched into a pair of men's trunk hose dated to 1567 that belonged to the Swedish count and statesman Svante Sture (figure 8). Arnold dubs this early version of a pocket a pocket-bag, indicating its transitional nature. But sixteenth-century people called them pockets (as I will here). Such pockets attached at the waistband and hung freely from it. Sture's pocket measured twelve inches in depth, while others could be as deep as twenty inches. They might be made of linen, stiff canvas,

Figure 9. *The Plow-Mans Prophesie*, ca. 1550s. In this ballad woodblock illustration, the man apparently reaches with some difficulty for the "pocket-bag" secured inside his breeches.

or more durable leather. Some had a drawstring closure, while others might be pleated and stitched to a side seam. In this early configuration pockets were not necessarily easy to access, as indicated by the stock figure in a contemporary woodcut ballad illustration who requires two hands to loosen his pocket ties and reach into the recess (figure 9).

Early users of pockets nevertheless appreciated pockets' attributes, if enthusiastic accounts in drama—which rivaled even those of the courts—are any measure. Like the suspect who tucked his whole household into his pockets, dramatists willfully exaggerated pockets' scope and scale. The clown Frisco, in a late sixteenth-century comedy, wishes that he were wearing the notoriously large, baggy hose of a Dutchman rather than his own English ones. Having tricked a trio of hapless adversaries and fearing an imminent beating, he frantically searches out a place to hide. "Oh that I had the Dutchman's Hose," he cries, "that I might creepe into the Pockets!" According to Shakespeare, Caesar was such an outsized personality that he "carried the moon in his pocket." In the imagination, at any rate, pockets' scale was not fixed. From storehouse to haven to the heavens, the pocket's boundaries seemed to extend to fit the circumstances.

A CODPIECE "LIKE A POCKET"?

A POTENTIAL ALTERNATIVE to early pockets arose in the codpiece, an emblem of procreative energy and masculine prowess. Derived from *cod*, the slang word for scrotum, the codpiece was a triangular, detachable piece of fabric that laced the trunk hose together at the groin, acting like the front fly of modern trousers (figure 8). Unlike the understated front fly, codpieces often protruded conspicuously, and when codpieces were de rigueur, critics pointed out that men appeared to have been more interested in stuffing the codpiece with straw to achieve the obvious effect. Women noticed. In his 1450s book of fatherly advice, Peter Idley warned his son about women's curiosity and brazenness. He condemned specifically the actions of women ogling and gossiping at church as they admired men's revealing clothes, hoping to get a look at how the stuffing of the codpiece "stands out." Ostentatious codpieces were stylish: Cornelius, the aristocratic gallant of Henry Medwall's 1490s *Fulgens and Lucres* (the earliest extant secular, vernacular drama in Britain), wears a notable one. Cornelius is introduced as "a new man of fashion" who must have "a codpiece before almost thus large." The line includes no stage direction, so just how far an actor might indicate was left to him to improvise.

Later codpieces were constructed over a rigid framework, sometimes leaving a hollow cavity in the interior. This cavity suggested to early modern historians that codpieces were used like pockets. According to a reference book of 1619, for example, when "unknit," the codpiece "made way to the Linnen bags tyed to the inside between the Shirt and Codpiss, these Bags held every thing they carried about them." The figure depicted in the 1510 *Young Knight in a Landscape* by the Italian painter Vittore Carpaccio wears a heavily padded codpiece as protection where armor was not feasible, and in what looks like a pocket housed on the *outside* of his codpiece, the knight has placed some sort of document, folded in quarters, with a reddish, quarter-round shape visible,

Figure 10. *Young Knight in a Landscape,* by Vittore Carpaccio, 1510.

perhaps a seal (figure 10). Evidence of using the codpiece as a container is extremely rare, however. And most assertions about function were made when men had taken to making fun of the apparent desire to "too much express our shameful parts." Others objected even to that notion: Cesare Vecellio asked if one would really want to store a piece of fruit in "so sweet a closet" and then unlace one's codpiece in public in order to proffer it to another? That this action in 1590 seemed "uncivil" to Vecellio (an artist and writer who had spent several decades compiling the most extensive catalog of fashions from around the world) marks a definitive turn against this accessory. Indeed, the idea that codpieces were at all utilitarian may have been a backhanded way to rationalize their century-long use after the fact.

POCKETS WERE CLEARLY less controversial than codpieces; they also surely carried more. Tailors, however, have been frustratingly mute about what precisely prompted them to commit to this possibility in the manufacture of clothes. The few sixteenth-century tailor's manuals that survive, most printed in Spain, do not mention pockets, nor do they highlight new styles or techniques. Without explanation or commentary, pockets start to appear in tailors' invoices, where they tend to be itemized separately. In 1581, William Petre's tailor sent him a bill for making up blue Venetian trunk hose that notes the half a yard of linen it took to make the pockets. The bill includes an additional charge "for [two] leather pockettes for his other hosen." As may have been the case here, pockets wore out and could be replaced as needed. By the 1550s, a date commonly used in encyclopedias of dress for marking the invention of pockets, pockets were still an emergent trend and far from universal. Of the few trunk hose that remain in museum collections, some include pockets and some do not. For example, the trunk hose of Svante Sture that Janet Arnold analyzed were discovered buried in an iron vault with those of his sons. The elder Sture wore the "conservative suit of an older man," Arnold notes, while one son wore a fashionable velvet ensemble and the other, a hunting suit of "hard-wearing" leather and wool. Yet it was the father's conservative trunk hose, and neither of the young men's garments, that held a pocket.

As integrated pockets became more common and expected in men's wear over the sixteenth century, they began to be called out by decorative trimmings. In a 1600 Dutch satirical print, the male customer who accompanies the woman to a shop wears breeches whose pocket is outlined in braid and punctuated by buttons (figure 11). Some women also attached pockets to the skirts of their gowns, likely at the placket (or skirt opening). The wardrobe accounts of Elizabeth I indicate that she had pockets sewn into a few of her more casual gowns and cloaks. But these were never decorative, and most women tended to rely on tried and true methods, continuing to carry a purse suspended from a belt, as does the

Figure 11. *The Vanity of Women: Ruffs*, attributed to Maerten de Vos, ca. 1600 (detail). The standing male figure at the right wears blowsy trunk hose, whose pocket opening at the side seam is outlined with topstitching and reinforced by braid and buttons.

female customer being fitted for a bumroll, a padded hip bustle, in figure 12. In this state of semi-undress, her suspended purse is visible.

POCKETS AND DEADLY POLITICS

WHILE MOTIVES FOR the pocket's inclusion in men's breeches have yet to be discovered, reactions and accommodations to them do appear in the historical record. Various edicts sought to limit the manufacture or distribution of some of the first objects intended to be carried in pockets: small-scale handguns. Perhaps for good reason, anxious rulers across Europe came to fear the potential of pocket pistols, also called "pocket dags," that were "carried privily." A dramatic

Figure 12. *The Vanity of Women: Masks and Bustles*, attributed to Maerten de Vos, ca. 1600 (detail). The female customer who lifts her skirts in order to be fitted for a bumroll displays a purse hanging from a cord in much the same way that women in the medieval era carried their purses.

Figure 13. Portrait Sir Martin Frobisher (1535?–1594), by Cornelis Ketel, 1577. The privateer and explorer holds a short-barrel wheel-lock pistol in one hand and rests the other against the handle of his sword.

wake-up call occurred on a winter night in 1549 when an intruder gained entry to the apartments of Henry VIII's heir, Edward VI, and, startled by the excitable barking of Edward's little dog, drew a gun from his pocket and shot it. A mere seven days later, Edward VI issued the first of repeated proclamations that attempted to create a protective bubble around the king. Fearing an actual assassin, he declared that no one could carry a pocket pistol within three miles of wherever the king happened to be in residence.

That pistols—until this point several feet long—could now fit in pockets was made possible by the wheel-lock mechanism, one of the significant technological innovations of the early sixteenth century. Older military firearms were cumbersome, heavy guns and required that a soldier pause and use both hands to light a tapering flare to ignite the gun powder. The wheel-lock pistol, in contrast, could be loaded ahead of time and then fired at will with one hand in a dramatically efficient and surprising motion. A game-changer for military combat, this kind of handgun was also appreciated for its ease in hunting and sport shooting, and aristocrats who served in a military capacity enjoyed them in times of peace. They spent large sums to purchase and collect these bejeweled instruments, and often displayed them or gave them as gifts.

In his 1577 portrait, the adventurer and privateer Sir Martin Frobisher holds his pistol at the ready, unsettling the decorum of elite portraiture in which most gentleman merely rested a hand on a sheathed sword or rapier, many of them "clogged" with gold and silver (figure 13). Frobisher understood that the "greatest gallant" wore the "deepest ruff" around his neck and carried "the longest blade" at his side—that tied up in any man's look were ideas about honor and his capacity for violence. (We still say, although rarely now, that a well-dressed person looks "sharp.") Yet Frobisher's image takes this capacity a step further than most, as his finger actually clasps the trigger of his gun. Placing the gun by the side of his sizable Venetian trunk hose, painter and subject seem to acknowledge the threat that pocket pistols posed.

In the meantime, the state began to limit handgun ownership and to qualify the conditions of their use. While rulers believed that elite men like Frobisher might be counted on for their loyalty, they were worried about armed insurrection by those with incomes lower than one hundred pounds a year. Their stated concern extended beyond their own safety to maintaining peace in general: with only a minuscule law-enforcement organization in England to thwart marauding troublemakers, urban violence was a major question of the day. In the monarch's name, and with Parliament in agreement, various proclamations were printed, read aloud in public ceremonies, and posted for citizens to see (figure 14). Noting that her subjects "are in fear and danger of their lives," Queen Elizabeth I asserted that no gun should be shorter than three-quarters of a yard. Anything shorter, in "a time of peace," could have only one purpose: to "execute great and notable Robberies, and horrible murders." A 1579 regulation updated the terms of the injunction, noting that small pistols were "commonly called pocket dags," and forbade the manufacture, import, and sale of any gun "that may be hid in any pocket or like place about a man's body to be his or carried covertly." Elizabeth I's successor, James I, observed darkly that "Pocket Dags" were "truly termed of their use . . . that are apparently made to be carried close, and secret."

In Britain, the state eventually banned the pocket dag absolutely, no matter the owner's rank (although the need to reissue the edicts periodically suggests that they remained ineffectual). Contemporaneously, the sovereign in France settled on a different strategy, focusing instead on those devious places "about a man's body"—that is, pockets themselves—rather than the dangers they might conceal. A 1564 ordinance of Henri III limited the bombast in men's trunk hose. It also explicitly banned placing pockets of a certain length inside them, presumably in an attempt to prevent the concealment of large guns. Of course, limiting the size of pockets rather than regulating the pistols at issue might seem a curious strategy. But this strategy would regain appeal in the late nineteenth-century United States, when state legislatures

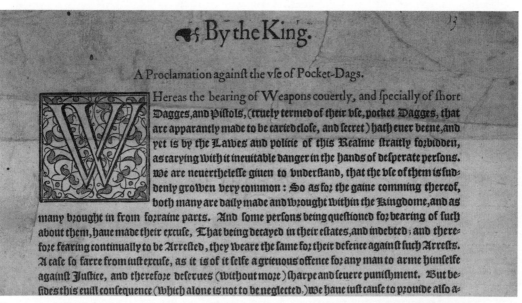

Figure 14. *A Proclamation against the use of Pocket-Dags*, issued by James I in 1613. Only desperate persons carried pocket-dags, as small-scale handguns were known, according to this edict of James I.

attempted to ban outright the new back or seat pockets on men's trousers, calling them "pistol pockets."

For all their inefficacy, early modern and modern regulatory efforts suggest the political view that pockets could enable deadly violence. According to James I, pocket pistols were "odious . . . instruments of mischief and murther." Not only did he lament that his peaceable kingdom had been "polluted with blood," but he judged covert weapons to be unmanly, an aspect of the general upset that we moderns have perhaps lost. In his published letters of advice to his son, James outlined how a ruler should dress and behave, and he took special care to distinguish visible and covert weapons. He admonished his son to wear only those weapons which were "knightly and honorable," and by this he meant "rapier, swords and daggers." The king expected that the aristocrats gathered round him at court or ensconced on their own estates would be armed. Weapons themselves were not the problem. It was concealing one's intentions that broke a long-standing social pact, signaling a general disintegration of chivalric codes. Pockets thus exacerbated a troubling turn. "Out with . . . your pocket-dagger," demands Duarte, the quarrelsome braggart in John Fletcher and Philip Massinger's 1619 play, *The Custom of the Country*, when he encounters Alonzo, his rival, on the street. He accuses Alonzo of the worst kind of cowardice: too timid is he to carry a sword with which to publicly defend his honor; rather, he sinks to the level of common criminal who pockets small-scale weapons with which to "murder men."

Only the smallest minority of men were murderers or robbers who relied on pockets for their dastardly schemes. But this early use of pockets as containers for covert weapons was certainly a sensational one, drawing pockets into political debate, and influenced the way early pockets were represented. The belief that valor should be discernable to all accounts for some of the breathless commentary that followed the first successful assassination of a political leader by a handgun. In 1584 Prince William of Orange (an ally of Queen Elizabeth I and an enemy of Spain) was assassinated by a wheel-lock pistol, which the

Figure 15. *The Assassination of William the Silent,* by Frans Hogenberg, 1584 (detail). Hogenberg's graphic depiction of the assassination included highlights of the action in sequential order. It acted like a news report, although one of limited accuracy, relying as it did on secondhand accounts and hearsay.

assassin, pretending to hand Prince William a letter, produced from his pocket (figure 15). Commentators kept coming back to this odd detail: the most unprepossessing of killers, dour in temperament and small in stature, had carried off a shocking assault, one that had the potential to tip the balance of power between England and Spain. Into one's pockets, the wearer might place articles that gave him an internal source of confidence. Bravery need not be visible with a pistol tucked in your pocket.

CRIME AND NEW SKILLS: "DIVING INTO YOUR STORAGE"

WHERE THE STATE saw danger, others identified opportunity. Pockets proved an irresistible temptation to criminals, so much so that with the advent of pockets an important subset of thieves required a name change and a new set of skills. Since the medieval period, *cutpurse* was the term for the thief who seized valuables directly from his victim. In Pieter Bruegel's 1568 painting, *The Misanthropist*, a cutpurse in a field of sheep simply grabs the old man's money bag and slices it free of its cord with a knife (figure 16). Most cutpurses, however, preferred to lurk in crowds, where the everyday jostle and noise helped to disguise their actions. Gaining access to pockets involved a greater degree of intimacy and a higher degree of risk. Capturing a shift in the relationship between criminal and vic-

Figure 16. *The Misanthropist*, by Pieter Bruegel, 1568. The figure of the misanthrope is hooded and withdrawn—he does not notice the cutpurse, and indeed, that was Bruegel's point. The theft is essentially the misanthrope's fault, so concerned is he with his own affairs that he does not notice the thief in the wide-open landscape.

tim, the first pickpockets were called "divers" in the colorful argot of the criminal underworld. The naive narrator who interviews a diver, among other various underworld characters, in John Dunton's 1685 allegory, *An Hue and Cry after Conscience*, takes this designation literally. He asks the thief whether his job is to "plunge into the water." ("Speak plain," he begs.) The diver reluctantly replies that his job is to "lift . . . your Cargo by insensibly diving into your Storage." Rather than cut at a cord, the diver plunged into private space.

According to Robert Greene's 1591 survey of criminal methods, the diver was a more respected criminal than the cutpurse. He was also something of a snob who "holds himself of the highest degree," refusing even to carry a knife with which to cut his meat for "disdain" of being mistaken for a cutpurse. "Nimble handed," the diver and pickpocket had to have the techniques and skill of a good surgeon,

Greene remarked. Prostitutes, too, were thought to have the specialized skills of the pickpocket, and a perfect excuse for the intimacy pocket diving required. As the "wandering whore" who narrates Peter Aretine's 1661 bawdy pamphlet, *Strange News from Bartholomew-Fair*, "dives" into the pockets of otherwise engaged customers, she manages to leave them "as clear as a room new swept." The writer figures the prostitute's successful foray as her domestication of the customer's personal space. Rifling through another's pockets was a real incursion into intimate parts.

POCKETS: A SOCIAL AFFAIR?

WITH THEIR DRAMATIC introduction, pockets seem to have traveled some distance from what the historian of technology George Basalla calls their "antecedent" artifact, the small bag or purse. All made things have antecedents, argues Basalla—and new things "are never pure creations of theory, ingenuity, or fancy." If we paid more attention to continuity rather than startling innovation, he adds, we could reconstruct "a grand and vast network of linked artifacts," a kind of artifactual family tree encompassing everything from existing artifacts to vanished ones. This network of object relations would better explain the diversity of the things we create and that surround us. On such a tree, pockets would be positioned as a mere offshoot of purses. And while pocket and purse share more qualities than not, their proximity belies the significance of small adjustments. Yoking bag to breeches in what looks like an improvisational "lash-up" created a tool demonstrably more private and personal than the public-facing purse whose uses and meanings could not have been foreseen.

The purse, important to one's overall look, is a satellite accessory, eminently detachable. And with millennia of lead time, purses acquired specific associations marked by their contact with gold and silver. From biblical Judas, whose infamous purse with its thirty pieces of silver marked his betrayal, purses have carried a certain burden. No matter the articles placed there, the purse remains a container overridingly identified with money and, by extension, the person's status, wealth, or lack thereof. In allegory and satire, purses might point out general qualities related to the person's care of their resources, from munificence to cupidity and miserliness.

Pockets, too, can be associated with money (as immigrant narratives that begin with some version of *and he arrived with only two dollars in his pocket* attest). But, at least relative to purses, one's money is the least interesting or remarked upon thing that people carry there. What did seem to capture people's imagination was the feature that distinguishes pockets from their antecedent, their integral construction. Once the wearer places something inside their pocket, that thing disappears, enfolded and seemingly absorbed into uncertain depths. The notion that pockets swallow their contents shows up in the first common expressions that used or expanded on the word *pocket*, many of which exploited a beloved quirk of the English language in which speakers turn nouns into verbs. According to the *Oxford English Dictionary*, the phrase "to pocket up" initially referred to situations in which one kept one's weapons and impulses in check. Rather than uphold one's honor by readying for a fight (and drawing, say, one's pocket pistol), one endured or swallowed some insult, circumventing a duel. The phrase's resonance can be attributed to the difficulty the nobility had in calibrating their responses to perceived social slights at court, where a once fiercely independent aristocracy increasingly depended on a ruler for status and privilege. In his 1611 lament about the loss of aristocratic power, Anthony Stafford observed that while at court the nobleman had to "crouch and bow." He had to appear unfazed as he confronted his enemies, putting on a "smooth front." He could never reveal his true feelings but must "lick the feet of the great." A gentleman, then, "must pocket up many a great wrong, to come to greatness." Honor might be something you wear at your side, but your pride was something you had to suck up to make it at court.

Figure 17. Portrait of Steven van der Meulen, Robert Dudley, Earl of Leicester, ca. 1564. Elizabeth's adviser wears a purse in which he displays a strikingly white linen handkerchief. After their brief appearance in men's purses in the 1560s, handkerchiefs were welcomed by pockets, taking on a very long compound name, pocket-hand-kerchief. Handkerchiefs are one of the few articles (other than pocket-watch chains) that are supposed to remain visible when held in pockets.

The nobleman's reputation now rested on an array of attributes that had nothing to do with his fierceness or bluster as a warrior. What you chose to reveal and what you chose to keep to yourself involved an entirely new kind of calculus—a new kind of clothing—and the recognition that everyday encounters might require concealment or dissimulation. As early conduct books explained, the important thing to do in social situations was to consider the impression that you made on others, and to keep separate those things you did alone from the ones you did in company. Conduct books considered pockets private space and counseled readers not to draw out a letter from one's pocket to read in the presence of others. Like checking one's mobile phone today, retreating to personal matters in public indicated that one was bored by present company.

Figure 18. Dior x Sacai collection, Spring 2022. Photograph by Brett Lloyd.

Because pockets were experienced as a quasi-extension of the person, the things held in them were thought to be especially revealing. In drama and literature, exploring the contents of pockets proved a kind of irresistible shorthand, a way to take another's measure. Prince Hal famously calls out the blowhard Falstaff for not being what he claims in Shakespeare's *Henry IV*. And no matter Falstaff's grandiose assertions, Hal need only search Falstaff's pockets, where a lint-covered piece of forgotten candy, "worthless tavern-reckonings, [and] memorandums of bawdy-houses" provide vivid proof of the knight's dissolute existence. Such pocket disclosures threatened to reveal the distance between the person one presented to the world and the far more messy or contradictory one kept to oneself. Could your pockets "speak"? asks Antonio in *The Tempest*. And if so, would they say you "lie"? You might wear "good clothes," as Thomas Dekker pointed out in a 1630 comedy, but carry neither "coin" nor "conscience" in your "torn pockets."

For most, guarding against torn pockets had far more to do with necessity. In pocketing an increasingly long list of necessary articles, wearers came to feel a new dependence on a portable storehouse. Pockets acted as a sort of reservoir that held those items so critical to maintaining one's equanimity, from coins to pistols to "bawdy house receipts." Their eventual proliferation spoke to the recognition that a person's sense of security was supported by a host of aids. As Joseph Hall observed in his 1598 book of satires, the social-climbing gallants who "still are poring on their pocket glass" did not seem to know how to get by without new artifacts of gentility such as small mirrors and handkerchiefs. Previously, people had used a sleeve to wipe their nose and had little way to see for themselves if they had done a good job. It is perhaps for this reason that Twain's unlikely knight felt so betrayed by what he experienced as his armor's bad design. Deprived of his pockets, he missed the assurance of those articles that had become his constant companions.

Why, then, didn't pockets and purses simply coexist in masculine attire? A revival of medieval-style purses in the 1560s clearly demonstrates that a gentleman could accommodate purse, dagger, and sword about his waist while wearing breeches that likely contained a pocket (figure 17). Yet as pockets came into general use over the next fifty years, they compelled a certain allegiance. By the end of the sixteenth century, the purse was more and more associated with out-of-date country fashions. Only the "plain country fellow" in a homespun coat wears a purse or "side pouch at his side," remarked Robert Greene. Few urbane gentlemen carried purses (or pouches) as the sixteenth century progressed. And if men's purses simply went out of fashion, then it is notable that this is one fashion that had been slow to experience a revival. Men had routinely carried handbags such as briefcases that belong in the luggage continuum, but it has taken some four hundred years after the demise of the purse for the fashion forward to experiment with what has been recently dubbed—and not without contention—the "murse" or "man purse," designed specifically for men (figure 18). They range from supposedly feminine clutch versions to elevated fanny packs to sporty messenger bags, yet wearing one remains something of a social experiment. Noting that the "luxe murse market" was expanding in 2019, a fashion journalist test-driving one nervously asked, "Could it work on a man such as myself? . . . Could I pull it off?" But for many others, there has been no need to experiment. Men's wear pockets have proved more than satisfactory, having faithfully kept the wearer's counsel. In welcoming pockets, men swapped spectacle for a private retreat, a secret territory of their own.

Figure 1. Illustration from Jonathan Swift's *The Adventures of Captain Gulliver, in a Voyage to the Islands of Lilliput and Brobdingnag*, 1776. In this children's edition of *Gulliver's Travels*, the castaway awakens in Lilliput.

CHAPTER 2

Pocket Proliferation:
Housing "the Workmanship of a Hundred Tradesmen"

The first pockets stitched into men's breeches in the sixteenth century proved popular, and enthusiasm for them led to a self-perpetuating momentum. Tailors, at any rate, found every opportunity to fold in more of them where space allowed. As women continued to rely on traditional methods of carrying articles of daily life, men enjoyed novel arrays of pockets that developed in conjunction with the three-piece suit.

The three-piece suit's basic format of coat, tie, and trousers surfaced in the late seventeenth century. This ensemble was worn, then as now, to business meetings and court appearances, to weddings and funerals. Notable for its longevity, and for recurring predictions of its demise, the suit is today discussed as being both a social and an aesthetic achievement, a uniform associated with sobriety, respectability, and civic virtue. But it was the suit's practical advantages (and a few of its impractical ones) that captured the attention of several commentators who witnessed its rise.

Perhaps no eighteenth-century cultural critic did more to demonstrate that pockets were a notable feature of the suit—and a necessary adjunct to the go-getting modern man—than Jonathan Swift. The suit worn by Swift's antihero, the obstinate traveler Lemuel Gulliver, receives special appraisal in a book Swift famously admitted to writing in order to "vex the world." When Gulliver unexpectedly washes up on the shores of Lilliput in the early pages of *Gulliver's Travels*, the diminutive Lilliputians are in equal parts curious and wary (figure 1), and they wisely decide to search his person. The Lilliputians' own clothes are "simple and plain," a "union" of Asian and European forms, and it is possible they had never seen anything like Gulliver's ensemble, with its myriad interstices. As the two court-appointed officers proceed with their search, they get to know Gulliver with an intimacy that might be disturbing if the specter of the two brave Lilliputians, clambering in and out of Gulliver's many pockets (they find at least ten), disappearing up to their heads, and perplexed by what they find, were not so funny and preposterous.

The Lilliputians' inventory of Gulliver's pockets is a long one and makes clear that he is well-equipped for his foray into unknown lands, as befits any would-be colonist. With his compass, pocket telescope, and journal at the ready, Gulliver can observe the landscape before him, measure and "compute" its attributes, while keeping a log and careful records. The insistent ticking of his pocket watch (like "a God he worships," according to the Lilliputian officers) drives him to even greater industry. Heavy gold, silver, and copper coins indicate that Gulliver has approached the venture amply funded, able to grease palms as need be. And if money doesn't allay resistance, Gulliver also carries in his pockets a knife, two pistols, a clutch of bullets, and plenty of gunpowder (in a watertight container meant to withstand the damp). A set of eating utensils ensures his refinement no matter the prevailing manners, and a razor, handkerchief, and comb allow Gulliver to keep up appearances. Should his spirits flag, a stash of snuff that the Lilliputians wade through up to their knees, sneezing, promises to focus the nerves.

With this more than ample store, Swift decisively lampoons the traveler's biases and misconceptions (as well as the idea that all the world was for the taking). But he also highlights the degree to which men's claims on adventure, not to mention an active public life, were supported by the effortless way their clothing accommodated it. That support did vary. Eighteenth-century men were not equal in their pocket bounty across rank and condition, nor yet "united by a fraternity of pockets." It was Gulliver's age that would see inset pockets become standard for men, but the adoption of pockets proceeded fitfully, in clothing made entirely by hand and in which the look and number of pockets were widely divergent. Intriguingly, men's mounting lead in pockets did not give women pause. Unlike today, women voiced little to no irritation over the imbalance—and seem not to have experienced any inconvenience; they continued to enjoy other methods of securing their everyday necessities.

RISE OF THE POCKETED SUIT

THE STRUCTURE OF the three-piece suit had coalesced only some years before Swift wrote *Gulliver's Travels*, and many experienced the new fashion as a dramatic break with tradition. Such breaks do not occur often, and dress historians disagree about their causes, including whether political pressures, social realignments, or a simple but widespread desire for the new are more to blame. In the case of the suit, there is some agreement that general unhappiness over the excesses of contemporary modes mingled with envy for the understated elegance of Eastern kaftans. Like the Lilliputians' clothes, the suit can be considered a hybrid that highlights borrowings across cultures that gave and still give rise to new forms—including, in this case, new pocket forms.

There were several factors at play in the move to the three-piece suit. Between the 1640s and 1660s many agreed that the two-piece doublet and breeches had reached absurd extremes. The doublet (a main jacketlike garment), which had once been substantial, had lost much of its rigidity and had also shrunk in size. The abbreviated doublet left a gap at the stomach, exposing the shirt at the belly button, and as a result, breeches could no longer be tied or hooked to the doublet and tended to sag around the hips. The breeches, meanwhile, had grown so wide they were likened to petticoats and, following French modes, were decorated with yards of ribbon. In such attire, the fashionable fop, the "English Antic" of the 1646 caricature, appeared disorderly to the point of undress (figure 2). In a 1661 pamphlet advocating fashion reform, the diarist and counselor to King Charles II, John Evelyn, complained that men in their beribboned petticoat breeches looked like maypoles, as if they'd "plundered" all the ribbon shops in town.

Figure 2. *The English Antic, or The Habit of an English Gentleman,* 1646. This satirical drawing pokes fun at the English Gentleman, dressed in the height of French fashions in his truncated doublet and wide petticoat breeches.

During this period of rising disgruntlement and dissatisfaction with men's clothing, King Charles II indicated his intention to introduce "a new fashion of clothes." Very rarely can one pinpoint the date a new style took hold, but the origins of the suit have been traced to a single day, Monday, October 15, 1666, when the king and a few of his courtiers followed through on his announcement and wore their new outfits to court on the occasion of the Duke of York's birthday. In what was perceived as a refusal to acquiesce to the dictates of French styles, witnesses reported that the king wore an ensemble that was stately, reserved, and "manlike," and, from the start, was understood to have been borrowed from the East. Charles had changed his doublet and petticoat breeches "for a comely vest, after the Persian mode, . . .

Figure 3. A more sedate gentlemen is depicted in a ballad illustration titled *Cupid's Kindness to Constant Coridon, or, Fair Silvia Wounded with a Dart*, 1675. The figure wears an early three-piece suit with two sets of vertical pocket slits decorated by buttons on his coat.

⚜ Aga Capitaine general des Ianiſſaires.

Figure 4. *Aga Capitaine, general des Jannissaires*, by Nicholas de Nicolai, from *Costume Engravings Made during Travels in the East*, 1587. The high-ranking Ottoman military officer places his hand in the pocket slit of his outer kaftan. The outer kaftan has detachable sleeves, worn hanging in back, which reveal the contrasting pattern of an under-kaftan.

resolving never to alter it," approvingly wrote Evelyn, who was a witness that day.

The vest itself was a notable innovation, as was the concept of layered pieces. Over the knee-length vest the king wore a knee-length coat. This ensemble, what is now recognized as the earliest version of the three-piece suit, offered a fundamentally different conception than doublet and breeches. Rather than tie a top (a doublet) to the bottom (breeches) with laces or hooks, the three-piece suit consisted of overlapping parts that provided wearers a more unified line. The garment, which Evelyn associated with Persia, had in fact a much broader geographic range. Versions of kaftans—long, unfitted coats layered in a series of under-coats and overcoats—were worn not only in Persia but throughout Turkic and Central Asian cultures, and Europeans had seen stunning examples of them worn, for example, by visiting Ottoman dignitaries, as well as depicted in costume books, tourist guides, on the stage, and at masquerades (figure 4). Long admired, this borrowed form provided Charles with decorously long cover. According to commentators, the king and courtiers appeared more understated and modest. The suit was "the most graceful, virile, and useful mode that ever appeared at court," proclaimed Evelyn.

This "useful mode" would become more useful when pockets migrated from breeches to coats and waistcoats—the point when their proliferation began in earnest. Following the kaftan, the first suit coats also included vertical pocket slits placed just below the waist. Sometimes two sets of vertical pockets, left open and surrounded by decorative buttons, were placed on each side of the coat (figure 3). It is unclear whether these earliest versions of suit-coat pockets had attached pocket bags. Sixteenth- and seventeenth-century kaftans did not tend to have integrated or sewn-in pocket bags—kaftans collected in the Topkapi Palace in Istanbul and connected to the reign of Sultan Süleyman, for example, do not. (The pocket slits in the kaftan, like the pocket slits set in the side seams of early medieval European gowns, allowed wearers to reach a bag tied at the waist.) Dissatisfied with this vertical placement of the pocket slits after about a decade, tailors shifted them to their now more familiar horizontal position. So placed, tailors could easily add envelope-shaped pocket bags set flat against the body.

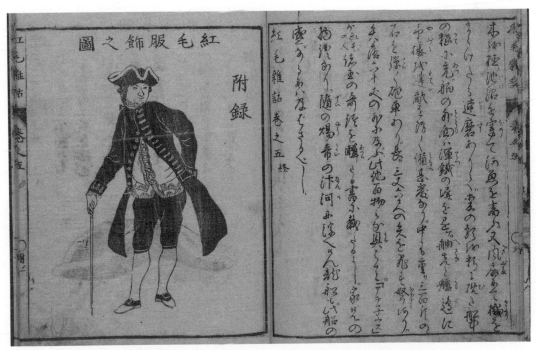

Figure 5. Illustrated page of Churyo Morishima's *Komo Zatsuwa* (*Red Hair Miscellany*), 1787. Morishima describes the suit worn by the Dutch, or "red hairs" as the Dutch were known in Japan.

Soon no one remembered the suit's source in the kaftan, and it came to be seen as a Western getup. The suit was among the articles of daily life that Churyo Morishima decoded for his readers in his 1787 *Komo Zatsuwa* (*Red Hair Miscellany*), for example. For Japanese readers otherwise cut off from firsthand knowledge about foreign dress and manners during the Edo period, Morishima's book was the first to offer relatively extensive description of the daily life of the Dutch residents within the confines of Dejima, the manmade island allotted to them in the Bay of Nagasaki. Japan's trade restrictions at the time allowed only the Dutch (who were not much interested in religious proselytizing) a limited trading outpost. Morishima claimed to have procured a full Dutchman's outfit, and sketched and described its notable features, including hat, overcoat, breeches, stockings, shoes, and belt. Defining the word *pocket* for readers who likely carried their personal possessions tucked into the belt or sleeve of a kimono, Morishima noted that in the Dutch suit, "there are parts to put things in."

IN *RED HAIR MISCELLANY*, Morishima also noted that "the [Dutch] dress system looks as if there were no distinction between the nobles and non-nobles." While it was true by the eighteenth century that across Europe and Anglo-America most men wore some basic form of the suit, Morishima did not witness a representative cross section of social classes at Dejima. Had he visited any European port, however, he would have seen that there were wide sartorial variations between social classes depending on whether one was free or unfree, one's rank (or the rank one claimed to have achieved), and the labor one performed. The cut of the suit mattered. A suit coat that followed the contours of a gentleman's shoulders and ran down the center of his spine indicated that a tailor had spent time measuring his body precisely. A suit coat that bunched or gaped suggested it had been made by an untrained amateur or acquired secondhand in some way, perhaps even pawned or stolen. Cloth mattered too: smooth silks and velvets as well as supple wools dyed in deep, vibrant colors suggested ample resources.

Figure 6. Court suit, densely embroidered, France, ca. 1810.

The coarser the textile and the lower its relative vibrancy (natural or dull colors often indicated fugitive dyes whose colors faded quickly after washing), the lower its value.

To a surprising degree, details relating to pocket distribution, placement, and decorative finish were the subjects of comment in the eighteenth century. At the height of wealth and privilege were highly ornate court suits, donned for official court audiences and other formal events, where pockets were a site of significant attention (figure 6). Professional designers produced two-dimensional patterns for the foliate embroidery that wound around pocket flaps and, in more opulent versions, up and down the coat's borders. Alternately, pockets, collars, and cuffs might be outlined with metallic braiding, borrowing a standard military motif. The single and double braids that delineate the borders of an unknown gentleman's suit in a portrait from the 1760s, perfectly symmetrical and orderly, give it an authoritative flair (figure 7).

Figure 7. *Portrait of a Man in a Green Suit*, by Pompeo Girolamo Batoni, 1760s.

Especially as the suit settled down into understated simplicity (or what seemed so compared to the ladies' furbelows and flounces), small pocket details on the suit gained importance. One hoping to stay in fashion had to pay attention to the smallest shifts in style, including the "various scallop of the pocket" (in other words, whether the pocket flap had one curved edge or two). A red superfine-wool suit from about

1760 demonstrates that great effort went into the subtlest of details (figure 8). The blue silk taffeta lining of the pocket flap (blue taffeta also lines the interior of the coat) has been eased around the edge of the flap so that it looks like a razor-fine line of piping. Even very plain and sober suits might be enlivened by decorative waistcoats, which remained a playful holdout of color and delicacy through the 1840s. A design for a gentleman's waistcoat pocket from 1765 includes sprightly little flowers and leaves that mirror the border design. Executed in pastels and jewel colors, the embroidery pops against its cream-colored silk background (figure 9).

The majority of suit coats and waistcoats neither achieved such a professional sheen nor were made up in fine materials. Set against the fine woolens and silks used by the wealthy was a mass of cheap linens in striped, checked, and speckled patterns. An unlined striped linen work jacket (also called a "waistcoat with sleeves" in this period), believed

Figure 8. Pocket detail on man's superfine-wool suit coat, Dutch, 1760–1770. Two operable buttons and buttonholes bookend a nonoperable button that hides just under the central point at the pocket flap.

to have been owned by Joseph Noyes of Rhode Island, is adorned with two flapped slash pockets that ingeniously create a decorative effect with a humble material (figure 10). The flaps are made from the same fabric but cut on the cross grain, creating horizontal stripes contrasting with the vertical stripes of the jacket. Even the alignment of the stripes on the fabric-covered buttons appears to play with the stripe theme.

And not all suit coats were visibly adorned with pockets. The hawker's suit depicted in a catalog of London types includes not a single pocket flap (figure 11). This figure wears the three hats he has to sell, but the rest of his stock of secondhand clothes is no more refined than his own very plain coat and waistcoat. The artist may very well have been exercising license to emphasize the ragged state of this tradesman. But the absence of pockets was also sometimes noted in the paragraph-long advertisements posted by employers and enslavers

Figure 9. Drawing, design for embroidery, gentleman's waistcoat pocket, by Fabrique de Saint Ruf (designer), ca. 1785.

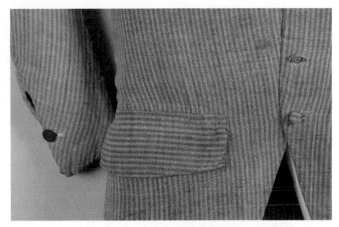

Figure 10. Joseph Noyes's jacket in the striped, blue linen typical of working garments from the eighteenth century. The vagaries of wear and use probably account for the flaps appearing to be set at different heights across the hips. While the buttonholes were hastily stitched, the maker was not an amateur: the stripes precisely meet at all the major seams.

who sought the return of servants and enslaved people who had fled their forced employ. In 1767, when the indentured apprentice James Axley ran away from a Williamsburg, Virginia, courthouse, a court official noted that Axley's leather breeches—the so-called blue jeans of the eighteenth century—were stained with turpentine and that he wore a "gray cloth coat, without pockets or flaps."

Other laborers, free and unfree, did not wear suits at all, pairing unfashionable trousers (indicative of proletarian status) with short hip-length jackets often acquired already made (figure 12). Sailors were members of one of the first trades that could purchase a version of ready-made clothes, or "slops"—particularly loose and poorly fabricated trousers with

Figure 11. *Old Cloaks, Suits or Coats*, by Marcellus Laroon, published in *The Cryes of the City of London*, 1687.

Figure 12. Illustration from George Bruce and Co.'s *A Specimen of Printing Types and Ornaments Cast by Geo. Bruce & Co.*, 1833. Block print commonly used to illustrate runaway advertisements appearing in newspapers in the United States. The runaway wears a short double-breasted hip-length jacket with long trousers.

jackets—to outfit themselves for long voyages. Pockets were not guaranteed. Nor were pockets guaranteed in clothes enslaved people endured. Many slaveholders took advantage of the emerging ready-to-wear industry, placing large-batch clothing orders with manufacturers, specifying that they use the cheapest cloths. Manufacturers likely would have avoided the extra labor and expense of stitching pockets into coats and jackets. Yet this was not always the case. On one Virginia farm, Nathaniel Burwell hired tailor John Grymes to make thirty-five suits for crop workers; Burwell paid an extra six shillings to put pockets into them. Sometimes either planters' or overseers' wives made clothing, but increasingly through the latter part of the eighteenth century, enslaved people took over the production of their own garments. A 1770 letter from an enslaver indicated that his male slaves "chose to have the Cloth given them and their Wives or Sisters to cut it out and make them up for them." Conceivably all sorts of indignities could be avoided—and features like pockets included—if a family member made up one's clothing rather than a slaveholder. In a 1930s interview, Shad Hall recalled that his former enslavers excluded pockets not just out of a desire for economy but as a sort of preemptive disciplinary strategy. As a boy his "first pants had no pockets so that it would be less easy for [him and other children] to steal eggs."

Yet there was enough confusion about social roles in the eighteenth century (and enough ways to procure secondhand or stolen goods) that clothes were often used to cross boundaries. Those who hoped to present themselves as genteel—or who more urgently hoped to pass as free—often knew how to manipulate appearances and perceptions. A runaway slave called Stepney from North Carolina was one such person. With his "knowledge of hair dressing," he was clearly attuned to style, and he wore his own hair "platted and turned up behind, and at other times cued," perhaps satirizing the hairstyles of white people in their cued wigs. Stepney was "cunning and ingenious," according to the man who was his enslaver and posted an advertisement for his capture in August 1794. The notice states that Stepney's coat was of fashionable make, for it had "a black velvet cape, cuffs and pocket flaps." Of course, conspicuous dress was not always best for escaping if a master's description could too easily identify you. But a runaway hoping to "pass himself for a free man" in a cosmopolitan port city like Charleston could take advantage of the fact that such cities included an increasingly skilled, mobile labor force that included free, indentured, and enslaved laborers. In such a context, slaveholders could not necessarily depend on skin color to mark servitude, and so a suit with all its parts could go a long way in upholding vital deceptions.

According to the enslaver James Walker, a runaway named Edom went to extraordinary lengths to alter his clothing on the eve of his escape from a Williamsburg, Virginia, plantation in 1770. Edom "dyed his cotton jacket brown," altering what was likely poor-quality undyed white-colored wool to a darker color that would read as a different textile (and importantly, not cloth reserved for enslaved persons' attire). Edom also "put pockets in and cuffs to it," indicating a knowledge of fashion. Another runaway, Dick, who escaped from a Virginia plantation in 1772, wore "a Beaver Coating short Coat"—a cheap woolen textile that had a long nap that he had "much altered." Dick lined this jacket, giving it more substance and warmth, and added "slash Pockets," horizontal pockets on the face of the coat. Through their stitching, runaways added functional space useful in flight while also critically transforming a mean livery of slavery—pocketless coats—into more distinguished, worldly garb.

BESIDES INDICATING THEIR worldliness, a person in a more or less well-made suit constructed by a professional or skilled amateur (even if it was purchased in a refurbished state) maintained an orderly relationship with the tools they carried. The integrated pockets in a man's suit were purposefully designed to differentiate belongings: various suit pockets allowed the methodical man to carefully separate items in his immediate possession. Accordion-shape compartments placed within a coat pocket, for example, offered space to further segregate disparate collections. Arrayed across the suit, some pockets had specific uses. Large side pockets in greatcoats, a kind of overcoat, were especially useful for documents. The fob pocket (a small chamber in the waistband) was a tiny but perfectly protected place to hold coins or a pocket watch. To "fob" is "to cheat, deceive, delude, trick," according to the *Oxford English Dictionary*, and in this case the trick was on the thief; sitting at the waistband, the diminutive pocket was hard to access and unlikely to be successfully breached without the wearer's knowledge. The Lilliputian searchers in *Gulliver's Travels* cannot climb into Gulliver's fobs, so snuggly does his belly press against them.

Thieves had their own trick pockets in which they might secret contraband. The "private pocket" engineered by postal worker and thief Timothy Robinson, charged on August 27, 1729 with stealing letters stuffed with money, almost escaped discovery. According to court records at the Old Bailey, when confronted by his employers, Robinson ostentatiously pulled out all his pockets to show his innocence. Not satisfied, his employers continued "feeling about his Pockets" and soon "felt a Lump, but could not find the Way into it." Finally, they cut and dismantled the entire coat, where they discovered a cleverly concealed secret chamber behind one of the pockets. Robinson attempted to deny owning the waistcoat, but "His Plea being incredible," Robinson was found guilty and sentenced to transportation to the colonies.

Following the proliferation of pockets, makers and tradesmen began to miniaturize useful instruments with the notion of portability in mind. While handguns had been among the first and most notorious pocket-size objects, most tools were not so contentious. The desire for compact devices encouraged the manufacture of minuscule hinges and springs, which resulted in even more accurate pocket watches and compasses. Mechanical upgrades like these inspired the development of ingenious tool sets with interchangeable heads and blades affixed to screw-on handles (figure 13). In a letter to a friend, Thomas Jefferson enthused about the calculations made possible via the science of the small, including determinations about latitude: "I have a pocket sextant of miraculous accuracy, considering its microscopic graduation." Called a "walking calculator" by his contemporaries, Jefferson also carried pocket-size scales, drawing instruments, a thermometer, a surveying

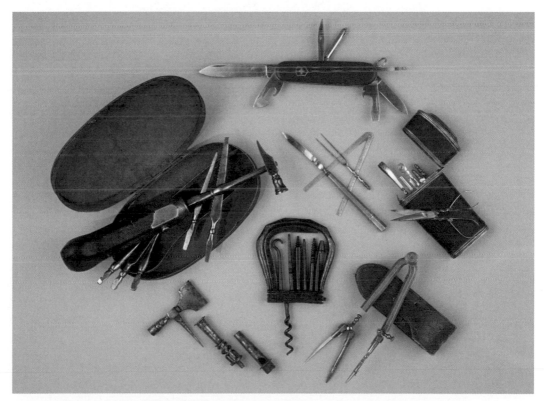

Figure 13. Pocket tool kits, clockwise from top: a modern Swiss-Army knife (shown for scale); a tool-kit etui (the knife, fork, and folding rule to the left belong to it); a pocket compass and case with a swiveling pen/pencil attachment; a snap-joint pocket tool; a gun tool (shown disarticulated); and a pocket tool kit retailed by Richard Dingly (with hammer resting on top). Dingly was active between 1768 and 1805.

Figure 14. Thomas Jefferson's ivory pocket notebooks, Monticello.

compass, a level, and a globe. He used these devices to record the temperature, wind direction, weather, bird migrations, and other seasonal changes, such as the appearance of flowers, jotting down observations throughout the day on an erasable ivory notebook (figure 14). Jefferson would later transfer his notes into his more permanent records at home. If Jefferson was a walking calculator, his suit was akin to a mobile laboratory.

While ivory writing tablets were relatively sturdy, many devices were rendered more delicate in miniature. Protective covers and cases became almost as important as the devices themselves. A set of playing cards from 1702 advertises pocket cases to keep safe instruments like sextants or drawing compasses for the artistically inclined (figure 15). Pocket flasks, if made of glass, might wear a protective leather sleeve, usefully insulating the object from its user, who might grow forgetful of its care, as has the drunken constable who stashes a bottle for his nightly rounds in figure 16. Sometimes exquisitely crafted cases were part of the allure of having things in your pockets. Bejeweled boxes, called *étuis* or pocket necessaries, were satisfying to look at and handle. These necessaries held everything from writing tools to hygiene must-haves, such as ear spoons, tweezers, and scent bottles. Snuff boxes, which held powdered, scented tobacco thought to have medicinal qualities, were also made of precious materials, such as silver, porcelain, and tortoise shell. Drawing out one's snuff entailed a whole ritual: there were ways to offer snuff and ways to take it—preferably with a dainty pinch of the forefinger and thumb of the right hand. One might, according to those paying attention to the rules of the ceremony, even indicate one's relationship to the snuff profferer via "the Careless, the Scornful, the Politick, [or] the Surly Pinch."

But even plain or handcrafted pocket cases might protect valuable artifacts, including various forms of identity, like passports and freeman's papers. Starting with an act of 1796, American sailors began to carry Seaman's Protection Certificates as proof of citizenship and to avoid impressment by the British Navy. Black seamen were additionally required by some US states to carry freeman's papers (or Certificates of Freedom), which declared them legally free. All such papers, which included only a description of the holder with perhaps a small official engraving or seal, were easy to forge or transfer, a fact that Frederick Douglass used to his advantage when he

Figure 15. Playing card describing pocket cases, ca. 1702.

Figure 16. *The Reforming Constable*, ca. 1750. The drunken constable leans against a post carrying a liquor bottle in his coat pocket.

borrowed a friend's seaman's papers and boarded a train heading to Philadelphia. When prompted by the conductor to produce his papers, Douglass, "rigged out in sailor style," retrieved them with a calm that belied his internal anxiety at this critical point in the deception. In his autobiography, he writes that he casually "drew from my deep sailor's pocket my seaman's protection," acting as if he were already a free man.

Paper itself was perishable, and while freeman's papers were legally binding documents backed by registers held at county courthouses, personal copies were subject to loss, theft, and destruction. Legally free and living in Virginia between 1852 and 1865, Joseph Trammell addressed those inherent flaws when he crafted a small tin pocket box with a specialized groove for a sliding lid. Here he secured his freedom papers and, with the reassuring weight and feel of the box jostling in his pocket, would have had continual knowledge of the document's presence (figure 17).

The need to carry more or less important paper documents (including paper money), and particularly printed information, resulted in all sorts of small-scale pocket books. The *pocket book* is a broad category of flat, often leather-bound cases that sometimes included printed material, like an almanac, ledger of accounts, or pages for memoranda. An accordion-shape paper container might be affixed to one or both ends for securing stray bits and was used much like a wallet is today. The term is a confusing one, in part because pocket books now denote women's much larger compartmentalized handbags. But before the twentieth century, the term encompassed any booklike container that was meant to be carried within a pocket.

The term also describes actual books of diminutive size, soon touted for their use in surprising contexts: The compiler of *The Soldier's Pocket Bible* (1643), for example, explained that convenient subheadings helped "supply the want of the whole Bible, which a Soldier cannot conveniently carry about him." Such a "useful" book could be turned to "both before the fight, in the fight, and after the fight." Miniature maps and a variety of other small-scale guides, sometimes called "Go With Me's," offered information and practical advice to travelers (listing hackney fares or common phrases in another language); to tradespeople and peddlers (with conversion tables for weights and measures); and to the socially anxious needing to check polite phrases and other rules of etiquette while moving through the parlor. They could be used to pass the time and show off one's erudition, as when a genial gentleman drew out his pocket Shakespeare to read aloud to his traveling

Figure 17. Handmade tin carrying box for Freedom Papers (certificate of freedom required by the state of Virginia), made by Joseph Trammell to be carried in a pocket, 1852.

companions. Abridgements and compilations became a predominant form; these books were not meant to be read but to be referenced. Pocket editions also suggested comforting physical limits—what you need to know or remember should be able to fit in the limited container you carry on your person.

AS MALE WEARERS distributed instruments of identity, measurement, faith, and vice across their bodies in a more or less organized fashion, the suit came to more closely resemble a cupboard or bureau with separate drawers—even locked or trick drawers—than a simple cloth covering. In France, furniture makers acknowledged the link between drawers and pockets when they added the *vide poche* (empty pocket) to the growing repertoire of specific furniture types of the eighteenth century. The *vide poche* was a piece of private bedroom furniture, usually a table with a deep rim around the top or a secret drawer underneath, on which or in which small objects taken from pockets could be placed at night.

Only a few asked whether all these pockets were necessary. In his immensely popular 1768 travel novel, *Sentimental Journey*, Laurence Sterne lampoons the well-equipped man who must now undertake pocket searches. Insisting that he is in possession of a certain letter, the narrator's serving man, La Fleur, performs a sort of pocket-patting pantomime, one that would become familiar over the next centuries. Because La Fleur does not want to disappoint the woman who has asked for the letter, or his employer (who should have by this time written the letter), or himself (why would he have agreed to work for a man who does not follow basic rules of politeness?), he sets about looking for it. "Oh yes," La Fleur responds to the expectant Madame L——, I have it right here, as he reaches first for the pockets on his left side, then "contrawise . . . then sought every pocket—pocket by pocket, round, not forgetting his fob." "*Peste!*" he exclaims. "*Diable!*" a moment later. "What thoughtlessness," he reproaches himself gamely when he surveys all the articles spread on the ground, minus the phantom letter.

Swift had less patience for this kind of rummaging. Whether undertaken by a hapless tourist or an ambitious merchant-adventurer, the search was evidence of a certain self-delusion. In *Gulliver's Travels*, the plethora of pockets in the three-piece suit reveals nothing so much as the traveler's overconfidence about his own preparedness. As the novel's hero travels beyond Lilliput, he gets into one scrape after another, often believing his pockets will come to the rescue. And while he is obsessively protective of them, he never actually has what he needs. The glasses that Gulliver hides in his "secret pocket" may help him see, but they rarely help him understand anything that he witnesses. Likewise, Gulliver's pocket compass never prevents him from getting lost. Nor does any potentially hostile stranger whom he encounters actually want the fake pearl trinkets with which he hopes he can "purchase [his] life." Pockets' multiplication, Swift concludes, had done nothing so much as result in a futile dependence on things. As a world-weary Gulliver complains when he finally returns safely back to England, "when I am at home and dressed as I ought to be, I carry on my Body the Workmanship of a Hundred Tradesmen." The suit, in Swift's estimation, was just as much an artifact of modernity as were the precision instruments commonly associated with the new and self-congratulatory rational age.

DIFFERENTLY POCKETED

WOMEN'S DRESS REMAINED unchanged in basic form as men's clothes underwent the radical transition to the suit. Women continued to wear some variation of the restricted bodice and full skirts that they had since the medieval era, and so a woman's dress did not appear, at first glance, to outfit her for adventurous travel. No pocket flap, for instance, to indicate that her gear stood at the ready. Yet for women in the eighteenth century, such distinctions mattered little. For a long period of time, women had perfectly serviceable methods of carrying what they needed. As they had done for centuries, women carried detachable containers, but starting in the mid-seventeenth century, instead of dangling a purse at mid-thigh from a cord attached to a belt, women brought the purse into closer proximity to the hand, adopting what historians call tie-on pockets. These pear-shaped pockets, either singletons or in pairs, were tied around the waist and lay flat at the hips. Worn under the skirt, tie-on pockets could be reached through a small opening in the overskirt. As Defoe's plucky con woman Moll Flanders remarks, a woman, too, could be "at home anywhere," that is, if she had money in her pocket.

In their history of women's tie-on pockets, Barbara Burman and Ariane Fennetaux have documented the ways women lavished attention on them. Tie-on pockets could be purchased premade but were often homemade; some were elaborately embroidered with patterns of flowers, and others were patched together out of scraps of fabric in ways that were nonetheless arresting (figure 18). Women gave them as gifts. Sewn for a friend or relative, they were often signed and dated. Yet all this care and work was not meant to be seen in public. The market and tradeswomen who sold various goods might keep their pockets over their skirts to have them readily accessible, but otherwise women wore pockets under the skirt, keeping them private. In dowries and washing lists, tie-on pockets were often categorized as underwear. Eighteenth-century scenes of undress demonstrate how they were worn. A caricature focused on the heroic efforts of two servants trying to tighten a woman's stays demonstrates a matching pocket tucked at the hip. The pocket rests snugly, easily accommodated in the folds of the petticoat (figure 19).

Tie-on pockets received hard use. That they frequently needed to be replaced is recorded in a hand-sewn diary made by Sally Bronsdson that lists the cast-offs and payments of clothing given to her between 1794 and 1800 by her Boston employer, Mrs. Davenport. In service to the Davenports from the age of fourteen, Bronsdson carefully recorded the "Clothes that I had of Mrs D," items that would have been considered part of the terms of her indenture. In 1794, Bronsdson lists twenty-two articles of everyday use, including gowns, chemises, a pair of shoes, a shawl, aprons, a straw hat, and "1 pocket." In her six years

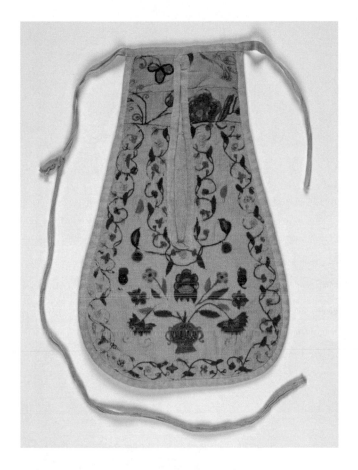

Figure 18. Tie-on pocket, eighteenth century. The maker appears to have mended the upper portion of the pocket, repurposing a piece of similarly patterned, embroidered linen.

with the Davenports, Bronsdson recorded receiving a total of eleven pockets, four "Old" and seven "New."

Tie-on pockets were far less secure than the pockets integrated into men's suits, and this was their major drawback. Lost and found advertisements include many rewards for lost pockets and detail their contents. Otherwise useful and perfectly convenient, women's tie-on pockets were nevertheless mocked by satirists. Caricature and pornographic renderings, for example, often linked women's tie-on pockets—womblike in shape with the very suggestive vertical slit outlined in ribbon—to female sexual anatomy. An illustration of a lascivious stays-maker who laces up his client while reaching into her pocket makes the point that tie-on pockets stood in for bodily spaces (figure 20).

Figure 19. *Tight Lacing, or Fashion before Ease*, by Bowles and Carver after John Collet, London, England, ca. 1770–1775.

Figure 20. Illustration by Thomas Sanders from Tim Bobbin's *Human Passions Delineated*, 1773. Women dressmakers had by this time gained professional recognition and claimed the right to produce women's and children's clothing. Stays (later called corsets) and riding gear, however, were still made by male tailors. As this satire makes clear, the male stay maker caused anxiety about the possibility of sexual liaisons between artisans and female customers.

More than their sexual suggestiveness, however, the ampleness of women's tie-on pockets garnered attention. Pockets that generally measured from twelve to twenty inches long and tended not to contain any further organizational compartments (although some did) allowed women to take advantage of the diversity of pocket-scale objects. Many of these objects were connected to domesticity: women often carried some kind of "housewife," a sewing kit that might include scissors, thimble, needle, and thread. But they also carried a range of items, from pocket knives to mementos, just as idiosyncratic as those of men. One Revolutionary War diarist in South Carolina complained that when her mother's pockets were forcibly searched during a raid, the looters took their entire contents, including sentimental treasures, two baby's caps, of value only to her mother.

Yet contemporary critics could not quite give up the notion that women's pockets constituted a repository of jumbled miscellany, a "dark closet" into which things disappeared, never again to see the light of day. Was there "no bottom to them"? asked a court officer at the Old Bailey in London, exasperated during a deposition concerning a theft. Such musings on the nature of women's tie-on pockets indicate the degree to which these containers had become something of a scapegoat, their scale and size inviting the very disorder that women were now accused of embracing. It is also possible that such expressions masked anxiety about this small but significant bit of privacy women had crafted for themselves. The rapacious rake, Lovelace, in Samuel Richardson's 1749 novel, *Clarissa*, desperately tries to access his quarry's pockets, hoping to discover intelligence in the letters Clarissa has written to a friend. But he despairs of finding what he seeks. A woman's pockets are "half as deep as she is high," he observes. Distracted from his plan, he remarks that pockets act like "ballast-bags" against women's long skirts in "full sail" on a high wind. Perhaps his real upset arises from the effectiveness of that ballast—the fact that women's ample pockets might act as a heavily guarded safe box for secrets.

Other critics emphasized the ways small-scale devices aided women's increasing forays into public spaces, highlighting the threatening potential of women's mobility. This observation was made in a 1750 narrative told from the point of view of a rented coat, which comments on the potentially subversive uses of notebooks in the hands of women. (Tales told by inanimate witnesses to human foibles enjoyed something of a literary boomlet at mid-century.) In this narrative, one lady, suffering from a "looseness of her soul," uses the type of notebook Jefferson so unproblematically carried for measurements to outline methods of romantic intrigue instead. In her pocket-scale ivory book, she jots down "a select number of extraordinary good *excuses* in case of *suspicion*, and some excellent *salvos* for *palpable discoveries*." In this case, readily available tools allowed women to maneuver successfully in a world that was constantly trying to limit their movement.

While women's tie-on pockets faced a degree of ridicule, any attempt by women to usurp masculine integrated pockets was met with outright hostility, most strikingly when women donned riding habits.

Riding large beasts with confidence and authority was more difficult in a dress, and women borrowed from the male wardrobe (usually the top half) for its greater ease of motion. Crafted by male tailors, this specialized sportswear resembled a suit coat and was worn over a matching skirt. In his 1688 proto-encyclopedia, Randle Holme included a definition of women's riding habits, remarking that the "long Coat buttoned down before like a Man's Jacket with Pocket-holes." Tailors had produced what could be called women's first power suit.

The outfit was immodest, even monstrous, complained Joseph Addison, writing in the London journal the *Spectator*. The two sexes appeared to have merged in this "amphibious" or "hermaphroditical" dress, he practically hyperventilated, although much of his upset came down to attitude. Witnessed along the highways, parading at Hyde Park, and even indoors at the gaming tables, these "female cavaliers" who "infected" the city with their presence strode about with "masculine assurance," remarked Addison. He was particularly incensed that one rider had insolently "cockaded her hat full in my face." Such masculine gestures were made on and off the horse. In 1712, an anonymous observer writing for the *Gentleman's Magazine* described a gaggle of young women chatting in an alcove. One of them openly yawned and flung her arms over her head while thrusting out her legs in order to "boldly lug out" her watch from the pocket of her riding habit "with a most officer like air." She enjoyed, in other words, the access pockets gave her to portable technology. (Women did not have built-in fob pockets in which to carry pocket watches and so wore watches like jewelry, around their neck or pinned to their dress by a chain.) Observing this vignette, the writer, his feathers clearly ruffled, concluded that when women are clad in their riding habits, "female delicacy is changed into masculine courage."

"Amazons" was the nickname that stuck to describe these apparently masculinized riders. To be dressed in a riding suit was to be, using the French lingo of fashion, *en tenue Amazone* (uniformed as an Amazon). For Richard Steele (Addison's journalist partner at the

Figure 21. Portrait of Mary of Modena when Duchess of York, by Simon Verelst, ca. 1675. The duchess wears a fashionable riding habit with a gaping pocket lined in pink silk.

Spectator), these riders who plunder our sexes' ornaments proved a symbolic threat to patriarchy. But for others the sight of a woman *en tenue Amazone* proved irresistibly attractive. Recognizing this allure, a number of elite women chose to have their portraits painted in their riding habits. The portrait of the seventeen-year-old Duchess of York, Mary of Modena, an accomplished horsewoman, represents such a riding habit along with a long man's wig, a magnificent cravat, and a whip (figure 21). The duchess is pictured in a pose of confidence and sly hauteur, holding her right arm akimbo, a gesture long associated with Renaissance kings and warriors. The painter deploys several cues, however, to confirm that the duchess's stance is but a slight tease. Not only does her waist narrow, but she thrusts forward a rounded right hip, emphasizing a welt pocket that gapes slightly open and is lined provocatively in pink silk. Men's welt pockets did not gape in late seventeenth-century portraiture and were often secured with buttons or displayed a finely woven handkerchief. The distorted pocket of this Amazon, in contrast, recalls her sex. Perhaps this delegitimization of the pocket of a power-suited woman was meant to indicate that the theft of men's clothes would be only temporary or at most playful and unthreatening.

Most efforts at masculine styling left no real question as to the sex of the wearer for very long, but cross-dressing occurred with regularity in, for example, "breeches parts" on the stage (figure 22). There were also occasions when cross-dressing to deceive was recognized as a useful strategy. Female warriors taking up arms to protect family or nation had been lauded in ballads and fiction in the seventeenth and eighteenth centuries. Women might also cross-dress for work if a male breadwinner became disabled. As Aphra Behn, one of the first British women to make a living from her writing, noted in a 1684 play, when a woman dressed in men's clothing, she enjoyed "a thousand little Privileges which otherwise wou'd have been denied to women."

Cross-dressing also aided in audacious escapes, and knowledge of the opposite sex's pocketing habits could mean the difference between a successful subterfuge and unwanted scrutiny. Harriet Jacobs attests to this in her autobiography, *Incidents in the Life of a Slave Girl*, which recounts her experiences during the 1840s in North Carolina. Before Jacobs could escape north, she moved between safehouses organized by friends and family wearing an outfit her friend

Figure 22. *An Actress at Her Toilet, or Miss Brazen Just Breecht*, by John Collet, 1779.

Betty was able to procure—a suit of sailor's clothes, "jacket, trowsers, and tarpaulin hat." Betty counsels Jacobs to put her hands in her pockets and to assume a sailor's "ricketty" walk. Betty approves Jacobs's impersonation, and as she moves through town, Jacobs recounts that she "passed several people whom [she] knew" undetected. "The father of my children," she explains, "came so near that I brushed against his arm."

Barring dire circumstances such as these, most women continued to tie their pockets under their skirts. One could say that women were not pocketless but differently pocketed. A change in fashion at the end of the eighteenth century, however, would ultimately threaten the tie-on pocket's existence. And only at that point would differences in pocketing begin to have more noticeable effects.

POCKET MONOPOLIES

SINCE THE SUIT'S introduction, men have held tight to their pockets and refused to relinquish them. They've lauded themselves as a group for refusing to suffer any embarrassments caused by that "fool" named fashion. When, for example, the mode for suit coats narrowed in the 1770s and young men about town hoped to emphasize a very long, lean silhouette, front flap pockets were dispensed with for a time. But tailors quickly made up for this loss, inserting an interior breast coat pocket that was secure and since that time has become a conventional member of the suit's pocket repertoire. It seemed to one nineteenth-century commentator that men insisted on first principles, on functionality and convenience in their dress, and that tailors complied. Evidence of that pact was apparent in pocketing: it appeared that "the man's pockets remain alike in size, shape and position, while the clothes change around them."

The sense that the conventions for men's pockets were stable and assured was confirmed in the first decades of the nineteenth century, when the men's garment industry took steps to modernize the process of clothing manufacture. The suit became even more standardized as the ready-made industry (formerly involved in selling low-quality slops) upped its game and began to produce moderate quality suits for all budgets. Whereas in 1824 one David Clapp, a printer's apprentice, devoted more than two-thirds of his income to a new suit, several shirts, an overcoat, a hat, pantaloons, and a vest, by 1850, he could walk into one of the ready-made "emporiums" like Brooks Brothers and purchase cheap, off-the-rack versions without having to make incredible sacrifices for a respectable appearance. Merchant tailors in the custom trade who crafted more expensive made-to-measure suits also took up the ready-made industry's recent innovations: tailors employed tools like the tape measure, invented in the 1820s, and more nuanced understandings of typical body proportions to obviate the need for, and the time and expense of, numerous fittings. In general, this burst of productivity meant that amateurishly sewn suits were a thing of the past. By the mid-nineteenth century, one was far less likely to encounter misaligned pockets or "a coat, without pockets or flaps." System and predictability replaced variety—and that included in pocket offerings.

Through this process of rationalization, it seemed that men had acquired what the humorist William Livingstone Alden, in an 1877 satire, dubbed a "pocket monopoly." Rather than acknowledge the success of ready-mades, however, Alden reiterated the notion that men had acquired their monopoly through natural inheritance. Responding to Carlyle's still widely remarked upon notion that humans wear clothing to compensate for the lack of marsupial pouches, Alden observed that people had come to consider pockets themselves as some sort of biological given. They were, in his satire, an element of dress that even more so than reproductive organs or facial hair distinguished man from woman. Taking on the neutral air of the scientist, Alden observed that pockets developed slowly, perfectly tracking a child's physical maturation. At about the age of five, trouser pockets sprouted in the male child of the human species. From there the boy gradually acquired coat, waistcoat, and fob pockets, while the arrival of pistol pockets (back trouser pockets) was delayed until the cutting of the wisdom teeth. Thus prepared by nature to carry guns and money and other tools "essential to civilization," he must be meant to deploy them.

Figure 23. *A Boy's First Trousers*, from *Peterson's Magazine*, 1860.

Alden turned to consider women's condition in this scenario. "Emulous" of men, women "boldly claim that the mysterious and unseen bags which they carry concealed about their persons are virtually pockets." But Alden playfully rejected such a notion. "Comparative anatomists," he pointed out, called tie-on pockets "plainly artificial and extraneous." Perhaps, Alden winks at his reader, nature herself suggest that "women are not designed to become the military or civil leaders of mankind."

Although Alden was joking, he exaggerates what was evidently true. Boys did recognize the acquisition of pockets as a privilege of approaching adulthood, a privilege young girls did not expect to enjoy. As depicted in an 1860 illustration for *Peterson's Magazine*, the metamorphosis involved testing out guises of power the boy would eventually grow into (figure 23). The young lad who tries on his first trousers plants his legs far apart while practicing that swagger that pockets allow him. Even if the show is only for his puppy, the implication is that he will lord over others as maturity permits. Via clothing he learns about the rights and expectations of manhood. As a writer observed in an 1894 issue of *Harper's Bazaar*, her son—his pockets "crammed to bursting" with objects of every description—was bestowed at an early age with the security of being well-equipped. A boy's pockets, she wrote, "are his certificate of empire. All through life, he will carry his scepter of dominion by the right of his pockets."

Men broadcasted their dominion with pockets that served both utilitarian and symbolic functions, taking pride in all the organizational capacity their pockets provided. In the long run, as they transitioned from a craft to an industrialized product, inset containers stitched throughout the suit have prepared men for public roles and private diversions. "I have only praise for my clothes," wrote the Viennese architect and sometimes fashion journalist Adolf Loos at the turn of the twentieth century, in an essay considering the three-piece suit. By that time, the form seemed to have "always been with us." Blithely ignoring Swift's caricature of Gulliver, Loos asserted that the "primeval dress" of men "is the dress of the self-reliant."

Homme de qualité en habit garny d'agrémens

Figure 1. *Homme de qualité en habit de garni d'agréments*, by Jean Dieu de Saint-Jean, 1683. Dressed in a casual suit without a waistcoat, the relaxed courtier depicted in this French fashion plate holds one hand in his breeches pocket, an early example of the familiar hands-in-pockets attitude.

CHAPTER 3

Pocket Attitudes:
"But What Do Your Hands *Do*
in Your Pocket?"

Since tailors first added accessible pockets into the breeches of the three-piece suit, hands have found their way into them (figure 1). Sometimes merely stowed and at others emphatically thrust there, hands seem to have a special affinity for pockets. On this affinity, just about everyone agrees.

Whether placing hands in pockets should be allowed in polite company, however, has been far more contentious. Should the man who puts his hands into his pantaloons while he saunters down the street be considered a graceful idler or an uncouth boor? Here, responses have been split, and for several centuries at least, the naysayers were the more vociferous. As Kitty Delicate, an indignant "lady," complains in an 1802 letter to a Philadelphia newspaper, the attitude amounted to "an *indelicate* fashion . . . universally adopted by those vile creatures, *men*."

If it was unfair to call out all men, it was true that the hands-in-pockets attitude was limited to them. Only men wore breeches or, when they became the mode after the French Revolution, trousers.

Insisting they enjoy exclusive rights to trousers and unrestricted access to them, some men ignored the imperative to "take your hands out of your pockets!" The recalcitrant included those who just could not help it: the awkward fellows for whom pockets acted as a refuge or shelter, a place to hide their nervousness. Others seemed more actively defiant, and over the course of the eighteenth and nineteenth centuries these "revolters against propriety" used their pockets to strike provocative poses. Ranging from cool hauteur to careless nonchalance, achieving such inflections depended upon the angle at which one drew one's hips and the degree to which one relaxed one's spine. The more languorous the overall stance, the better.

Such small revolts are part of what gives fashion, with its propensity to "mock" the proprieties and "moral pretensions of the dominant culture," its energy and subversive edge, historian Elizabeth Wilson observes. Yet to this day, long after the retreat of formal deportment, putting hands in pockets remains a pose assumed by debonair sophisticates, troubled loners, and hipster wannabes alike, and employed in fashion spreads, advertising, and various forms of self-promotion. What makes the gesture so expressive? And what explains its continued allure? Gesture is among the most elusive of historic topics, so fleeting that it is difficult to recover a sense of the ways people have held their bodies, indicating their ease or discomfort. The hullabaloo over the flippant and swaggering attitudes of men, however, makes tracing this particular "bad habit" possible—and tells us a lot about pockets themselves. While commonly regarded as useful containers for the stuff we carry about, as harbors for the hands, pockets fulfill their most surprising functions.

HE CARRIES HIS HANDS IN HIS POCKETS "JUST SO"

SUSPICION OVER HANDS preceded the arrival of pockets and had to do with their promiscuous explorations of self and the world. People's inclination to use their hands to tend to their bodies, in particular, inspired the very first etiquette guides to pay special attention to them. Hoping to instill a new and far-reaching kind of self-consciousness about how to act and behave, these texts admonished readers not to pick or scratch or hunt for irritants like lice. One 1460 guide offered particularly frank advice: "Put not your hands in your hose, your codware for to claw." (*Codware*, like *cod*, was medieval-era slang for scrotum.) Such cautions against "clawing" seem sensible considering that they were directed toward young pages, whose duties included serving food at the dinner table. Yet the tone of such advice grew almost paranoid, especially as it was elaborated by Giovanni Della Casa in his influential 1558 book of manners, *Il Galateo*.

At the beginning of his treatise, Della Casa was concerned with demonstrating that acquiring good manners, and the resulting social skills and prestige, was not a matter of merely avoiding a list of forbidden behaviors. One had to understand the nuanced messages that the body might convey. Gesture, he argued, separates "pleasing" from "unappealing" acts. In the category of behavior to be avoided was every word or conversation that "brings to mind unpleasant matters" and any movement that evokes the "dirty, foul, repulsive or disgusting." After concluding his preamble, Della Casa then invoked his first rule, a precept that regards the hands: "It is an indecent habit practiced by some people, who, in full view of others, place their hands on whatever part of their body it pleases them." One wonders precisely what he meant—he included this suggestion before a host of other behaviors that might seem more evidently rude. Della Casa's sensitivity to hands was nevertheless so acute that he returned to them several times in the book, noting that even hand washing in view of others after returning to the table from urinating should be avoided, because *the reason* for washing would be clear to onlookers.

And what reasons did men have to put their hands in their pockets? This was the operative question and one that would continue to be debated long after Della Casa thought he had settled the matter. In Jean Racine's 1668 comedy, *The Litigants*, a lawyer who is preparing his client for trial has some difficulty with his coaching. Despairing of producing an acceptable witness, he asks, "But what do your hands *do* in your pocket?" Like the lawyer, we tend to imagine the worst in such situations as our minds travel low, linking pocketed hands to masturbation and to licentious desire. William Hogarth does just that in his depiction of the lecherous gentleman who ogles Moll and the other women who have come to the city, apparently to be led into a life of prostitution (figure 2); the gentleman's leer is as suggestive as his pocketed hand. Much of the insistence on carefully monitoring the hands can be traced to a desire to avoid any suggestion of the untoward, that is, to Della Casa's belief that the hand's projected path was as meaningful as any other discernable motion. By the eighteenth century, etiquette manuals specifically mentioned pockets and included reaching into them in their lists of behaviors to be avoided. Only "vulgar Boys" dared "thrust" their hands into their pockets, warned the compiler of a 1758 etiquette guide.

Civilized boys, in contrast, knew not to use any gesture that signaled their animal appetites for food, sex, or violence, and replaced open expression with restraint and self-control. Making open reference to the body was not only "ungenteel," as Kitty Delicate objected in her 1802 letter, but was "adopted by the very lowest class of people." Delicate's letter was addressed to Samuel Saunter, a pseudonym for the *Port-Folio* editor Joseph Dennie, whose long-running American Lounger series took up "the fleeting topics and manners of the day." In printing the letter, Dennie chided Delicate for her concern about men's deportment, highlighting the writer's inconsistencies. Was this habit of "stuffing" hands into breeches "before ladies" really practiced only by the lower classes, as Kitty Delicate charged? If so, how could it be a universal or fashionable practice? She could not have it both ways, relegating *all* men to the category of the "vile."

Delicate's contradictory position reflected larger cultural concerns over what constituted a fashionable attitude. Manners were supposed to separate the elite from the "rude rustik," yet here were gentleman

Figure 2. *A Harlot's Progress*, plate 1, by William Hogarth, 1732. A notorious procuress and brothel-keeper welcomes young Moll to the city, hoping to induce her into a life of prostitution. The gentleman in the doorway holds one hand in his pocket, eyeing Moll, as well as the other women sitting in the carriage, expectantly.

making a show of cramming their hands into their pockets as they entered the ballroom. Dennie disregarded all of Delicate's many objections, and as editor, he had the last word. All this worrying over the hand's whereabouts, he seemed to scoff, was—reflecting the letter writer's pseudonym—overly delicate.

From Dennie's point of view, there was nothing offensive about the hands-in-pockets attitude. Dennie, aka Saunter, bragged that he had "formed himself upon the model of some of the fashionably *nonchalant*," by which he seemed to mean all those idlers with aristocratic pretensions who made a show of doing nothing rather beautifully. These men had every reason to consider putting their hands in their breeches' pockets to be an elegant gesture, as the attitude could be traced to early courtiers who first embraced the three-piece suit. Courtiers ignored the

Figure 3. *Portrait of William Shirley*, by Thomas Hudson, 1750. Long before Napoleon Bonaparte was pictured with his hand in his waistcoat, other men who sat for portraits did the same.

idea that hands should always be visible, demonstrating how consistent rules of etiquette came into conflict with material possibility. New clothes invite and even compel new ways of holding one's body: one overlooked effect of the way coat and waistcoat are layered over one another and button down the center front was the suit's accessibility.

The most common of the hand-in gestures was to tuck one's right hand into the waistcoat, which would be casually unbuttoned to the belly. By the 1680s, this hand-in-waistcoat pose surfaced in engravings and fashion prints depicting the casual but elegant entertainments in the court of the Sun King, Louis XIV. Standing about, enduring a reception or ceremony, was a physical accomplishment, much like bowing or retiring gracefully from a room. The act required considered strategy, and courtiers came to rely on the advice of the professional dance masters, whose remit had grown beyond dance steps to choreographing the small but important movements of the everyday. In order to stand firm "yet easy and without Affectation," dance masters advised gentleman to withdraw one hand into the waistcoat. In a pose promulgated by fashionable people and upheld by professionals, the aristocrat standing at his ease appeared as if he had wrapped himself in a loose embrace. In Britain, painters seized on the hand-in-waistcoat gesture as a popular portrait formula, believing it depicted qualities of modesty and reserve (figure 3).

Men did not confine their hands to their waistcoats, however, and soon found their breeches' pockets. Especially as ceremony at court began to wane in the last years of Louis XIV's rule, it was considered more attractive to demonstrate some independence from all that rigorous training, and courtiers led the way, modeling what would become an eighteenth-century ideal of casual effortlessness that spread across the channel. As Addison noted in the *Spectator* in 1711, "the fashionable world is grown free and easy; Our manners sit more loose upon us. Nothing is so modish as an agreeable negligence."

During the first decades after the suit's introduction, Anglo-American commentators linked the hand-in-pocket attitude to the French courtier and his imitators, and critiqued it for being too slick. Soon, this attitude served as a shorthand for identifying a new urban type, fops and beaux on the make who followed preening French fashions. Spoofs of London life included detailed descriptions of the deportment of these aspiring men. In one sketch, an observer spied a "fellow Powder'd from Top to Toe, his Hands in his Pocket, *à la Mode de Paris*, humming a new Minuet." George Farquhar's 1707 romantic comedy, *The Beaux Stratagem*, included stage instructions that the young beau working a scheme to hoodwink marriageable heiresses should "[walk] in a French air." The beau, notes a bemused observer, "carries his hands in his pockets, and walks just so." In these accounts of early

Figure 4. *Print Shop*, by J. Elwood, 1790. A crowd gathers to view caricatures of widely recognized social types, including the macaroni.

eighteenth-century life, this attitude had nothing to do with unschooled rudeness and everything to do with following *la mode de Paris*.

The hand-in-pocket attitude's link to the elite is further suggested by late eighteenth-century British caricature, which included a surprisingly large number of prints depicting macaroni with pocketed hands. The macaroni were a conspicuous subculture of young men who had picked up the affected fashions and manners of foreign courts during their Grand Tours of the continent, taking their name from a dish they had tasted in Italy. Ever on the lookout to deflate "French airs," caricaturists, who posted their wares in windows for passersby to see, hit a chord with their depictions of these men (figure 4). They were drawn wearing outrageously tall powdered wigs and colorful silk suits, and they seemed to spend an inordinate amount of time in the boudoir looking in mirrors. When the Yankee Doodle Dandy of the British colonies stuck a feather in his cap (and called it macaroni), he too attempted to imitate their fashion sense.

Besides ridiculing Francophile looks, the caricaturists lampooned the macaroni's artifice in posture and affect. In a 1772 print titled *How D'ye Like Me*, such a figure points his toe in ballet's fourth position, suggesting that he had been under the tutelage of a French dancing master (figure 5). He manages aristocratic accessories, including a hat tucked at his elbow and a sword hanging behind his hip. The artist, however, seems especially intent on lampooning the widely decried sexual profligacy of the courtier, using visual plays on body parts and clothes to indicate the macaroni's suspect sexuality: the macaroni's loose breeches imply the folds of the vulva, while the phallic sword hung diagonally across his rear is notably decorated with elaborate ribbons and tassels. This confusion of parts indicates the figure's connection to the hermaphrodite (a term often used in this period to label men who engaged in same-sex sexual activity). Most evocatively, the figure has deliberately slid his hand into a gaping breeches pocket. That the pocket has no very precise bodily analog does not seem to matter; the hand-in-pocket attitude at the very least helps exaggerate the figure's unrestrained impulses and sexual excesses.

The hand-in-pocket attitude was not associated exclusively with maca-ronis or people who might today iden-tify as queer. Satirists taking a broad view of men's foibles used it to high-light any vain display that employed sexual posturing. Female critics, who had begun to contribute to a lively press culture, also attempted to punc-ture that vanity with notably barbed quips. An 1810 article published in an American women's magazine, the *Lady's Miscellany*, objected that men appeared to undress in public as they reached for their pockets:

Figure 5. *How D'ye Like Me*, 1772.

It is but too common, whenever a man of fashion meets a lady in his walk, as soon as he has addressed her, for him to unbutton, if not done before, one side of the fall of his small-clothes [breeches], put his hand into his pocket, and standing on one leg, with the other swinging about, enter into conversation.

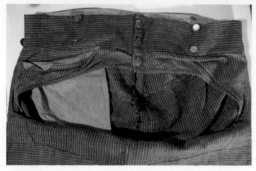

Figure 6. "Full falls" breeches. The "falls," or front flap, could be unbuttoned (breeches did not have a center fly).

Eighteenth- and early nineteenth-century breeches did not have a center fly but instead buttoned up across the waist band. To access a pocket set in a front panel across the hips (rather than at a side seam as in modern trousers), men might unbutton one or two buttons of their breeches, seeming to strip (figure 6). In an 1803 letter to the *Philadelphia Repository*, a writer taking the pen name Ann Lively charged that the "beaux of Philadelphia" meant to cause a stir; they were intent on drawing attention to themselves by "shewing their fine persons." The first thing they did upon entering a room was to "seize hold of their breeches . . . chattering and grinning, buttoning, and unbuttoning, unbuttoning and buttoning again."

Men who brazenly fiddled with their breeches alluded to the desired outcome of a flirtation, putting the "lady of modesty . . . to the blush." Like the letch depicted by Hogarth, the man in a 1778 print, *The Beauties of Bagnigge Wells*, cruises the female prostitutes of a popular park and strolling avenue in London known for such assignations. He telegraphs his intent via his preoccupied hands (figure 7). The young man's invitation is explicit, while the female prostitute crosses her arms, considering. The same gesture might shift the tenor of the most delicate of courting rituals. While at first glance the couple in an 1808 French fashion plate seem to be strolling demurely, viewers know the amorous content of the "mysterious conversation" of the plate's title (figure 8). As they walk in close proximity, her dress is pulled by the pressure of their touching hips, and his hand bulges in his pocket.

"SWINGING ABOUT" IN conversation with a lady with one's hands deeply buried in one's pockets also established that one intended to ignore the imperative to be polite. Overt references to sex, something that had been lampooned as self-involved in the macaroni caricatures, came to be seen as oppositional in the revolutionary era of the late eighteenth century. The young fellow who walks into the coffee house and, with a defiant look, "gropes his breeches with a monarch's air," as one incensed observer put it, understood this principle. Expressing freedom from social obligations and restraint was one way for young people to assert their status, especially in public gathering places where men vied with other men for influence. As we were reminded again in the #MeToo era, masculine prestige often relishes such flagrant expressions of bad behavior.

The insight that a man's position depended to some extent on his bodily attitude and the kinds of poses he could master marked a major shift. For as long as anyone could remember, rank had been recognizable at a glance, and deference to one's "superiors" was required. Figuring out if you had to doff your hat or give way to a passerby on the street, or in what order you could sit at the dinner table, depended on knowing your relative status and correctly identifying any person of "greater quality" in a gathering. As rigid social hierarchies began to crumble, however, navigating the social scene caused great confusion. Many looked for help, consulting the Earl of Chesterfield's extremely

Figure 7. *The Beauties of Bagnigge Wells*, 1778.

Figure 8. *Conversation misterieuse,* by Philibert-Louis Debucourt,
plate 50 in *Modes et Manières du Jour,* 1808.

influential etiquette guide. In it, the British aristocrat explored in vivid terms the unstated rules at work in the ruthlessly competitive arena of the drawing room.

Chesterfield's guide began as a series of private letters to his illegitimate son, later collected and published. Hoping to ease his son's path as he traveled around the courts of Europe, Chesterfield sent off anxious missives, reminding him about everything from his clothes to how to make conversation. He emphasized that it was important to play it cool, to indicate one's composure and self-assurance, when in the company of others. To avoid losing ground in the social pecking order, it was imperative to demonstrate that you were "not dazzled" by anyone in a position of power. How many men have I seen, Chesterfield confided, who "trembled" in the presence of superiors? Trembling was not just embarrassing from Chesterfield's point of view but resulted in a kind of social "annihilation" from which one might never recover. The ability to demonstrate one's refusal to be dazzled centered on the body— one needed to appear relaxed and unruffled, to hit on that "extremely engaging . . . easiness of carriage and behavior."

Chesterfield cautioned that it was easy to take shows of indifference too far. (You should not "loosen your garters" and "lie down upon a couch," Chesterfield admonished.) Once engaged in the high-stakes game of impression management, though, many a young man erred in this direction. What better way to demonstrate your confidence than to establish that you could manipulate your clothes to your own advantage—to loosen your garters and show that you were undeniably the "proprietor" of your clothes and not their "prisoner"? So much plays out in a 1797 comedy of manners, *The Heir at Law*. After coming into an unexpected inheritance, young Dick Dowlas tells his father that he knows how to move in his newly acquired fine clothing: "slouch is the word, now, you know." The fictional Dowlas, like the editor of the Philadelphia *Port-Folio*, Joseph Dennie, comes from humble origins. He too has modeled himself on the "fashionably nonchalant," in Dowlas's case, the self-made dandies and fops he has seen strutting along Bond Street in London, men who claimed an elevated social position based solely on superior style. Dowlas has confidence that he can pull off the look, knowing that "lounging lazily along" with his hands "cramm'd" into his pockets designates him as up to date, as "quite the dandy" (figure 9). As he explains to his doubtful parent: "That's the fashion, father; that's modern ease."

CRAFTING "MODERN EASE" FOR DEMOCRATS: WHITMAN AND THE LOAFERS

THE ARISTOCRATIC CARRIAGE of dandies and fops, although long admired, became increasingly suspect by the early decades of the nineteenth century—especially in the newly minted and fiercely egalitarian United States. Any attempt to put on "airs" was "laughed at," as the "silver-forkishness of pretenders," James Fenimore Cooper noted in an 1830 essay on American deportment. In trying to devise what *The Perfect Gentleman* in 1860 called "an American code," one that acknowledged the promise of democratic access to public life while rejecting outright pompousness, predominantly middle-class authors of a new spate of etiquette guides attempted to school a nation of immigrants on how to act and behave. They argued that Americans should not preen in the positions so favored by the dancing masters, and instead should replace affectation with undemonstrative sobriety. The grave figure depicted on the title page of *The Young Man's Guide to Knowledge, Virtue, and Happiness* has taken this advice to heart: he has rejected the languor of the earlier fop or dandy (figure 10). He is erect and holds his hand in his waistcoat, very deliberately borrowing the gesture of the restrained eighteenth-century gentleman.

Many men, however, continued to experiment with careless and otherwise "negligent guises." And no figures did so more appealingly than the loafers. The term *loafer*, widely believed to be an Americanism, was coined in the 1830s and encompassed a wide variety of social

A FASHIONABLE FOP.

Figure 9. *A Fashionable Fop*, 1816. The fop ambles out of a textile or tailoring establishment. Like the dandy, a consummate consumer, he knew how to "regulate his hands and gait after the fashion of the glories around him."

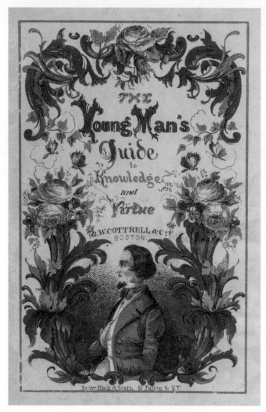

Figure 10. Title page illustration from Frank Fergurson's *The Young Man's Guide to Knowledge, Virtue, and Happiness*, 1853. The young man of "virtue" is the model of middle-class respectability and self-control with his hand in his waistcoat.

types, from the dock loafer to the literary loafer, loosely grouped together by nineteenth-century observers for their nonconformist sensibility. But it was the loafers' most influential proponent, Walt Whitman, who managed a notable feat when he demonstrated that one could channel the careless grandeur of the aristocrat, and something of his authority and presence, without being ridiculed for acting like him, with silver-forkish pretention. From the attraction of loaferism—and from the way that Whitman co-opted and transformed his gestures—came twentieth-century variants of the insouciant hand-in-pocket attitude.

LOAFERS WERE INITIALLY associated with the down-and-out. During his travels in the United States, Charles Dickens complained of the two or three half-drunken loafers who inevitably came "loitering out with their hands in their pockets" during stagecoach changes. Dickens had in mind the loafer who holds both hands in pockets and slumps in dejection, as does educationalist George Caleb Bingham's *Village Character* (figure 11). This version of the hand-in-pocket attitude clearly marked untutored country people and was also typically used in popular illustrations to indicate unsavory urban figures: drunks, failed businessmen, and shady characters who lurked on street corners.

Not all loafers slouched in dejection and failure, however. The illustration of a loafer who unconcernedly leans against a post held some intrigue for middle-class observers, who recognized in him a certain kind of admirable dignity (figure 12). Such loafers stood apart.

One journalist sensed something "glorious" in the hostility and contempt the loafer shows a world that has rejected him, something romantic about his degree of "go-to-hell-impudence." His attitude seemed to take direct aim at a culture that celebrated the ambitious, striving world of self-improvement and industry promulgated by the likes of Benjamin Franklin. Whitman very clearly aligned himself with this refusal, writing in the opening lines of his landmark book of poetry, *Leaves of Grass*, "I lean and loafe at my ease . . . observing a spear of summer grass."

Whitman also demonstrated just what the glorious hostility of the loafer might look like (figure 13). The famous frontispiece image in *Leaves of Grass* came about serendipitously. One hot July day in 1854 Whitman sauntered down the street in his work clothes—canvas trousers and shirtsleeves, formalized by neither vest nor suit coat. He worked as a carpenter with his father and brothers that year, taking a break from journalism, sometimes showing up to plane and hammer, other times simply wandering off to daydream and write. Spying the carpenter-bard while watching the passersby from the door of his Brooklyn photography studio, Gabriel Harrison called out to his friend. "Come!" he said, inviting Whitman into his shop. "I'm dying for something to do." The product of Harrison's boredom and Whitman's willingness to be diverted, the resulting portrait would end up being iconic—a treasured image of a successful American rebel.

Figure 11. *Village Character,* by George Caleb Bingham, 1847.

Figure 12. *The Loafer,* from *Prisoner's Friend,* 1847.

Figure 13. Portrait of Walt Whitman, used as the frontispiece to the first edition of Whitman's *Leaves of Grass*, engraved by Samuel Hollyer after a daguerreotype by Gabriel Harrison, 1855.

Whitman loved the resulting image: "It is natural, honest, easy: as spontaneous as you are, as I am, this instant, as we talk together." Harrison's daguerreotype was later engraved, and for the remainder of his life, Whitman used some form of it in every edition of *Leaves of Grass*. Whitman did not include his name in the front matter of the book. Readers were instead confronted with a frontispiece portrait unlike any other. What he later called the street figure appears to have been captured in an outside setting, as his hat is still on. The image centers on Whitman's torso, presenting the poet as an earthy, working everyman, "disorderly, fleshy and sensual," as Whitman described it. Rather than stand upright, Whitman tips hat, eyebrow, and hips at a similar rakish angle, letting his weight fall unevenly. He holds one arm akimbo and thrusts the other hand "lazily into his pocket." A paragon of self-assurance, he balances a thoughtful intensity with a barely restrained sexuality.

Figure 14. Portrait of Ralph Waldo Emerson, by Elliott and Fry, 1873. Emerson's is the expected author photograph.

Yet even Whitman experienced moments of self-doubt, worrying that the portrait could be misinterpreted and that he had set the wrong tone. He regretted its provocation. According to Whitman, it looked as if he were "saying defiantly, to hell with you!" Early readers and reviewers agreed. They found the portrait disturbing and in some critical way distasteful. Typical was the pronouncement of a *London Critic* reviewer: "The man is the true impersonation of his book—rough, uncouth, vulgar." As Whitman recalled, "War was waged on it. It passed through a great fire of criticism." The persona evoked by Whitman's hand-in-pocket pose was nowhere near the refined literary one represented in a later photograph of his enthusiastic supporter Ralph Waldo Emerson, who admitted that he read *Leaves of Grass* despite an "unpromising frontispiece portrait" (figure 14).

To contemporary twenty-first-century observers, Whitman's frontispiece portrait feels familiar, and it is the Victorian sitters in their

Figure 15. A "Bowery Boy," Sketched from the Life, published in *Frank Leslie's Illustrated Newspaper*, July 18, 1857.

respectable uprightness who seem slightly alien. How did Whitman pull off this prescient bit of cultural readjustment? While Whitman suggested there was nothing very considered about his self-presentation, it does seem he engaged in some strategic and very democratic borrowing. As critics and he himself noted, Whitman had rejected the staid posture of the refined gentleman. He held himself much more loosely, aligning himself with the loafers, streetwise toughs, rowdies, and "Bowery Boys," cult figures of working-class culture (who, as the nickname suggested, hung out around the Bowery neighborhood of lower Manhattan). Like the Bowery Boy depicted in *Frank Leslie's Illustrated Newspaper*, Whitman emphasizes his earthy physicality with his pocketed hand (figure 15). Evidence suggests Whitman actively worked to illustrate the sexualized persona he presented in his poetry. In what had long been a mystery, the "one or two trifling alterations" to the original engraved portrait that Whitman requested during the first printing were centered on accentuating the bulge in Whitman's pants. The desired increase reflects Whitman's claim that he indeed was "one good shaped and well hung man."

While Whitman embraced what was sexually provocative and intriguing about the Bowery Boys, they were not the only source for his frontispiece portrait. As he demonstrated in different ways in *Leaves of Grass*, Whitman explicitly sought "to find a new unthought-of nonchalance with the best of Nature!" With his nonpocketed hand, Whitman does not make a threatening fist. His entire postural stance is more relaxed than that of the Bowery Boy; his hip juts not with aggressiveness but with a kind of lolling ease that recalls Greek standing nudes like *The Leaning Satyr* (figure 16). Bringing the rough into

Figure 16. *Anapauomenos* (*Leaning Satyr*), usually attributed to Praxiteles. A Roman copy of a Greek original from the fourth century BC.

conversation with ideal beauty was one way to model alternative modes of grace, something mid-century etiquette guides supported. Since the court had been discredited and the dance master was now blamed for advancing an effeminate posture, perhaps it was "in the unconscious statues of the old Greeks" where one could discover "the true bearing of a gentleman," surmised the 1860 *Illustrated Manners Book*.

Other sources for apparently "unconscious" poses existed much closer to home in time and place. Children had not yet learned the manners inherited from the courts and promulgated by traditionalists. Boys, especially, had trouble mastering the rules; impertinent and unruly, boys' supposed freedom from restraint was celebrated throughout Anglo-American culture, as their autonomy and confidence came to signal the health of the nation. Eastman Johnson's 1860 *The Barefoot Boy* (which Louis Prang adapted into one of his best-selling popular prints) is typical (figure 17). The child is oblivious of the very social expectations Whitman aimed to forget in his life as in his poetry. As Whitman admitted, he hoped to "[drop] disguise and ceremony, and walk forth with the confidence and gayety of a child."

Tellingly, these are the very terms Whitman had used in his appraisal of his frontispiece

Figure 17. *Whittier's Barefooted Boy*, printed by L. Prang and Company after Eastman Johnson and based on a poem by John Greenleaf Whittier, ca. 1868.

portrait as "honest, easy and spontaneous." Whitman's attitude seems natural and spontaneous in part because of its evident rudeness, the key sticking point for upholders of middle-class respectability. Do not "abandon" yourself "to the fate of a loafer," etiquette guides warned with increasing urgency as it became clear that here was "a style in all respects remarkable, picturesque, and with a certain air of careless grandeur." In the face of these earnest warnings, Whitman and the loafers nevertheless managed to make the case that loafer style was worthy of both admiration and imitation. Through his reference to the Greeks and to the "confidence and gayety" of children, Whitman crafted a modern ease for democrats. With his hand in his pocket, one could say he is "nature's aristocrat."

FASHIONABLE ATTITUDES IN THE MODERN ERA

ALARM ABOUT THE hands' placement, inherited from sticklers like Della Casa, had considerable staying power. Anxious mothers and school-masters stitched boys' trouser pockets closed to prevent them from the "trick of putting their hands into them" through the end of the nineteenth century. At the British boarding school Harrow in 1895, all boys' pockets were still sewn up, something James Joyce referred to when, in his 1916 *The Portrait of the Artist as a Young Man*, Stephen "carried his arms stiffly at his sides like a runner and never in his pockets." But as the Victorian period drew to a close, it seems that everyone let out a collective sigh of relief, and the absence of formality that Whitman and the loafers had so joyfully modeled gradually took hold. People wore less restrictive clothing, sprawled across the new, overstuffed easy chairs, and "strode" rather than "glided" across the dance floor as if on a golf course, complained the doyenne of twentieth-century American etiquette, Emily Post, in 1922. And while gentlemen hung about the drawing room chatting in mixed company, more and more of them had their hands in their pockets. Rearguard upholders of tradition warned gentlemen to forego this "obnoxious habit." But despite the warnings, a growing number of men affiliated with neither the loafers nor bohemian circles came to rely on the gesture to look fashionably at ease.

It was at this time that some jealousy surfaced. Women began to ask why this attitude of "slangy nonchalance" was unavailable to them. Strutting young fellows were not "nature's aristocrats"; they relied on gendered clothing traditions, which until then had *seemed* natural. Unless they donned trousers, ladies would remain unable to achieve a similar effortless ease.

Demonstrating that the hand-in-pocket gesture relied particularly on the features of masculine dress, three young "fellows" from White River Junction, Vermont, posed for the camera in an 1890 photograph (figure 18). Perhaps commemorating their masculine roles in a collegiate or amateur theatrical, the friends spoof the clothing and mien of young masculine types. With breezy aplomb, they pose in ways that seem less imitative than simply automatic. The women who stand on either side of the faux tree stump hike their legs up onto it. Each finds a pocket and slides her hand in. With their cross-dressing, these women gained access to an arrogant sensibility difficult to achieve when corseted and dressed in the full-length, usually pocketless skirts of the 1890s. These cross-dressers' evident delight arises

Figure 18. *Fellows*, cabinet card, White River Junction, Vermont, ca. 1890. Three women pose for the camera wearing pants.

Lead Pocket Eggs

Figure 19. "Lead Pocket Eggs," by Jonathan Bonner, part of the series *Front Pockets*, 1999.

not from getting to wear the pants but from the poses and attitudes discovered once in them, indicating that the hands-in-pockets attitude was too useful to remain free from female poaching. Many a young woman wanted to "strut down the avenue with her hands in her pockets, just like her brother," as the *New York Tribune* reflected in 1913.

WHILE THE HANDS-IN-POCKETS attitude is no longer called out as the "indelicate fashion" of men, still, people have remarked on its indelicacy into our own period. The relationship between hands, pockets, and genitals continues to give us pause on occasion, a phenomenon the sculptor Jonathan Bonner demonstrates in his deadpan work of 1999, *Front Pockets* (figure 19). In the series, Bonner crafted pairs of functional-looking but whimsical objects that, he explained, were "made to be carried in the front pockets of your trousers." These imaginary

products were meant to discomfit their owners, like Pocket Air Bags that pump up and expand and Ice Pocket Mounds that cause an embarrassing melt. In the accompanying photographs that document these tools in use, Bonner emphasized the awkward ways they disrupt the silhouette of flat-front khakis. Just like one's hands or bulky wallets, Lead Pocket Eggs cause unsightly bumps (figure 19). Bonner demonstrates how the objects protruding from front pockets shift the body's profile dramatically, changing the front that wearers present to others.

Distracted by unseemly reminders of the body, we forget that the way we interpret placement of the hands draws from domains other than etiquette. Since antiquity, people have understood hands to be a critical adjunct to speech, second only to the face in expressiveness. Orators at the lectern, pulpit, and political rally, as well as actors and painters, have made specific studies of their articulations, hoping to capture just the inflection to persuade or represent emotion. Anthropologists, linguists, and psychologists, meanwhile, have mapped the hands' rhythms as interlaced with speech, analyzing the impact of nonverbal communication in social interactions. Practitioner and academic alike distinguish two major types of hand gesture: emblematic, such as the thumbs-up sign, or more "imagistic," comprising the balletic, abstract hand motions that punctuate speech. To gesture in either category, it goes without saying, the hand must be visible. And so one wonders whether a hand-in-pocket gesture that stills and conceals the communicative hand even qualifies as intentional expression. Yet it has certainly stood out to viewers. People pay attention to others' gestures and attitudes to discern their mood or receptiveness; if someone of interest sits "bolstered up, with his back against his chair, his hands in his pockets," people notice (what arrogance!). Perhaps because our expectations for their aid in communication is so great, the hands' absence turns out to be as equally rich in associations as any movement.

Critically, the hands-in-pockets gesture derives its meaning from the hands' interaction with clothing. This collaboration is highly unusual: for the most part, hand gestures do not utilize objects or require props. People in conversation tend to ignore or consider incidental the way a partner tugs on or rearranges their clothes or brings a coffee cup to their mouth. Yet when the person positions hands in pockets and as a result changes the slant of the hips and the spine, we read their overall pose as intentional, evidently constructed, sometimes mannered. In the fraction of a second it takes to assess another person's body language, we observe and appraise any number of specific nuances as we try to decode them. Understanding that the hand is contained, we translate that sense of containment to other registers and, in an imaginative leap, surmise that the attitude reflects the person's emotional inaccessibility or disengagement.

Demonstrating one's inaccessibility may be an especially useful approach in a crowd, something the sociologist Georg Simmel pondered in his investigation of city life. Intent on characterizing the "metropolitan blasé attitude" he observed at the turn of the twentieth century—the way that people collectively decided to ignore one another in public—Simmel identified the methods urbanites used to insulate themselves from the expectations and demands of others. One key strategy was not to attend, for example, to the faces of the strangers whom one encountered. Inattention can take on various forms, and one could say (although Simmel does not himself mention it) that putting hands in pockets, too, helped to shape an imaginary "sphere of indifference."

That indifference has long been understood to be political. As Chesterfield advised his son in the eighteenth century, it was better to look nonchalant than to bow too low to a social "superior." Updating that notion, the sociologist Pierre Bourdieu agrees that how one holds oneself or rearranges the body in the presence of others should not be dismissed as an innocuous component of everyday interaction. A person's bearing reflects, and can either perpetuate or resist, the social order. When W. E. B. Du Bois posed for his picture at the Exposition Universalle International of 1900, he pointedly refused deferential modes (figure 20). In Paris to debut his collection of photographs documenting the accomplishments of African Americans, he wore the height of fashion in his Astor and Prince Albert waistcoat. Unlike Whitman, Du Bois embraced formality and wore a starched collar that Whitman likely would have disdained. But with both his hands tucked deeply into his pockets, he also emphasized his easy composure.

Du Bois's attitude in this photograph reflects entitlement and emphatic self-possession. For many, their attitude became a protective armor that was often characterized as cool. Holding one's hands in one's pockets was a bit like wearing sunglasses at night and on stage, as did (for the first time) the legendary saxophonist Lester Young, who coined the modern usage of the word of *cool* in the late 1930s. Rejecting the genial persona of Black musicians like Louis Armstrong, Young embraced blankness and impassivity, modeling a rebellious style that was widely admired. This rebel sensibility emerged from Black American innovators connected to the jazz scene, and it soon spread as

Figure 20. Portrait of
W. E. B. Du Bois at the
Exposition Universalle
International, 1900.

other musicians, artists, film stars, Beatniks, and youthful rebels incorporated elements of it. These "cool figures" represent the "cultural
aristocrats" of a secular, democratic consumer society, writes historian
Joel Dinerstein, one that has elevated individuals who have crafted an
individual aesthetic approach or artistic vision, romanticizing stylistic
pioneers from Humphrey Bogart to Prince.

Aloofness is a recognizable component of those outlaw poses, and
pockets are a critical accessory. Resting one's hands in one's pockets
"just so" helps underline a person's sexual charisma and mystery. As it
oscillates between sexual and psychological registers, the attitude has

evolved, gaining, rather than losing, meaning over the centuries. While tucking one's hand into one's vest over the breast would now appear hopelessly quaint, the hands-in-pockets attitude remains current. It is pervasive in all sorts of media, perhaps foremost in fashion imagery, where it first emerged. A model's blasé attitude in some ways feels more distinctive than any one piece of clothing that they wear. The figure in Helmut Newton's famous 1975 photograph featuring Yves Saint Laurent's "Le Smoking" suit presents herself with gaze averted and hand in pocket—the embodiment of distant, scornful remove. Saint Laurent's muse, Catherine Deneuve, believed "Le Smoking" encouraged confidence, sexual empowerment, and the striking chance to "change" one's gestures.

Even those of us who do not aspire to fashionable distinction find our hands in our pockets. Without consciously wanting to express anything at all, there they go as one confers with a neighbor or colleague. Pockets give you something to do with your hands. That can be a boon when you find yourself at some gathering and realize that your hands are likely to betray your nervousness. If the gesture feels reflexive, most people seem to know how to shift it closer to the realm of pose when required, as courtiers, loafers, and fashionistas did before us. This knowledge does not often rise to the level of conscious decision, but it is the reason that putting your hands in your pockets should not be understood as merely a casual or relaxed attitude. However faint or distant, the attitude recalls the allure of aristocratic distinction, the shock of open sexual expression, a studied indifference to decorum, and a refusal to defer to one's fellows.

Figure 1. Portrait of Harriet Campbell, by Ammi Phillips, ca. 1815.

CHAPTER 4

Pocket Sexism:
"Why We Oppose Pockets for Women"

W hen self-taught itinerant painter Ammi Phillips advertised his skills to prospective clients across small town New England, he stressed not only his ability to produce a credible likeness but his knowledge of (and ability to provide) cosmopolitan fashions and accessories. He made good on those claims, outfitting seven-year-old Harriet Campbell of Albany, New York, with a pink Empire dress, beribboned slippers, a parasol, and a reticule—the first incarnation of the fashion handbag (figure 1). He provided another Harriet, a teenager named Harriet Leavens, with the exact same costume that year, attire that seems to us more appropriate for the older girl. But Phillips treats young Campbell with seriousness and respect: she certainly does not look as if she has discovered her mother's discarded handbag and too-large slippers in a dress-up bin. She appears preternaturally contained, regarding the viewer with a steady gaze, one eyebrow slightly raised, grasping what suffragists would later call a "badge of servitude" with practiced ease.

Harriet's high-waisted dress was to blame for endangering those reliable companions, tie-on pockets. The early nineteenth-century ideal in women's wear exalted those dressed like Greek goddesses in thin, gauzy dresses that fell in columnar lines mimicking the architecture of Grecian temples. The most risqué of these dresses tended to cling to the body, and as a result the number of underclothes were gradually reduced. With this turn, bulky tie-on pockets lost their place. To compensate, women began carrying tiny purses called reticules—from the French *réticule*, derived from the Latin *reticulum*, a diminutive of "net." Like their namesake, the first reticules looked like the drawstring net purses worn by Roman ladies. They dangled from a woman's wrist, sometimes all the way down to the ankle. As a Londoner marveled in 1817, women now "walked with their *pockets* in their hands."

Women had long been differently pocketed. But when women adopted handheld receptacles to carry everyday articles, people suddenly took more notice of the difference. Remarking on the "great interest" in the "pocket question" in 1828, the women's journal *La Belle Assemblee* reflected that these "serious articles . . . have given rise to serious dissentions." Though the accounts of pocket disparity were (and still are) often cloaked in humor or slight condescension, at their core there is a serious question: why is it that men's clothes are full of integrated, sewn-in pockets, while women's have so few? As women made the transition to modern dress, and still did not achieve anything like parity, they began to ask the question more insistently. The suspicion that there was a sexual politics around preparedness, that privilege was something that could be stitched into one's trousers, fueled a proxy battle of the sexes that has continued to simmer for over two centuries.

WOMEN'S POCKETS COME AND GO

THE EARLY NINETEENTH-CENTURY press offered readers dismissive accounts of new fashions, specifically scolding women for their "silliness" in acquiescing to "the very inconvenient custom of being without pockets." Women were more willing to relinquish their free agency as consumers than to challenge fashion, so the charge went. Reporting on the tribulations of one such follower of fashion in 1806, the *Weekly Visitor* ran a story about a young woman intrigued by the sight of a peddler's wares. She was hoping to make a purchase but had to admit she couldn't because she didn't have any money. The reason? She hadn't worn a pocket. Desperate for a customer, the peddler was forced to follow the unprepared woman home to collect his payment. A 1789 sketch was less indulgent and forgiving in tone. Titled *Fashionable Convenience!!*, it depicts a young child asking for money to buy cakes. Mamma replies, "How can you be so vulgar, child, have not I told you a hundred times I never wear pockets!" (figure 2). Women conformed to fashion's dictates at the expense of convenience, sacrificing even those little but meaningful things like treating their youngsters to sweets.

The mockery got no better for women when they sought a practical alternative in reticules. In carrying reticules, women were essentially exposing their pockets, a once-private accessory. Pockets were previously classified as undergarments, so these displays were an unseemly spectacle to many. An illustration from 1800 makes that connection apparent while ridiculing women for their impractical dress choices (figure 3). Fashionable ladies are shown in their winter dress wearing floral hats that impede their sight, transparent dresses that show off their nakedness and hardly protect from the cold, and reticules that swing lower and lower down their stockingless legs. The English promptly chose to mispronounce the French word for

Figure 2. *Fashionable Convenience!!*, by G. M. Woodward, ca. 1789. I cannot give you money for cakes, the mother tells her child. "I told you a hundred times I never wear pockets!"

the fashion accessory and referred to it as a "ridicule," or, perhaps further punning on its tiny, impractical size, an "indispensable."

Tie-on pockets came to be associated with the habits of more traditional women, industrious housewives, and "old ladies." In them housewives carried everything they needed. They were an "honest" and useful receptacle, according to various laments on their demise. A 1796 letter from a mother to her son indicates the politics involved: don't marry one of those reticule-carrying women, a so-called "Anti-Pocketist," warns the prominent Mrs. Ridgely of Delaware. To make her case she compares the young man's sisters with an attractive, "simpering" young visitor who professed herself astonished to find the Ridgely sisters busy sewing. The simpering visitor self-righteously claimed that she never carried scissors, thimble, needle, or thread about her, "for it was terrible in a Lady to wear a pair of Pockets—the French Ladies never did such a thing." The disuse of tie-on pockets by fashionable women constituted a disavowal of traditional women's crafts and, for Mrs. Ridgely, a strike against any young woman hoping to marry into her family.

The infatuation with narrow goddess dresses was brief, however, and women's skirts widened by the 1820s. Some women returned to wearing tie-on pockets (which happily fit again), but many women began to experiment with integrated, masculine-style pockets sewn into

Figure 3. *Parisian Ladies in Their Winter Dress for 1800*, by John Cawse. The sight of women carrying the handheld reticule inspired mockery: "While men wear their hands in their pockets so grand, the ladies have pockets to wear in their hand."

Figure 4. Fashion plate titled *Les Modes Parisiennes*, published in *Peterson's Magazine*, November 1885.

dresses at side seams on the hips. For a time, inset pockets fit under the voluminous skirts of the 1850s and 1860s. But this tentative exploration did not gain traction. When bell-shape hoop skirts went out of style, women's pockets migrated in haphazard and unexpected ways. By the 1870s and 1880s, dresses flattened in the front and skirts were pushed to the back, forming an enormous bustle at the rump (figure 4). Dressmakers did the best they could and, seeking the area of greatest volume, placed a lone pocket in the folds of the cantilevered bustle.

Artfully tucked under all that drapery, pockets seemed to be buried "in some innermost recess" of one's being, complained one writer. They were more difficult to locate than "paradise." One woman reported salvaging material from one of her used gowns: to her surprise, she discovered an entirely unworn pocket so cunningly hidden away that she had never known it was there. Reaching such pockets involved

THE NEW YORK TIMES, MONDAY, AUGUST 28, 1899.

iously of making common cause with the Bonapartists. It is the general opinion among the dissatisfied supporters of Prince Henri that Prince Victor Napoleon is no more an ideal pretender than the Duc d'Orléans, but what is said to be drawing a good many Orléanists and Bonapartists together is the future of Prince Louis Napoleon, who is at present at the Czar's Court. Royalists of both parties declare that in him they have a strong man—one who possesses the qualities necessary in a French pretender, and which are lacking both in Prince Victor and the Duc d'Orléans.

SCARCITY OF DIAMONDS.

De Beers Syndicate Takes Advantage of Transvaal War Scare to Limit the Output and Raise Prices.

The possibility of a war between Great Britain and the South African Republic has already had a disquieting effect on at least one industry in this country. The diamond market is in a condition which could almost be described as one of panic. The market value of stones is now 40 per cent. higher than it was a year ago, and, from present indications, there seems to be no prospect that the high-water mark has been reached.

This fact of itself would, of course, not cause the diamond importers and dealers any anxiety. But there is in addition a remarkable scarcity of stones, and it is probable that the coming season will find a good many traders unable to make good their contracts, except at heavy loss.

It is the great De Beers syndicate which is responsible for this state of things. The syndicate is controlled by Cecil Rhodes and half a dozen other men, and they have apparently determined to limit the output of the Kimberley Mines—which, in reality, means that the output of the world—to an infinitesimal quantity. It is customary for the representatives of the large importing houses of the United States, England, France, and other countries where there are large markets for the sale of precious stones to visit South Africa in the Summer in order to make their purchases. Frequent ...

WORLD'S USE OF POCKETS

Men's Clothes Full of Them, While Women Have But Few.

CIVILIZATION DEMANDS THEM

A Tailor Tells the Queer Purposes Pockets Are Made by Some Men to Fulfill.

"Assuming," said the Philosopher of Small Things, "that Adam and Eve both began life without any pockets, it seems to me that the difference in the progress of the sexes toward pockets illustrates and proves the superiority of the male. Man's pockets have developed, improved, and increased with the advances of civilization. Woman is actually retrograding—losing ground and pockets. They tell me the women have fewer pockets in their clothes now than they had two generations ago.

"Our grandmothers," continued the philosopher, "used to have big, deep pockets in their skirts which they could get at somehow and in which they usually carried the household keys, a ball of yarn with knitting needles stuck in it, a little smooth-worn gourd for darning operations, and very often a few doughnuts or cookies or apples and a pair of spectacles. Then the big, long gingham aprons had pockets, and later young housekeepers and even unmarried women wore dainty little white frilled and tucked aprons with the most absurd and charming pretenses of pockets in front.—gave the girls the opportunity to show how small their hands were by sticking their tiny white fists into them, and were very fetching.

through life and unnumbered suits. Careless men scatter things everywhere through their clothes. All of us have seen men of that kind turning one pocket after another inside out looking for something they wanted.

"But," said the philosopher, "there you touch one of the greatest blessings of many pockets as a source of hope. Because he has many pockets the average man is never quite sure that he is flat broke or utterly without matches. He will go for days every now and then turning out his pockets, picking out the lint that gets wadded in the corners, hoping that he has stuck away a small coin; and no other joy like the joy of finding forgotten or unexpected money in a remote and unsuspected pocket. Many times I have packed dollar and two-dollar bills in pencil or fob or hip pockets, hoping to forget them and then some time in an emergency, but I always remember them and catch myself banking on them with my second sub-consciousness.

WORLD DEMANDS MORE POCKETS.

"The world demands more pockets than it has. The women have none, and if they ever got within hailing distance of equality with men must have dozens. The fact that men need more than they have is evident every day. We see small packages slipped into umbrellas and papers carried in hats. The surface road conductors use the sweatbands of their caps for extra pockets and pack transfer tickets into them. The only useless pockets are those in the tails of a frock coat. You can't carry anything in them that you can afford to sit on, and even a handkerchief there gives a hanging bustle effect.

"The desire for pockets has become by process of evolution a fixed sex trait. As soon as a boy gets on trousers with pockets he begins to swagger and assert his superiority, and feel that he is in business, sure enough. Watch a boy stick his hands in his trousers' pockets and spread his legs apart and argue a point of family difference, and you'll see his older and younger sisters, and very likely his mother, cower before him. I tell you it's all a matter of pockets.

"No pocketless people has ever been of since pockets were invented, and the female sex cannot rival us while it is pocketless. The boy who carries pieces of string, marbles, fishing worms, bits of crockery, sections of partially masticated chewing ..."

Figure 5. "World's Use of Pockets," from the *New York Times*, August 28, 1899.

struggle and contortion. Pockets were "practically inextricable" when needed, observed the writer T. W. H. in *Harper's Bazaar* in 1893. She reported an exasperating experience involving an impatient horsecar conductor waiting to take her fare. As she twisted around, fumbling at her bustle, trying to locate her money, he and a lengthening line of waiting passengers demanded that she accelerate her search. "How can I possibly hurry up when my pocket is in South Boston?" she indignantly retorted.

T. W. H. further wondered whether contemporary clothing limited the mobility of an *entire* sex: What if one were to undertake a "statistical inquiry" comparing the pockets of men and women and boys and girls? What would one find? An 1899 *New York Times* article confirmed the writer's hypothesis: the "world's use of pockets" was strikingly uneven (figure 5). The headline made the situation clear: "Men's Clothes Full of Them, While Women Have But Few." The article notes while men's pockets had "developed, increased and improved," women were actually "losing ground" after having jettisoned tie-on pockets.

The effects of this lost ground were sketched with more detail in popular fiction. In one of his many adventures in the 1908 book *The Wind in the Willows* (now considered a children's tale, although Kenneth Grahame meant it for adults), Toad dresses up as a washerwoman to escape from jail after stealing a motor car (figure 6). His experience cross-dressing is a "nightmare" because he misses the vest pocket "eternally situated" over his left breast. Unable to access his wallet and thus the money he needs to make his escape, he finds his options severely limited when it matters most. Wearing women's clothes, Toad observes with surprising frankness, leaves him "unequipped for the real contest."

SUFFRAGISTS DEMAND EQUALITY IN POCKETS

IN THE MEANTIME, a number of women had begun to "agitate with much earnestness in behalf of the right of women to have and enjoy pockets," fervently believing, unlike Toad, that a woman *was* "undoubtedly made to be a pocket-wearing person." The most sustained attention came from women's rights activists, who made women's clothes in general—particularly unwieldy skirts and debilitating corsets, as well as pockets—a political issue. With barely contained irritation, activists published cogent analyses

Figure 6. Frontispiece illustration by Arthur Rackham for the 1940 edition of Kenneth Grahame's *The Wind in the Willows*. Unable to reach his wallet dressed in women's clothes, an unhappy Toad realizes that the world is divided between the "many-pocketed animal" and the "inferior one-pocketed or no-pocketed productions."

of sartorial inequity. Their demands for "equality in pockets" sound disconcertingly familiar, just like the demands made in the present day.

Women's rights advocate Elizabeth Cady Stanton was incensed by the contrast between the utterly encumbered woman walking down the street—one hand holding up a majestically sweeping skirt, the other clutching an umbrella, pocketbook, and other small necessaries—and the man who charged down the same street "free as a lark." A dearth of pockets was one of the "unrecognized disabilities of women," claimed other progressive women commenting at the turn of the century. It was her "greatest lack." Feminist writer Charlotte Perkins Gilman pointed out that the design of the material world had marked social implications. Ready access to tools and devices enhanced one's practical and psychological "preparedness," giving one the confidence "to meet all emergencies." Without pockets, women really were "unequipped for the real contest," as Toad had opined.

In her 1915 sociological study, *The Dress of Women*, Gilman observed that the pocketless, cheap calico housedresses worn by the majority of housewives and women laboring in other people's homes neither prepared them nor protected them from wet, dirt, grime, or the fire hazards of the pre-electrified kitchen. Under these conditions, what women should really have been wearing was a protective "leather apron" or a waterproof "oilskin cloak," she argued. That housewives did not shored up the fiction of happy domesticity while it denied that women were performing actual work. Gilman made a point of outfitting the characters who inhabit her all-female utopia, *Herland*, in costumes that readied the wearer for any kind of work, including the important business of administering a nation. Emphasizing the wearer's personhood above their gender, Gilman stepped away from the trouser and skirt binary to propose a garment stripped down to the essentials: a bodysuit "fairly quilted in pockets." These pockets "were most ingeniously arranged, so as to be convenient to the hand and not inconvenient to the body, and were so placed as at once to strengthen the garment and add decorative lines of stitching." Gilman's fiction was not widely recognized in her time, but in it exists a challenge that remains relevant: pockets could be integral to anyone's clothes in ways that served structural, aesthetic, and practical ends.

Conservative commentators for the most part scoffed at the notion that pockets made a difference, that but for lack of pockets women would be the titans of Wall Street. Such arguments were easily brushed off as so much nonsense, and as one reporter wrote in the *San Francisco Chronicle* in 1913, suffragists were "now dragging the pocket into the female emancipation problem." According to these mostly anti-suffragist critics, it seemed as though women had been easily lead astray by an unimportant, irrelevant side issue. Some hoped that women would remain lost in the weeds. Perhaps all those upstart suffragists who "clamor" for the vote should just demand pockets instead—that was the "real grievance," according to one cynic.

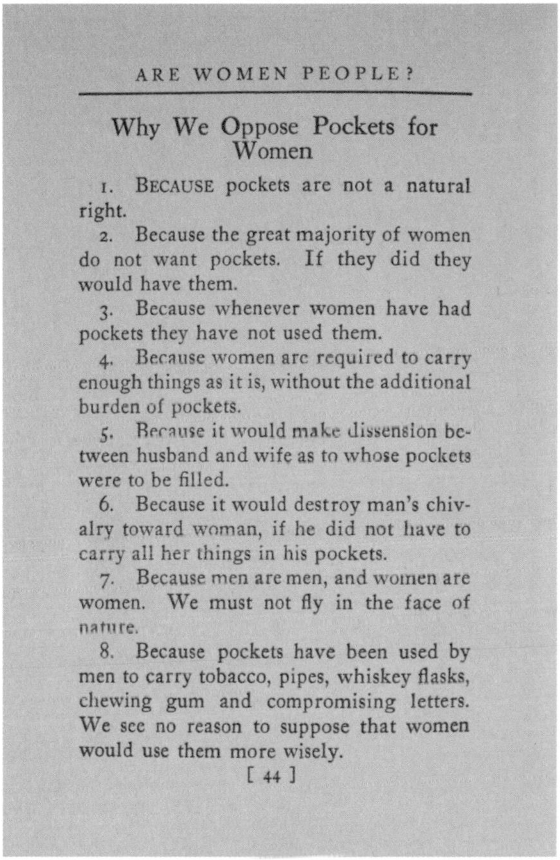

Figure 7. "Why We Oppose Pockets for Women," by Alice Duer Miller, published in *Are Women People? A Book of Rhymes for Suffrage Times*, 1915. Copying the arguments of the anti-suffragists, but substituting "pockets" for "votes," Miller illustrated the ludicrousness of calling either pockets or the vote a right belonging exclusively to one sex.

But in the midst of making major social and political advances, women *also* wanted the flexibility and assurance pockets provided, and they worried about the dangers of acquiescing to the no-pocket tradition in women's clothes. "By-m-bye, no pockets for the female sect will settle down into hard and fast law," warned a contributor to a domestic magazine in 1907. The worry seems well-placed: several social traditions were being reconceived as natural by conservative forces opposed to change, from the notion that mothers were not fit for careers to the design of clothes. In a lighthearted but insightful satire, the suffragist Alice Duer Miller pointed out the circular reasoning involved in invoking either tradition or biology to reaffirm the status quo. If women really wanted pockets, they would already have them! Ergo, suffragists must not "fly in the face of nature" by demanding pockets, Miller wrote in her 1915 poem "Why We Oppose Pockets for Women" (figure 7). If you could claim tailor-made pockets as a natural right, you could do so for just about anything, including the right to vote.

Miller's humor was lost on all those detractors who felt acute anxiety about maintaining traditional gender roles. Conservative voices tended to identify all suffragists as gender-nonconforming, singling out queer female suffragists in particular as deviant. The lawyer, activist, and president of the National Federation of Business and Professional Women's Clubs, Gail Laughlin, for example, was chided in the *St. Louis Star* for her refusal to appear in a dress that lacked pockets. "Only on rare occasions does Miss Laughlin take off the mannish garb that she usually wears," the reporter noted. The journalist mocks Laughlin for being arrayed in a brand-new gown for a federation event and having made it to that point in her life without realizing that such "creations" typically did not offer them. Pointing out her intransigence, the journalist wrote: "Miss Laughlin declined to wear the thing until a pocket was sewed on."

Anti-suffrage cartoons and propaganda were just as negative, representing suffragists as starkly unattractive. The plot of Charles Hoyt's 1899 musical comedy, *The Contented Woman*, involves a wife who runs for mayor against her husband as comeuppance after he rudely tears off a button she has diligently sewn onto his suit, if in the wrong color. The wife's impulsive retribution, satisfying in the moment, has lasting consequences, according to Hoyt's play; the image on the cover of the playbill alludes to the changed demeanor of any woman engaged

Figure 8. Playbill for Charles H. Hoyt's *A Contented Woman: A Sketch of the Fair Sex in Politics*, 1898. Suffragists were satirized for wearing masculine-style jackets and vests and stuffing their hands in the pockets of their "suffragist skirts," which had side pockets set into the seam like men's trousers.

in the "vulgar clamor for rights" (figure 8). Among the many "horrid" habits she might pick up, the "speechifying" suffragette would need someplace to stash her hands "like a man," adopting one of his worst mannerisms. But for the suffragette, "pockets mean business," from being "equipped for the street" to enjoying a gesture considered a bad habit that, because it was defiant, just so happened to be authoritative as well. As one lawyer lamented, she could not approach the jury with the same commanding nonchalance as did her lawyer husband. "Is anything so convincing as that easy attitude a man takes when he plunges his hand deep in his pocket and says, *Now, gentlemen of the jury?—*"

EXPLANATIONS FOR THE pocket discrepancy that did not blame nature tended to blame women's vanity and their submission to fashion. Women made "no fight" for pockets and instead let themselves be ruled by dressmakers, who made the majority of clothing until the late nineteenth century. (Dressmakers produced custom, made-to-measure garments; the tight fit and elaborate styles of women's dresses made them too complicated to transfer to industrialized methods as men's wear had a century earlier.) From an account of her dealings with her dressmaker that Stanton published in 1895, it is clear that makers and their clients negotiated over the finished product. Describing her demand for a pocket, Stanton pointed out that even a fight didn't guarantee

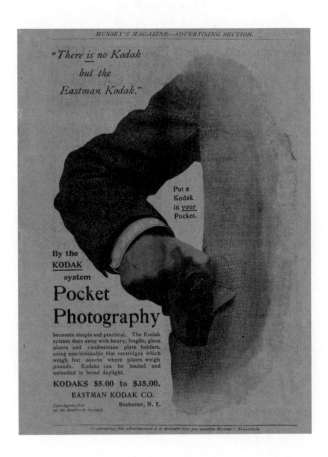

Figure 9. Kodak advertisement, "Pocket Photography," from *Munsey's Magazine*, 1899.

results: the dressmaker "manufactures excuses," tells her there is "no place" for one, and informs her that a pocket "would bulge you out just awful!" During a long back and forth, the dressmaker insisted Stanton follow her expert advice, which she delivered with pitying condescension. Stanton nevertheless believed she had won her case—only to receive, upon its completion, a dress without a single pocket.

The worry that pockets would "bulge you out just awful" for the most part trumped concerns about the lack of function in women's dress. Not even excitement over new, pocket-scale technologies pressured dressmakers or manufacturers to consider women's adventurous forays away from home. In hoping to introduce the first amateur, hand-held portable camera, Eastman Kodak marketed it with the catchy tagline "Put a Kodak in *Your* Pocket" (figure 9). The company intended

Figure 10. Kodak advertisement, "Take a Kodak with You," from *Ladies Home Journal*, 1901.

to attain as wide a market share as possible and introduced the Kodak Girl to demonstrate that photography was easy enough for women to handle too (figure 10). Advertisements that featured the Kodak Girl, however, tacitly admitted that the camera was an accessory, equivalent to the parasol. You could certainly "take" a pocket Kodak with you, but you'd have to hold it in your hand. Just as women improvise today when carrying their mobile phones, amateur women photographers of 1900 also had to make do.

By the eve of World War I, the flowered hats, parasols, and trailing skirts worn by the Kodak Girl began to disappear. The entire genre of difficult clothing that Stanton and many others had long complained about had finally lost its allure and had begun to look downright incongruous in the context of the machine age. Women began to have more options and could visit department stores to purchase good quality, ready-made clothes distinct from high-fashion confections. The first of these were tailored jacket, shirtwaist, and skirt combinations that allowed all classes of women, from college graduates to secretaries and shop girls, to look turned out and smart at the workplace or when undertaking errands about town. Theodore Dreiser's Sister Carrie longs for one of these "nice little jackets" she sees in a shop window, believing it will help her make the transition from country girl to city sophisticate. Modern women's dress, it seemed, could finally adhere to a more practical, sensible scheme. Not only had dress become less difficult and confining, but it accommodated women's expanding roles and activities. In 1909 *Vogue* noted approvingly that dress had come "in touch with modern needs, views and demands." News circulated that women who had "yearned for a pocket" could now "rejoice."

Such reports were far too optimistic. Even ready-made separates could not be counted on for usable pockets. Interviewed by a journalist about the pocket question in 1910, one working woman, identified as a stenographer, asked rhetorically: "Where is the ready-made suit that shows anything deserving the name of pocket?" Women's clothes *did* become more practical, and certain sports ensembles, like the bicycle bloomers pictured in a 1895 *Harper's Bazaar* fashion plate, were equipped with pockets (figure 11). But manufacturers were less concerned about providing women with functional means to navigate the world than they were about achieving the simplification necessary to enable mass production. They experimented drafting patterns that required uncomplicated pieces and fewer pieces per garment, producing suits, separates, and, by the 1920s, dresses that were streamlined in comparison to Victorian ruffles. Critically, throughout this process of simplification and standardization, the notion that "women's clothes aren't made for pockets" prevailed.

Figure 11. Illustration of more functional walking, traveling, tennis, and cycling costumes, from *Harper's Bazaar*, June 1895. Note the women wearing a "travelling suit" (far left) and a bloomer outfit (middle), who place their hands in their pockets.

This did not have to be the case. "Woman's dress is so admirably suited to sly concealment," wrote one commentator in the *Independent* in 1912, that it should be "full of pockets." Yet useful pockets would continue to come and go in the modern era, as they had in the Victorian one. They made vivid appearances with the outbreak of World War I, when designers and major department stores hurried to market civilian dress that allowed women to take on a more brisk and erect attitude in a difficult time. In the context of military khaki, tailored suits, and important belts, pockets that signaled efficient preparedness became de rigueur. Skirts, coats, and dresses sported pockets as large as "young knapsacks," as *Women's Wear Daily* observed. How wearers should interpret the sudden abundance was harder to discern. Was the pocket bounty that season in Paris "the result of the feminist movement, or merely a whim?" *Vogue* asked in 1916. *Vogue* decided it was mere whim and warned readers not to take the unprecedented interest in pockets all that seriously. Admitting that the fashionable Parisienne might need those pockets for her knitting or "to harbor letters from the front," the editor suggested that she might just as well favor them "wholly without a reason."

According to *Vogue* contributor Virginia Yeaman, writing in 1918, useful pockets might appear when they supported some style or look, like that of sober efficiency in wartime, "and then, presto, they were gone." Even if "pockets should follow on the heels of suffrage," they were certain to remain fickle, Yeaman believed. In light of this uncertainty, it seemed unlikely that women would "vote" for pockets. And should women really mind not having pockets all that much?

Yeaman argued that women should not blame men for women's pocketlessness. While she reprimanded men for engaging in quite a bit of unseemly crowing over their pocket monopoly and noted that they would be rendered "cross as bears" without them, she reasoned that the blame game was a complicated one. Yeaman suggested that "impersonal, severely logical forces" might be at play, by which she seemed to mean the interests of the clothing industry, and, more shockingly to pocket advocates, that women had in essence denied pockets to themselves when they decided against unsightly bulges. While she envied men their pockets, Yeaman proposed that women could get by admirably without them. They could now look to a far more reliable companion: the modern handbag. The "average woman," Yeaman predicted, cared only that she had some means to ensure her economic independence; she "seems content to take the cash and let the pockets go."

UNLIKE THE RETICULES of the 1800s, which were cloth bags very much in the textile tradition, the modern handbag derived its form from the handheld luggage carried by men in the last third of the nineteenth century. Framed handbags were sturdy, often made of leather with metal fastenings, compartmentalized interiors, and robust handles. If clothes would not consistently outfit women for activity in the world, perhaps handbags could compensate. Handbags soon came to be seen not just as fashionable accessories but as a sign of independence. As the generations of statement or otherwise fashionable bags that have followed demonstrate, handbags have garnered devotion and engendered desire.

Yet even in the face of this love affair with handbags, a significant number of women still longed for pockets. In 1913 journalist Helen Dare noted that suffragists hoped to do away this accessory, calling it that "shameful handbag." Radclyffe Hall, author of one of the first openly lesbian novels, *The Well of Loneliness* (1928), refused to carry a handbag and instead had extra pockets sewn into her skirts. Maybe there really was no "average woman" as Yeaman had theorized; many wanted *both* the money and a pocket to stash it in. The handbag, its name an unimaginative compound noun, requires the use of the hand and almost constant vigilance. Some bit of psychic energy is needed to keep track of its whereabouts throughout the day. Any purse owner has to remember where they have put their purse down—preferably before they've walked out of the restaurant or the taxi has sped off.

While easily lost, purses have nevertheless been hard to get rid of, and women have carried them into all sorts of situations, some more surprising than others. Did anyone really want to drag a handbag to war? As volunteers for the Women's Auxiliary Army Corps (WAAC, later WAC when the auxiliary status was dropped) during World War II, thousands of women did just that. And although the purse was carried slung over the shoulder rather than held in a hand, it still looks out of place on the leader of the phalanx of marching women pictured in a recruitment poster from 1942—as though she's leading them to the supermarket rather than to dangerous outposts (figure 12).

To outfit the new recruits, the Office of the Quartermaster General of the US Army relied on inadequate knowledge of women's wear, having supplied only a limited number of nurse's uniforms during World War I. Yet the quartermaster's office soon began to brag to the press that it could make uniforms that "lasted," and suggested that

Figure 12. WAAC recruitment poster, 1942. The WAAC volunteer wears her handbag across her right shoulder, in the approved manner, so that it will not slip. Snaps used to affix the bag at the shoulder had been tried by military designers but did not work.

military service would afford women their first real experience wearing high-quality, functional, and durable clothing. As the development of the WAC uniform demonstrates, however, military decision makers seemed just as unwilling as nineteenth-century dressmakers to challenge cultural expectations about women's clothing. Former WAC member Mattie Treadwell described the purse's adoption with wry humor in her 1955 history of the corps, noting that military handbags were one of many compromises born out of the struggle to avoid hostility and resistance to women serving in the armed forces. Worried that masculinized dress would substantiate the rumors that Wacs were Amazons in disguise, lesbians, or prostitutes hired to offer enlisted men female company, the corps initially opted for skirts over trousers. Those skirts had no pockets. Nor, in short order, did Wacs' coats have any working breast pockets. Experiments with carrying necessities at the chest "quickly produced a rule against even so much as a pack of cigarettes in that location," Treadwell reported. One wonders what those experiments looked like and what the possible objections could have been (Treadwell does not elaborate). Did even a pack of cigarettes threaten to disfigure the breast, making it lumpy and misshapen, a sort of metaphor for servicemen's worst fears—that after joining the army, women would no longer be recognizable as women?

At any rate, working breast pockets in the women's coats were judged to be unsuitable, an embarrassment that upset the delicate balance between correct military appearance and femininity. The rule prohibiting carrying anything in the breast pocket led to the eventual adoption of a pocket flap without the attached pocket. Someone must have thought it better to remove the temptation than to try to enforce the rule against using it. This left Wacs with fake breast pockets and without the means to carry much of anything, consigning military designers to a dead end that they had created for themselves. It forced the long and tedious development of a bag with a shoulder strap, which involved problems with sourcing materials and long debates about how to carry it.

DESIGNING "HOLD-EVERYTHING" POCKETS

IN 1937, DIANA Vreeland, a fashion impresario and a fashion editor of *Harper's Bazaar*, declared she wanted to abolish all handbags. "I've got the best idea!" she apparently said to another editor passing in the hall soon after she arrived at *Harper's*. Vreeland happened to be wearing a chic Chanel shirt with pockets tucked on the inside, where she carried lipstick, rouge, powder, comb, cigarettes, and money. Bitterly complaining that the "bloody old handbag" was a nuisance, she announced her plan to eliminate them all and suggested devoting a whole future issue of the magazine to "just showing what you can do with pockets." Not only could you carry what you needed "like a man, for goodness sake," but placed in the right positions, pockets could improve the silhouette: the pockets might be bigger, but they'd be "rather chic," she imagined. And freed from carrying a bag, one's posture and gait would be unencumbered: "there's nothing that limits a woman's walk like a pocketbook," she observed.

The other editor, somewhat astonished, ran right to the editor in chief, who later cautioned Vreeland that she sounded like she had lost her mind. No fashion magazine could risk the advertising revenue from bag manufacturers. *Harper's Bazaar* fashion pages nevertheless consistently and wholeheartedly praised "hold-everything pockets." In a 1940 essay on trends to watch, the magazine confessed, "We're interested in pockets—enormous pockets on wrap-around skirts, deep pockets in shirt-jackets, inner pockets in evening skirts, flat pockets on the fanny side of shorts." Not a designer herself, Vreeland actively supported the careers of a number of women in that field, including the American sportswear designers responsible for practical ready-to-wear, the casual clothes (eventually including slacks) that replaced dresses in the "modern dress code." Designers understood that women wanted pockets in order to feel emancipated, and they demonstrated the possibility of integrating useful pockets without disrupting the idealized slim silhouette.

One of these designers was Claire McCardell. Responding to a challenge proposed by Vreeland to design an attractive housedress that would meet the needs and budgets of the American housewife during the lean World War II years (while complying with wartime textile restrictions), McCardell designed the "Pop over." A simple, wrap-front denim dress, McCardell's innovation may be difficult to recognize now, but she pulled off a remarkable feat in reconfiguring the dowdy housedress into something chicer. Typical housedresses were frilly simulacra of fashionable dresses made in cheap, washable cottons unsuitable for work or transition into public. (Charlotte Perkins Gilman had complained about just these aspects of women's clothes years earlier.) Wearing a housedress could be demoralizing: one woman complained that they inevitably made her feel "pot-and-pannish" rather than "woman-of-the-world-ish." Countering this state of affairs, McCardell offered a dress that could be worn to cook dinner and run errands. Its most striking feature was a large, off-center, accessible patch pocket that anchored the skirt. It looked something like a working apron pocket, its puffy, quilted pattern enhancing its size (and obscuring any potentially lumpy thing stashed there) (figure 13). A former curator of the Costume Institute, Richard Martin, observed that this generation of American women sportswear designers tended to create "visible, spacious" pockets that were "purposefully conspicuous." In fact, they "flaunted" them.

Figure 13. Sketch for the "Pop over" dress, by Claire McCardell, 1942.

Figure 14. Purse-pocket skirt (and detail), by Bonnie Cashin, 1954. Figure 15. Adlers publicity material for Bonnie Cashin, 1952. The first of Cashin's coats with a purse-shaped pocket. "To steal the purse, you have to steal the girl," Cashin noted.

Another designer who raided the female wardrobe and repurposed it was Bonnie Cashin. Cashin was critical of Paris fashions that failed to respond to women's needs. "I really have contempt for clothes that do not combine practicality and attractiveness," she claimed. Calling herself a "nomad by nature," Cashin said she designed "for the woman who is always on the go, who is doing something." Walking in the Los Angeles hills with her sketchbook one hot day during the early 1940s, Cashin got tired of lugging around her painting equipment, and upon her return home, she had her mother, a dressmaker, sew a large purse directly onto her coat. What looked like a snap-closure coin purse embedded into the clothing became her signature design. Cashin patented the hands-free purse-pocket in 1950 and included it in coats and skirts throughout her career (figures 14 and 15). The purse-pocket was inserted at the hip in a way that accentuated the hip and narrowed the waist. Pockets, as McCardell, Cashin, and others demonstrated, could serve both functional and aesthetic ends. It was certainly not the case that the "woman is without pockets because pockets do not become her." Including pockets in women's clothes just took a certain commitment.

That commitment should be extended to garments for professional women as well, *Harper's Bazaar* argued when it commissioned Cashin to design a smart and attractive shift dress that could generously equip women for the "day shift." More specifically, Cashin was asked to devise a garment for the emerging field of digital computing at a time when an IBM mainframe took up whole rooms. In this act the magazine emphasized the importance of the new careers women might pursue: the programmer must inform and instruct the machine; she was the computer's "Svengali." Her work enabled the "flights of calculation" computers could achieve, and she therefore deserved to be thoughtfully prepared for it.

Cashin's resulting shift turned out to be more of a smock, as sleek and well designed as computers themselves, according to *Harper's*. As illustrated by Andy Warhol, before he turned to a career in the fine arts, zippy arrows point out every well-considered pocket, ones for punch cards, printouts, and other dispatches (figure 16). Even eyeglasses and clip pens look rakishly stylish in their nesting patch pockets outlined in stripes of topstitching. Accompanying the Cashin-Warhol design was a letter to the future. Composed in the winter of 1958, just as Sputnik had returned to Earth's atmosphere and thoughts had turned to galactic possibilities, it outlined a few other, more improbable goals beyond versatile smocks: cities without traffic, easier air

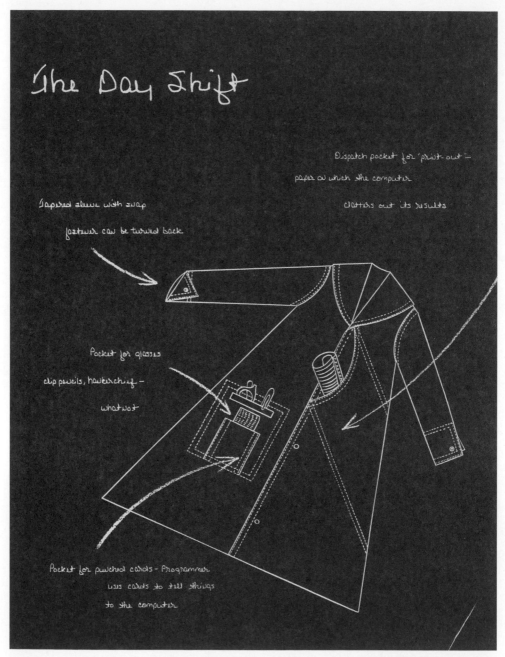

The Day Shift

Dispatch pocket for "print-out" —
paper on which the computer
clatters out its results

Tapered sleeve with snap
fastener can be turned back

Pocket for glasses
clip pencils, handkerchief —
whatnot

Pocket for punched cards — Programmer
uses cards to tell things
to the computer

Figure 16. Bonnie Cashin's speculative design for an IBM programmer's garment, illustrated by Andy Warhol, published in *Harper's Bazaar*, February 1958.

travel, packages that arrived when they said they would, and divorce laws that did not require lying. Replacing fussy, difficult clothes with those that enabled efficient action seemed, in contrast, totally doable.

THE CONTINUING FIGHT FOR POCKET PARITY

MORE THAN FIFTY years on, who would have thought that no-fault divorce would beat out dependable pockets for women? The interventions of sportswear designers during the mid-twentieth century provided key ideas and material for future work. Generations of designers after McCardell and Cashin have referred to their innovations and added new ones. But their commitment to pockets could not eradicate the deeply held beliefs about gender that created the pocket disequilibrium in the first place. Underlying many protestations about fit and fashion were real questions about whether women actually needed pockets. A scathing 1940 piece in *Life*, for example, ridiculed the reappearance of pockets "large as pouches" in women's wear, arguing that soldiers, hunters, mailmen, mechanics, little boys, and their fathers all *used* their many pockets. Men act and do, as this list of male-dominated professions implies, and his clothes should reflect and prepare him for the diverse range of his activities. Women "will wear pockets" if fashion decrees, "but no one expects" women to make use of them.

Here, then, is the crux of the pocket problem. Only one sex requires functional clothing because only one sex is truly expected to use and demand it. Very old ideas about women's place, about the more limited social and economic contributions they are expected to make, remain with us and are reflected in the clothing we create and agree to wear. If clothes are a "social product," as Gilman insisted in *The Dress of Women*, then the lack of pockets in women's dress reveals what we think women should do and the things women need. Blaming some inhuman, abstract force called nature or fashion for women's lack of pockets has been too easy an out, a convenient way not to think seriously about the lack of functionality in women's clothing. What is more, such explanations neatly avoid deeper anxieties that surfaced as women came more frequently into public space. What might happen if women *did* make use of perfectly functional pockets? What might they carry or conceal in "their garments of emancipation," as one tailor dubbed the 1890s bicycle bloomers that allowed women to sit astride their bicycles? Interviewed by the *New York Times*, the tailor had his suspicions about the large pockets lined in leather he had been asked by female bicyclists to fit inside the accommodatingly large bloomers. "Not all of them want to carry a revolver," he said, "but a large percentage do and make no bones about saying so." A widely republished poem appearing in the *Kansas City Daily Journal* spelled out the threat: in their bloomer pockets women "stowed away" pistols, gum to fix flat tires, and "woman suffrage speeches." The more women could carry, the more freedom they potentially had to act. Reports that there were also "plenty of pockets in suffragette suits" suggest that society was worried about women's ability to hide an expanding range of necessaries. Writing for *Vox*, Chelsea Summers surmised this worry arose because, like men's, "women's pockets could carry something secret, something private, or something deadly."

OVER THE COURSE of the twentieth and twenty-first centuries, women's pockets have continued to follow a familiar pattern, stylish one season and gone the next. Women's clothing has co-opted more and more from the male wardrobe, including jeans in the 1950s, tuxedos in the 1970s, and power suits in the 1980s. But by and large pockets have remained an unessential extra. Pockets don't require much fabric, but they are a trick to insert well. They increase the cost of manufacture, and while that cost is accepted as part of doing business for anyone working in men's wear, it is rejected as an undue burden for those working in women's wear. During her time at the New York firm Townley Frocks, Claire McCardell, for example, had to repeatedly argue for their inclusion with her cost-cutting production manager. The increased time and expense is one reason that so many fake pockets exist, and the number of those has increased with the rise of fast fashion. The look of a pocket flap might be nice, but putting in a working pocket to go with it is just the kind of incremental cost that gets scrapped in the name of global efficiency.

Far more exacting data than the informal inventories conducted at the end of the nineteenth century convincingly illustrates that when they appear today, women's pockets are decidedly smaller and less useful than men's. After measuring pockets in eighty pairs of men's and women's jeans from the top twenty brands in the United States in 2018, Jan Diehm and Amber Thomas discovered that on average women's pockets are 48 percent shorter and 6.5 percent narrower than men's (figure 17). They also determined that women's hands do not fit in their own pockets past the knuckles and that more than half of the women's pockets examined couldn't hold wallets, cell phones, or pens. Such findings support the contention that midrange fashion is at times driven entirely by aesthetics rather than consideration of wearers'

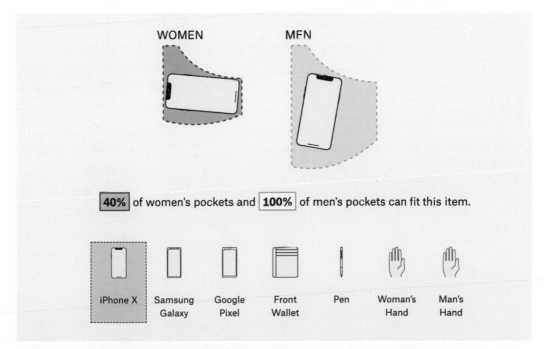

Figure 17. Illustration from Jan Diehm and Amber Thomas's "Someone Clever Once Said Women Were Not Allowed Pockets," published online at *The Pudding*, 2018. Average front-pocket size in jeans in 2018 and objects that fit into front pockets.

needs. Diehm found the difference between hers and her male partner's pocket size "political": "Pocket size is another thing that's policing women's bodies and limiting our independence in what we can carry."

Diehm and Thomas's work is among some of the most convincing recent analyses of "the pocket question." Indeed, the second decade of the twenty-first century marks a notable—although not unprecedented—uptick in commentary concerning the gendered politics of pockets. What in 1800 caused "serious dissention" had by 1900 resulted in pointedly political "agitation." By about 2016, attention to pocket inequity, never resolved, appeared again in a spate of journalistic pieces in the *Atlantic*, the *Washington Post*, *Vox*, and *Medium* along with programming from *The Today Show*, *CBS Sunday Morning*, and National Public Radio. These commentaries accompany rawer expressions of outright irritation on social media, with hashtags like #PocketInequality, #HerPocketsSuck, #wewantpockets, and #givemepocketsorgivemedeath trending in the thousands on Twitter and Instagram, all of which characterize inadequate pockets or the lack of pockets as an infuriating swindle. Pocket memes that circulate across the Internet illustrate a recurring theme, featuring side-by-side comparisons of pocket cornucopia and pocket desolation. One pocket tweet posted by Delilah S. Dawson in 2018 imagined a conversation between a clothing executive asking "what women want" while ignoring his female customers' sensible requests (figure 18).

Another inventive demonstration involved asking how men would feel and act if they were rendered

Delilah S. Dawson ✓
@DelilahSDawson

exec: So what do we think women want in fashion?
women: Pocke--
exec: Cold shoulder tops in pastels. Got it.
women: Pock--
exec: Clothes with pre-made holes in delicate fabrics.
women: Po--
exec: Cut-outs in flabby areas. Good.
women: POCKET--
exec: Shapes that require new bras!

♡ 24.7K   12:24 AM - Jun 20, 2018

💬 7,880 people are talking about this   boredpanda.com

Figure 18. Pocket tweet, by Delilah S. Dawson, June 20, 2018.

pocketless. In 2017 an editor at the online magazine *BuzzFeed* decided to conduct a real-world experiment to test out that event; she found four male volunteers from her office and sewed their pockets shut. Experiencing pocketless pants for the first time was something of a surprise: the volunteers not only left their work badges behind and forgot their wallets, they also had difficulty ordering food and getting takeout back to the office. "It's stressing me out," one volunteer confessed at midday. "I'm going to lunch, carrying my wallet and keys in one hand, and it's so frustrating to know that I might lose my things." One volunteer could not figure out how to navigate the urinal while holding his cell phone. By the end of a trying day the male volunteers unanimously agreed that women's pockets were inadequate and unfair. One likened the experience to knowing electricity had been invented yet being forced to live in the dark.

Advocates pointed out that this fashion double standard doesn't just affect adult women; it also takes a toll on younger generations, reinforcing ideas about women's ostensibly limited range. Author Heather Kaczynski never expected to go viral for a tweet about her toddler's pants, but that's what happened in 2018 when she wrote, "PLEASE PUT POCKETS ON GIRLS PANTS! omg. My 3yo is SO ANGRY when she doesn't have pockets or the pockets are fake. She has THINGS TO HOLD, like rocks and Power Rangers. She's resorted to putting stuff down her shirt. come on. pockets for girls please." The international response from other mothers of young girls followed soon thereafter. Stories accumulated about how little girls wore their shorts backward to access working pockets or painfully stuffed things into the sides of their shoes to compensate. Nurse Alison Chandra replied, "My girl refuses to buy shorts in the girl section because 'they don't have any treasure pockets.'"

SINCE PRESCHOOLERS ARE unlikely to consciously choose a slim silhouette to flatter their figures or to make a statement about their independence, the arguments against offering them pockets weaken considerably. "Pockets are a small symptom of a larger inequality," Kaczynski concluded, some of which she witnessed in the negative responses she received, which questioned why she allowed her daughter to play with Power Rangers in the first place.

In a similar spirit, Eleanor Hanson from West Yorkshire, England, who cited her age as "8¼ years old," took matters into her own hands. She wrote a letter to the FatFace clothing company after realizing she needed to wear their boys' shorts to help collect eggs at her family farm. The girls' shorts she'd been looking at with her mother were described by the company as "stylish yet practical," yet they only had room for one egg in the tiny pocket. In contrast, the boys' pair she ended up getting—labeled "tough, durable, and ready for action"—could fit seven eggs. She asked them to explain their reasoning, ending with "Girls need pockets too!" Hanson's letter and subsequent letters from other young customers, including one from a seven-year-old from Bentonville, Arkansas, to Old Navy asking for "real pockets" in jeans, have been covered in the press, prompting responses from corporate CEOs who have allowed that "a gap" in girls' pocket offerings might exist—and who have promised reform.

Agreeing with young Eleanor Hanson that clothes should be "ready for action," a number of design firms focused on women's workwear have made a point of including useful pockets and make it a key advertising pitch and promise to their customers (figure 19). Of course, there are a scores of women who embrace the pocketless look for their own satisfaction, who prefer sleek lines or clothing that accentuates their figure, especially in evening wear. But until the time that pockets find a more secure place in garments designed for the day shift, pocket sexism is something to take seriously. As the men in the *BuzzFeed* pockets-sewn-shut experiment and Toad in *The Wind in the Willows* discovered, our ability to range freely can be determined by our ready access to those things we need to get by in the world, articles necessary in a range of interactions. Women do not count on that ready access. Instead, they have been conditioned to expect inconvenience, a lesson

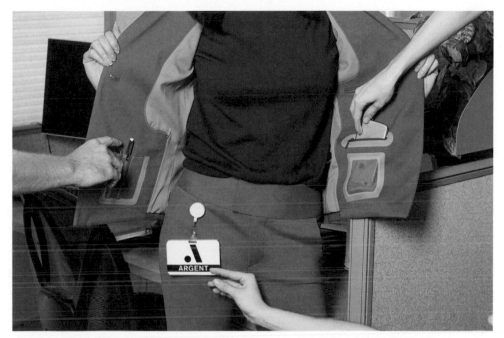

Figure 19. Pocket bounty in women's workwear brand Argent, 2019. Manufacturers have rarely utilized interior suit-coat pockets in women's wear. "When I try on a women's blazer and find no inside pocket, I want to be true to the name and set fire to it!" commented Erika Hall on Twitter in 2014.

that begins when little girls are shooed to skinny jeans while little boys can expect mini-paratrooper pockets that button and snap. In adolescence, teenage girls are forced to find alternative ways to conceal things like menstrual pads by taking a backpack for a trip to the restroom, for example. Such charades end up excruciatingly highlighting rather than concealing the reason for the trip. Everyone makes a mental checklist before walking out the door, but that list may require more contrivance if you also have to think about exactly where you will put what you need.

WHEN THEY WALK out the door with a bag at their side, women do not receive the same *legal* protections as men who are furnished with pockets. So much was confirmed in the 1999 Supreme Court case *Wyoming v. Houghton*, which involved a debate over the Fourth Amendment protection against unreasonable search and seizure: does it necessarily apply when a person carries a handbag? The plaintiff in the case, Sarah Houghton, was a passenger in a car legally stopped because the driver was suspected of drug possession. A police officer rummaged through her purse even though she herself was not a suspect, as frequently occurs during traffic stops when a passenger is asked to leave their purse behind. In contrast, a passenger not under suspicion with pockets instead finds protection from such invasions of privacy. Pockets lie somewhere between clothing and the body, and searching them constitutes a violation of the Fourth Amendment recognition of "the unique, significantly heightened protection afforded against searches of one's person." In authoring the majority opinion in *Wyoming*, Antonin Scalia equated purses with other containers in the car in question, such as briefcases or knapsacks, asserting that they were all subject to search. Justice Scalia, in other words, denied the societal understanding that a purse is as private as a billfold carried in one's pocket. Justice Breyer, in a concurring opinion, was troubled by Scalia's equation of a purse with other receptacles holding property. "Purses are special containers," he noted, admitting he was "tempted to say that a search of a purse involves an intrusion so similar to a search of one's person that the same rule should govern both." He added, "it would matter, if a woman's purse, like a man's billfold, were attached to her person. It might then amount to a kind of 'outer clothing' . . . which under the court's cases would properly receive increased protection." In *Wyoming v. Houghton*, the plaintiff's purse had been discovered some distance from her body, having been tossed into the backseat. In the end, Breyer decided to uphold previous precedent. He wrote that he might have come to a different conclusion had she been holding the purse at her side.

Design matters. The simple distinction between integral pockets and satellite handbags has repercussions, and not only in terms of privacy questions, as the Supreme Court case demonstrates, but in terms of agency, as women have maintained for centuries now.

The poet Emily Dickinson, the famous recluse and "myth" of Amherst, had some sense of that. In a prose fragment discovered among her papers, Dickinson envisioned "domains" within her pocket, a conceit that celebrates the small territory we hold close and whose future yield is hard to measure. Dickinson was among the women in the nineteenth century who won their arguments with their dressmakers, enjoying a single patch pocket (protected by a secure flap) that was stitched on the right side of the glittering white dresses she began to wear in her thirties. Dickinson used her victory to full effect: in her pocket, Dickinson kept a short pencil and scraps of paper on which she committed, in handwriting one admirer likened to "fossil bird-tracks," fleeting thoughts and observations from the rounds of her days. Those observations she might later rework or reject, amend or polish, during the evenings when she undertook most of her composition, sitting at the desk in her room, where she would not be disturbed.

Dickinson had a room of her own—and a reliable pocket.

Figure 1. *One Year's Dungaree Debris*, by Ralph Morse, published in *Life*, April 8, 1957. Bobby and Peter Paulding of Millwood, New York, pose with the objects their mother collected from their pockets over the course of a year.

CHAPTER 5

Pocket Inventories:
"Not a Penny Was There in It"

In 1957 *Life* magazine hoisted two brothers by their ankles, turning them upside down and their pockets inside out (figure 1). Artfully scattered across the floor underneath them were the marbles, charms, bottle caps, and spent shells that comprised a "whole year's shakedown." "Like small boys everywhere," Bobby and Peter Paulding of Millwood, New York, picked up and carelessly stashed away the small-scale things they came across on their wanderings. The boys' mother was fascinated by the discoveries she made as she emptied her sons' pockets before laundering their clothes, and she began saving the "dungaree debris." The magazine's editor noted that some 476 "major, identifiable objects" had been retrieved and listed them in no particular order in an inventory to the right of the photograph.

In their mission to document American life, and believing that pictures were more eloquent than statistics, *Life* staged a number of these sorts of photographic analyses, some more serious than others. How much had the diet of a typical working-class family improved since 1900? Picturing the four-member Czekalinski family of Cleveland in front of the two-and-one-half tons of food they would consume in the year 1951, including 698 quarts of milk in glass bottles perfectly aligned in rows, the answer—a lot—could not be much in doubt. Nor was the larger point in doubt: that at the start of the Cold War America was experiencing "a remarkable picture of plenty." But what lessons were readers supposed to draw about less edifying objects, like the plenty that comprised Peter's and Bobby's dungaree debris? Admittedly lighthearted, *Life*'s tone nevertheless evoked the analytic lingo of science, comparing the year's collection to an experimental "yield" while carefully documenting its component parts, including an empty .22 shell, a letter to Captain Midnight, and a rabbit's foot charm. There was *something* to be learned from pocketed collections, even if the editors of *Life* were not entirely sure what that might be.

Life's pocket inventory was unusual only in that an image accompanied it and it comprised a cumulative accounting of the many days' explorations of two boys. Otherwise it followed a long tradition of such tallies that have survived in myriad press accounts, rhyme and fiction, and even museum collections, where curators have marked objects as belonging to a pocket group. These inventories reflect the tenacious belief that pocketed stashes constitute a special type, that the ephemera temporarily gathered on the person must be qualitatively different from other significant collections. Unlike artifacts gathered in homes, libraries, and museums, the things people carry are not usually curated with considered thoughtfulness, nor for recognition or posterity. Pocket caches are instead weighted toward incidental and accidental finds: a perfectly round stone plucked from a mass of its irregularly shaped fellows, a scribbled phone number on the back of a restaurant matchbook, a receipt temporarily stuffed out of the way after a new purchase.

If one acknowledges feeling somewhat indignant at having to empty one's keys, lip gloss, and forgotten candy wrappers into a plastic bin when moving through security checkpoints at airports or federal buildings, how does one justify perusing another's pocket trove?

Intriguingly, the pocket shakedowns on record tend not to be presented as a trespass but rather as offering intrigue and edification. Detectives, real and fictional, have pondered the significance of pocket clues, as does the sleuth in Agatha Christie's *Pocket Full of Rye*, who wonders what the murdered businessman's mysterious stock of seeds had to do with his failed business venture, Blackbird mine. Amateur sleuths of all sorts have joined the game, hoping to satisfy their curiosity about family and strangers alike, allowing nosiness to overcome discretion in order to uncover some unguarded or authentic truth about the person in question. The resulting exhibitions that unceremoniously spread out a person's secret store for all to admire, satirize, or theorize double down on that old axiom: tell me what you eat—or, in this case, what you carry—and I will tell you who you are.

THE "GREATEST CURIOSITY": BOYS' POCKETS

WHILE THE PRESS has tended to pass over girls' pockets in disinterest (more about this omission to come), boys have become famous for gathering a kind of cornucopia of the mundane that in its extravagant excesses proves incredible. According to press accounts that begin around the 1850s, and lasted for over a century, boys do much more than keep a modest few articles in their pockets for safekeeping. These reports often lead with a common gambit: have you ever turned a boy's pockets inside out? According to the *New England Farmer* in 1861, a boy's pocket "defied reason"; it was just about the "greatest curiosity" to be met with in "a hum-drum, everyday world." In 1885, a grown-up man ruefully admitted in *Puck* that boys' pockets "challenged the wonder" of anyone who had never been a boy or whose memories of boyhood were too distant. The conundrum: "*theoretically*, a boy's pocket is a contracted sphere; *practically*, it embraces everything." Like a boy's stomach, his pockets could always expand to fit in just one more thing, "strange" as it might be.

Nineteenth-century commentators agreed that "the variety and number of articles that find their way into a small boy's pockets are not to be cataloged." His stash could not rightly be called a collection, in that no selective criteria could be said to have been at work. Instead, boys' pockets were frequently likened to places where order had failed, like curiosity shops, junk shops, or flea markets, chaotic storehouses all. Some also saw a close analogy to sites where human order had never sought to interfere: warrens, suggested one observer who heard and then found a live rat in the pocket of a friend's son. The youngster had put it there hoping to feed it to his dog.

But the impulse to catalog was too strong, and just about every writer produced an expansive list that constituted the central feature of these reports (figure 2). An 1862 contributor to *Maine Farmer* explained that he and his wife had "caught our devil and made him disgorge." He proceeded to report the results:

> one eel skin, a piece of chalk, a stub of a lead pencil, seven marbles (one a blood-alley,) a steel pen, an odd mitten, a chunk of taffy candy (very dirty,) an iron screw, a piece of hard putty, four peanuts, a lot of dried orange peel, a comic song (very much worn,) a kite tail (various colors and fabrics,) a reward of merit (dated July, 1860, and quite dilapidated,) a stem of tobacco pipe, portion of a horse shoe, a leaden ten cent piece (showing marks of teeth), one wooden skewer, a lucky bone, and, to cover and protect the whole, an extraordinary dirty pocket handkerchief, the original color of which could not be determined.

The parent-narrator of the *Maine Farmer* takes on the neutral objectivity of a court-appointed trustee making an inventory for probate or a jailer recording the belongings discovered in the possession of a prisoner at his conviction. Adopting the as-you-come-upon-it quality of these records, the father in the *Maine Farmer* milks this incongruous list for full comedic and sentimental effect. In his son's

CONTENTS OF A BOY'S POCKET. (SEE PAGE 499.)

Figure 2. *Contents of a Boy's Pocket*, from *Every Saturday*, August 1870. The father holds up a live turtle that he has just discovered in his sleeping son's trousers.

pockets the natural mingles with the social and man-made; things still potentially useful mix with others hopelessly past their useful life; and the magical rubs elbows with the banal. The father remarks on particulars—the leaden ten-cent piece shows "marks of teeth"; one of the marbles is a special "blood-alley," so called because it is made with alabaster streaked with red veins—and insists on a rigorous specificity, accounting for "four peanuts" that wouldn't usually deserve enumeration and the "odd" mitten lonely without its match. Such exactitude makes the failure to account for the bits of orange peel especially notable. Consigned with others like it to the general term "a lot" (a slang expression in the mid-nineteenth century), the father throws up his hands, emphasizing their considerable number.

As the list unspools the reader has no sense of when it will end. As such it comes close to overstepping the "load limit of what a list can skillfully hold," according to Robert Belknap in his study on literary lists, the point before which a reader falls over in utter boredom. But the cataloging finally does end, and the father wraps up the whole with what Belknap calls an effective anchor, the object that signals the end of the list and that receives special attention, in this case, an "extraordinary dirty pocket handkerchief, the original color of which could not be determined." Under any other circumstance a soiled handkerchief would not be the least bit charming, but here it serves as a worthy coda, its dinginess a testament to the devoted, albeit hygienically lackadaisical, care with which the boy has protected his treasures.

Some parents and writers stop here. Producing the list is testament enough to the strange phenomenon of a pocket's contents. However, many others have not resisted making hypotheses about the single mind responsible for the items, and have tried to divine a future career or something else meaningful from the exercise. Perhaps the bits of wire and wood and "queer contrivances" might indicate a "mechanical turn," wrote a contributor to the *Monroe City Democrat* in 1917. One father, writing in the *Boston Daily Globe* in 1923, took the pocket search as an important process of getting to know one's son, for in them the attentive parent could find "an accurate index to his interests, his habits, his future and his problems too." Yet for most, attempting to discern anything from a motley pocket collection was as difficult as decoding a mysterious "cipher."

Thus the overwhelming tendency was to celebrate a "trait" shared by "all boys" rather than try to detect what each pocketed collection might mean about the boy who created it. Noting that her boy "never has pockets enough," one mother indulgently remarked on her son's hoarding in an 1894 essay. Rather than condemn his disregard for order, she celebrated his bulging pockets, believing his altogether "promiscuous taste" was a sign "of a genuine loveable all-round boy." Pockets, this writer suggests, reveal some key proof or testament to the boy's very boyishness. That bulging pockets could be construed as a biological or developmental trait tells us that these pocket inventories did much more than entertain readers with endearing anecdotes about children. In all this anxious surveillance perhaps parents were looking for confirmation that the kids were all right.

LIKE ANXIETY ABOUT too much screen time for the young in the digital age, worries about excessive civility plagued late nineteenth- and early twentieth-century adults and parents who worried that the comforts of urban life and lack of physical challenges had rendered boys soft, weak, and effeminate. Childhood labor was no longer essential to family survival, as it had been on the family farm, and children instead spent more time in age-graded schools (high schools proliferated by the end of the nineteenth century), engaging in other kinds of activities organized by adults, from scouting to sports clubs to church outings. Middle-class white parents now believed they had to prepare their children for a world of bureaucratic employment requiring different kinds of socialization.

In the process of accommodating a far more regimented life, it seemed boys were losing touch with just what made them "genuine loveable all-round boys." Famous American male writers made this critique and populated their fiction with scampering mischief-makers who reminded readers just "what a boy of forty years ago was like." Initiated by Thomas Bailey Aldrich's *Story of a Bad Boy* (1870), they included Twain's *Tom Sawyer* (1876), William Dean Howells's *A Boy's Town* (1890), and dozens of others. These so-called Bad Boy authors remind readers that "real boys" were not "good boys"; they did not sit quietly in the parlor or church pew, obey their mamas, or pay attention to their lessons as did the wooden characters in children's didactic fiction and Sunday school primers. Real boys roamed about in the world without constraint, free from adult supervision as they traversed the territory from the river's edge to the sawmill while carefully skirting school and the domestic interior. A 1901 ditty in the *Detroit Free Press* made clear that a "natural boy" was "a Robinson Crusoe reading boy, whose pockets are filled with trash."

As the Bad Boy authors had it, childhood was such a world apart that parents could not "penetrate" it with any understanding. So parents looked where they could for reassurance, including into boys' pockets. And those in the know about boys, Aldrich admonished in an essay on pockets in *Every Saturday*, "should not be astonished at finding anything" there. Parents should especially not worry about all the "trash" boys seemed to acquire, one of the central mysteries regarding boys' collecting. As inventories appearing in the press had made clear, boys stuffed their pockets with broken, dirty, soiled, and utterly useless articles, bits of string, "keys that opened nothing," sticky crumbs, and wasps' wings. Paradoxically, as Twain acknowledged in *Tom Sawyer*, to the boy this trash constituted "treasures of almost inestimable value."

More than anything else, boys' value system seemed "inexplicable" to the adult. Why did boys attach equal importance "to a juvenile mud-turtle and an old door knob?" asked a writer in 1870. Making such equivalences without any sense of incongruity reaffirmed that boyhood had its own culture with its own manners and customs, as well as some kind of functioning, if eccentric, economic system. Apportioning value to things—deciding what things are to be treasured, and what things do not count—constitutes one of the ways cultures help to make sense of the world. Upon reflection, the neighborhood friends of Tom Sawyer might have admitted that Tom had pulled a fast one when he got them to pay for the privilege of whitewashing Aunt Polly's fence. But they would all agree that either "a dead rat and a string to swing it with" or a "piece of blue bottle glass" were currency of equal value.

Such norms seemed irrational to adults, however. "Diamonds have not half the value in his eyes" as the junk and "curiosities" he collected, one observer wrote in 1867. Boys seemed to pick up anything that caught their eye during their wanderings, and a preponderance of those curiosities were specimens of the natural world. Frogs, turtles, rats, worms, crabs, snakeskins, beetles, and mice—dead and alive—are overrepresented in boys' pocket inventories. As are other vegetable and mineral substances, including spotted chicken feathers, chestnut hulls, colored pebbles, tree bark, and shells. According to the Bad Boy authors, such stores represented the boy's wide compass and his sustained involvement in agrarian rhythms. In *Boy's Town*, Howells devotes a chapter to boys' foraging, describing its seasonal patterns and products, from unripe mayapples to the variety of "nuts and acorns, and hips and haws" found along the roads and on the riverbanks, in the woods and the pastures.

Evident in these and other depictions by the Bad Boy authors is their nostalgia for the country boy's life and their desire to preserve the rural traditions that were fast disappearing in a modernizing world. But by the last quarter of the nineteenth century, with the commercialization of childhood in full swing, it is likely that boys' pocket treasure included fewer acorns and more penny whistles. The contents of their pockets eventually looked more like the ones represented by the artist Grace Albee, a mother of five boys, in her 1937 print, *Contents of a Small Boy's Pocket* (figure 3). The only found object pictured among the riches spread over a pristine handkerchief is a single flint arrowhead, an artifact that might or might not indicate the boy's exploits far afield. Counterfeit arrowheads had flooded the market beginning in the late nineteenth century for collectors of all kinds.

The pocketknife, by far the most prized pocket object, was manufactured, and it was also the only item (other than a pocket watch) that

Figure 3. *Contents of a Small Boy's Pocket*, by Grace Albee, 1937. Resting on an improbably clean handkerchief are a Norton Subminiature camera (approximately 3½ inches wide, 2½ inches deep, and 2 inches tall), a skate key, a Sears STA Sharp pocketknife, an arrowhead, a pocket watch, and a toy airplane (likely a model of a Douglas DC-2, circa 1935, the first airplane to allow commercial passenger air travel).

made the transition from boyhood to adulthood. When Tom Sawyer receives a "sure-enough" Barlow pocketknife as a gift, "the convulsion of delight that swept his system shook him to his foundations." The knife, costing only twelve and a half cents, could not cut anything, but that did not matter. It retained its "inconceivable grandeur." Discussions about pocketknives and other gear filled the pages of *Boy's Life*, the monthly journal for the Boys Scouts of America that was started in 1911 and was supported by advertisers like Remington, a company that hawked both knives and rifles. "Every fellow [had] a little of the Robinson Crusoe in him—*on his own*—out in the open" if he carried a Remington knife with the official seal of the Boy Scouts. In such advertisements, the small-scale knife's potential for trouble was carefully downplayed. Instead, the knife was seen as a tool that encouraged the hand skills and grit that could produce better, more risk-taking men. A boy without a knife "is to be pitied," judged a journalist in the *Independent* in 1912. "You cannot make a man out of such a boy." The pocketknife was far more important than either a spelling or grammar book because "doing" remained the better "teacher." In his authoritative 1922 study, *Boyology or Boy Analysis*, Henry William Gibson reminded adult readers that while the pocket knife was a boy's most valuable possession, a boy's pockets (and all that they contained) were an "index" of his wealth.

GIRLS' POCKETS: ELEGANT THIMBLES AND DO-GOODERS' TRACTS

WHAT WAS THE index of a girl's wealth? Discussions of the contents of girls' pockets just do not show up in the nineteenth-century press. "From time immemorial," journalists and others have had a great amount of fun over the contents of boys' pockets, observed one "newspaper paragraphist" in an 1876 piece. In considering why the fun did not extend to girls' pockets, this writer admitted to a sudden squeamishness. The writer claimed that, presumably, male journalists were just so unfamiliar with the female pocket form that they did not know what it could hold.

Considering the lavish attention paid to the contents of boys' pockets, this lack of curiosity is notable. Perhaps the most famous girl's pocket did not even belong to a girl at all but rather a grown woman, Lucy Locket (figure 4). While the precise origins of the nursery rhyme remain a matter of debate, what can be said for certain is that the

Lucy Locket, lost her pocket,
Kitty Fisher found it ;
There was not a penny in it,
But a ribbon round it.

Figure 4. Illustration by Kate Greenway for "Lucy Locket," from *Mother Goose; or, The Old Nursery Rhymes*, 1888.

rhyme has nothing much to do with children's experiences, desires, or problems:

> Lucy Locket, lost her pocket,
> Kitty Fisher found it.
> Not a penny was there in it,
> Only ribbon round it.

One widely held contemporary reading has it that Kitty Fisher, a noted courtesan living in late eighteenth-century London, took up with a man—the pocket—that Lucy had cast away when he became insolvent. The whole imbroglio was the topic of excited gossip around town. That a woman called Locket did not secure her lover was the apparent punchline for adults. But young readers likely took the rhyme at face value when it innocently showed up in various editions of *Mother Goose*. And they were left with a merely banal fragment of an incident that, as tie-on pockets became obsolete over the course of the nineteenth century, became a perplexing one: How could you lose an inset pocket? The rhyme offered no lovely nonsense to ponder, no cow jumping over a moon, but disappointing evidence that girls did not carry much of interest. Lucy Locket's empty pocket, with "not a penny in it," appears a most unsatisfactory inheritance.

Like their mothers, girls did not have many pockets at their disposal. "My daughter has only one pocket in her frock," observed one mother at the end of the nineteenth century, while her son had several "crammed to bursting with odds and ends." Inexplicably, in this piece, the writer does not return to her daughter's comparative shortage, nor does she consider taking any kind of action. However, some girls did confront their mothers. In an 1894 remembrance, Sarah Sherwood recalled that getting a single pocket in her dress was her "first and greatest ambition." Her mother had long resisted her pleading, explaining that "there is no use in little girls having pockets. They put everything in them, and tear their dresses off the belts." Receiving a new dress and discovering that her mother had ignored her request yet again, she inexpertly added her own pocket, a lumpy one that hung crookedly. To her credit, Sherwood's mother finally capitulated to her daughter's desires; she fixed the pocket, and "on that day," Sherwood reported, "began the growth of a purer, more unselfish love between mother and me."

When as here girls' pockets are mentioned, descriptions of their contents tend to be brief and to confirm that girls stock useful things. Alice of *Alice in Wonderland* carries a box of comfits, sweets all wrapped up neatly in a box, not moldering and dusty. These sweets come in handy in Wonderland when Alice is unexpectedly asked to distribute prizes to all the creatures who have participated in the caucus race. "What else have you got in your pocket?" asks the Dodo after Alice has given away the last of the candy. "Only a thimble," Alice replies sadly, which the Dodo takes and solemnly presents back to Alice as *her* prize. Trying not to laugh, she accepts the "elegant" thimble out of politeness. Of course, it is no prize at all but rather a reminder of her future role as a thrifty and conscientious housewife. As it turns out, thimbles were as overrepresented in girls' pockets as pocketknives were in boys'. Already pleasingly small in scale, thimbles came in child sizes during the nineteenth century. In her 1817 guide, *Eighteen Maxims of Neatness and Order*, Theresa Tidy advised that girls carry a full complement of sewing devices, the idea being that you should "always have a piece of work to take up at a spare minute."

Among the useful articles girls were expected to have on hand were things that allowed them to do good works. The charitable ideal, giving alms and performing other generous acts, was described extensively at the pulpit, in school, and at home. It was also pictured, for example, in William Beechey's 1793 portrait of the young Mary Ford, where Mary hands a clearly distressed beggar boy a coin that she has retrieved from the tie-on pocket under her apron (figure 5). So pervasive was this ideal that Louisa May Alcott felt the need to expose it as a burden. Had Jo March of *Little Women* been "the heroine of a moral storybook," Alcott wryly remarked, she would have "gone about doing good in a mortified bonnet, with tracts in her pocket."

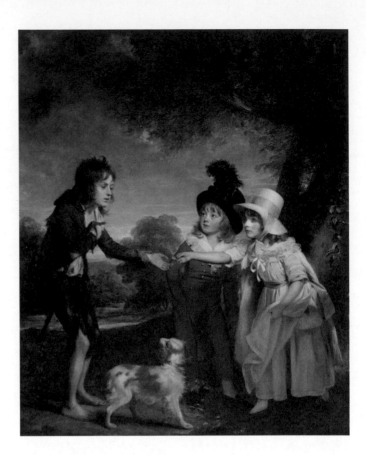

Figure 5. *Portrait of Sir Francis Ford's Children Giving a Coin to a Beggar Boy*, by William Beechey, exhibited 1793. The girl's full, pale-blue tie-on pocket peeks out from under her apron.

Jo does accompany her family when they give the family's Christmas dinner to a poor neighbor. But she does not wear a bonnet, much less a "mortified" one that conceals her face; nor does she carry, think, or say only good things. Alcott eloquently explains that Jo was "only a struggling human girl like hundreds of others, and she just acted out her nature, being sad, cross, listless, or energetic, as the mood suggested." According to Alcott, being good took continual effort and should be expected of everyone.

For Alcott, a spunky girlhood is tomboyish. Jo ignores thimbles. She has professional ambitions, and in what must have been a large pocket (either a tie-on or an integrated one sewn under the voluminous skirts of the 1860s), she stashes manuscripts, rather than sewing projects, to work on in her spare time.

Surely, there must have been avid girl-collectors, matching their male counterparts, who secreted their finds as they galivanted across the prairies or perused interesting corners of the domestic landscape. But as in the periodical press, they were mostly passed over in novels. It was as though everyone just assumed that little girls *were* good, that they carried useful and generic things, and that, in effect, they were made of "sugar and spice and all things nice" as Robert Southey insisted in his 1820 nursery rhyme "What Little Boys Are Made Of." Sugar and spice were gratifyingly positive attributes, to be sure, but attributes whose cloying sweetness effectively dampened further inquiry.

SECRETS NOT INTENDED FOR YOU

ARMED WITH THE "right of search," nosy parents have shown little compunction about their snooping. However, looking back with affection on their own period of unrepentant boyhood hoarding, grown men began to admonish other adults to respect children's privacy. Do not try "to discover secrets not intended for you," wrote Frank Cheley in a 1923 reflection on "the job of being a dad." Do not "empty his pockets and mix their contents," wrote another father in 1912. "Do not undertake to put his things in order." Order would eventually come, these writers supposed, and when it did, boys would continue to enjoy the privileges pocket systems provided. Boys would leave behind childish things, picking up a billfold or a memorandum book instead and discovering that every object had its rightful place, as many a man boasted with evident pride and satisfaction.

That satisfaction was rarely challenged. At least, nineteenth-century press accounts found nothing much to satirize vis-à-vis men's pocket stores. For the most part, men of that century revealed a few key items they *wanted* to show, a bit of colorful pocket handkerchief, for example, or a pocket watch, newly affordable in the 1860s. The watch itself was usually nestled in a pocket, but a chain of gold, silver, leather, or even braided hair announced its presence and helped to keep the watch safely in place (figure 6). Men's pockets, their ubiquitous watch chains seemed to signal, were protected space. They could effectively be secured, like a locket, in ways that children could only dream of.

Only rarely, such as in the event of death, did that protection falter. In his caption to what became one of the most famous Civil War photographs, *A Harvest of Death*, the photographer Alexander Gardner observed that the dead often had no shoes, and their pockets were "turned inside out." He ascribed this desecration to the "pressing need of survivors," who, however, abhorred the practice. In his memoir of the Civil War, a Massachusetts private, James Madison Stone, wrote of the obligation soldiers felt to one another, explaining that it was an "unwritten law" that they would never rifle through the pockets of their "own dead." "Our own dead were sacred, and inviolate, and any man found breaking that law was despised," he asserted. Stone described a recruit who was ostracized after others in his regiment witnessed his theft of eight gold watches from his dead comrades.

The most famous and poignant failure to preserve a kind of pocket integrity took more than a century to unfold. In 1937, the Library of Congress received a strange gift from Lincoln's granddaughter, Mary Lincoln Isham: the articles President Abraham Lincoln had carried in his pockets on the night he was assassinated at Ford's Theatre. Soon after the artifacts that the family had long saved were donated, one enterprising librarian placed them out of public view. They were wrapped in brown paper wrapping with a label that said "Do Not Open" and stashed in a closet-size wall safe adjacent to the head librarian's ceremonial office. The artifacts remained there concealed for almost forty years.

The identity of the librarian, and their motivation, is unknown. Perhaps it was professional pride and a desire not to be associated with other institutions that held and regularly displayed sensational remnants of Lincoln's death. Perhaps the motivation was more personal, and the librarian felt an ethical commitment to preserve Lincoln's dignity. Whatever the case, only much later, when historian Daniel J. Boorstin took over as the Librarian of Congress in 1975 and discovered the mysterious box, was whatever trust had kept the contents hidden broken; the library publicly turned out Lincoln's pockets. Gathering library officials and journalists for a press conference, and choosing Lincoln's birthday as the date to do so, he inspected the contents for the first time. Boorstin explained that the library "should try to human-ize" a man who had been "mytho-logically engulfed." Boorstin also stressed that the items were quite ordinary. They included two sets of eyeglasses; a linen pocket hand-kerchief; a pocketknife; a button; a watch fob but no watch; a recently worthless five-dollar Confederate bill; and newspaper clippings, some with favorable reviews of Lincoln's 1864 presidential candidacy. These clippings demonstrated to Boorstin that Lincoln "was very much like the rest of us": this man Americans so revered for holding steadfast to his principles in the face of unfath-omable loss also needed reassurance on occasion and relished (keeping for years) kind words of a press not always on his side.

Figure 6. Union soldier seated with pistol in hand and watch chain in pocket, ca. 1860–1870.

The circumstances were too tragic and the person too venerated for the inventory to have ever been made the object of fun. But visi-tors still valiantly try to decode their meaning. In a transformation that Boorstin did not foresee, the artifacts, rather than humanizing Lincoln, have "become like relics," as the library itself has observed with some discomfort. They remain the artifacts visitors to the Library

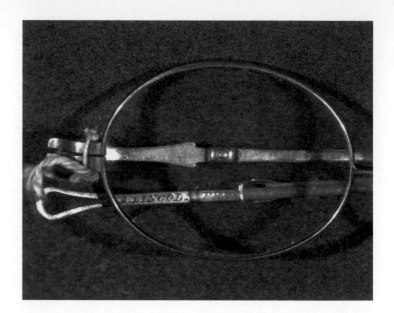

Figure 7. A bit of string holds together the broken hinge of Abraham Lincoln's glasses, undated, one of the objects found in his pockets on the night of his assassination.

of Congress most frequently ask to see. Through these humblest of intermediaries, visitors hope to experience that electric shiver of connection made possible by their onetime proximity to Lincoln's person, to access Lincoln in an unselfconscious moment, dressing for the theater, remembering with a mix of habit and special intent to take what he thought he might need. Lincoln, we learn from his pockets, bowed to convention when he carried a handkerchief, his initials stitched by hand in red thread. But he also demonstrated a quirky resistance to it, appearing in public without having had his glasses fixed and instead using a bit of string to secure a broken hinge (figure 7). More endearing proof of Lincoln's lack of vanity would be hard to come by.

"TALK ABOUT A BOY'S POCKET!" TREASURE AND TRASH IN WOMEN'S HANDBAGS

THE VOLUPTUOUS LISTS and inventories of boys' pockets that had long delighted readers appeared with less frequency over the course of the twentieth century. "Huck Finn Era Gone, Boys' Pockets Show; Cash and Bankbooks Crowd Out Eels, Gum" was the snappy title of a 1950 *New York Times* article mourning the change. While boys might not have demonstrated the same zeal for pocket collections as they once did, they became a useful foil for a new type of collector when this "trait" of "all" preadolescent boys was recognized as one shared by grown women. "Talk about a boy's pocket!" exclaimed a clerk at a busy newspaper desk in 1905 as he listened to an "excited" woman recalling the contents of her lost handbag to place an ad in the Lost and Found section of the classifieds. The clerk suffered through a number of digressive histories as the woman recalled the provenance of each lost article, divulging information that elicited a web of associations and memories. For his patience, the clerk is allowed the punch line: "a boy's pocket ain't in it with a woman's purse when it comes to infinite variety in the way of contents."

This bit of reported conversation made a point that would become familiar as women, increasingly resigned to the on-again-off-again presence of integrated pockets in their clothes, took up the handbag, interchangeably called a purse or pocketbook. The more duties imposed on handbags, the more they increased in size, blossoming from the tiny change and handkerchief holder of the late nineteenth century into what critics likened to a bulbous sack, an omnipresent trunklet, a suitcase, an ashcan, a millstone, and a burden. Observers soon faced the same conundrum they had with boys: *theoretically*, a woman's purse is a contracted sphere; *practically*, it seemed to embrace everything.

Such comments echoed the accusations directed at women over their eighteenth-century tie-on pockets—like them, handbags were disorganized pits in popular representation. A century on, women still could not distribute objects over and around their bodies, neither enjoying nor understanding "the science of pocket equilibrium," according to one satirist reflecting in 1903 on the misunderstandings and dissensions caused in one marriage by the pocket/purse distinction. While the husband crows that he can distribute several pounds of things "and scarcely realize that he was loaded," he worries his wife may have no capacity for rational organization. He reflects that this must be the reason she "jams" all of his pocketed collection back into a single pocket after mending a button on his coat, leaving him to list dangerously.

Some celebrated the intriguing possibilities that a generously sized bag offered, however. In her 1934 children's book, *Mary Poppins*, P. L. Travers describes the severe but lovable nanny who arrives from the sky carrying a distinctive umbrella and a carpet bag hooked on her elbow like a handbag. To the children, the bag appears empty. After peeking inside, each claims that "there's nothing in it." But it appears empty only to nonbelievers. Poppins proceeds to unpack a starched white apron, tying it on to signal her readiness to bring order to the Bankses' household, and then retrieves a number of other necessaries in a list that recalls the furious miscellany of a boy's pocket inventory. Between a bottle of scent and a package of lozenges, Poppins casually produces a folding lawn chair. Travers acknowledges the playfulness of the boys' pocket inventories and one-ups it, adding objects of discordant scale to the mix.

Disney's 1964 film adaptation of Travers's book further exaggerates this scene by renewing the bag's contents. As Poppins surveys her new room, a plain adjunct to the nursery under the eaves, she comments that its "not exactly Buckingham Palace." She remedies this condition by pulling from her bag a hat rack, mirror, potted plant, and highly decorative standing lamp with a shade full of tassels. These are the very household accoutrements that employers denied servants as a way to underline their lowly status in the household (figure 8). Was the bag some kind of trick? Michael Banks wonders as he looks under the table on which the bag sits, searching for a false bottom. He will come to learn that imagination extends the limits of daily life, that Poppins is not tricky, as he suspects, but "wonderful," as his sister knows already. Celebrating Poppins's magical powers, the film nevertheless pokes fun at her for the qualities she supposedly shares with all women; as she continues unpacking, Poppins has trouble locating an item she wants in her capacious bag, a magical tape measure with which she can evaluate the children's height and character. "Funny, I always carry it with me," she muses as she stamps her foot in frustration and submerges her arm and shoulder into her bag all the way up to her chin.

Figure 8. Mary Poppins unpacks a hat rack from her carpetbag. Still image from Disney's 1964 film adaptation of *Mary Poppins*. © 1964 Disney.

A woman rummaging in a handbag had become a familiar sight at once perfectly reasonable and apparently perplexing. When a woman cradled a bag that *Vogue* suggested was "as full of tricks as a magician's" and peered inside it, she accessed private space to which every onlooker was barred. Absorbed and "busy" with their bags, women thus signaled that their attention was elsewhere. Perhaps it was inevitable then that the handbag posed a kind of irresistible challenge. Solely associated with women, the handbag promised to reveal intriguing evidence about femininity. As boyhood seemed a world apart with its own cultures and rules, so too seemed womanhood.

Picking up on this challenge, the editors at *Life* promised "to throw light on the mystery of what a woman crams into her handbag." Believing that a mere photograph would not suffice and channeling popular interest in the new medical (and science fiction) uses for X-rays, *Life* sent out a handbag to a radiographer to "penetrate" its "messy interior" in the fall of 1939 (figure 9). *Life* placed the X-ray image adjacent to an ordinary photograph in which, to orient the viewer, the frame of the handbag had been sketched on paper and the objects arranged as they had appeared in the purse. The resulting comparison between photograph and X-ray is more confusing than illuminating, a silly visual stunt, as the X-ray shows quite a bit *less* than the photograph. A reader casually paging through the magazine would have come across the x-rayed handbag just after a spread focusing on the newest bag designs (figure 10). The implicit message from *Life* is that you can buy this great new bag, but watch out: we see through you! Taken together all this suggests some ambivalence about fashion's role in manufacturing sleek exteriors. Women may have appeared aloof and unapproachable, perfectly in command, but just a

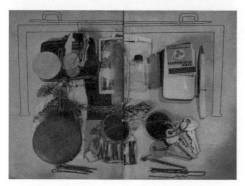

Figure 9. The interior of a woman's handbag, photograph by Ralph Morse (with radiographer Dr. H. Volmer-Pix, top), published in *Life*, November 1939. Figure 10. Fashion photograph by Ralph Morse, published in *Life*, November 1939.

little digging revealed a hopelessly chaotic interior. Women themselves lugged around "impediments" to their own functioning; in this case, sixty-one of them, to be exact, according to the X-ray.

Even though *Life*'s X-ray was not illuminating, reports in various media attempted their own accounting. Inventories of the contents of women's purses began to appear in newspapers and journals and made it onto daytime TV. Journalists accosted women on the street and waiting in the local subway station; interviewed confidants and friends; conducted informal or random surveys among high school students, suburban housewives, and businesswomen; and set up celebrity interviews asking their informants to disgorge the contents of their handbags. In the early 1950s, the charming and attentive TV host Art Linkletter convinced members of his mostly female studio audience to divulge intimate details of their lives in live broadcasts of CBS's *House Party*, an audience-participation-based talk and variety show that had originated on radio. Linkletter had "a sort of psychiatrist's effect on his audiences," the *Saturday Evening Post* commented, and so it was perhaps not surprising that his audience described things like their most embarrassing moments and opened up their handbags for inspection. In what became a recurring "ritual," as the *Post* dubbed it, Linkletter peeked inside some volunteer's purse and commented on the dentures, rum flask, and unpaid telephone bill he held up while guilelessly inquiring, "Why on *earth* would you have *that* in there?" Women began to arrive on *House Party* "with their purses loaded," Linkletter recalled in his memoir, evidently hoping to stump him.

Although evidence varied widely, a portrait emerged over the twentieth century of the average woman as an unrepentant purse stuffer. Journalists had ready frames of reference. Toward the ephemera they encounter over the course of a day, women "exhibit the same acquisitiveness which small boys generally confine to marbles, or pack rats to shiny objects," *Life* magazine charged in 1945. Having raised the specter of pack rats, it did not take long for the idea that women's purses were rat's nests to become proverbial. Boys certainly mistreated their pockets, creating spaces more like actual rat's nests when they prepared them with bits of straw, grass, and dirt to accommodate their pocket menageries. But they were forgiven their slovenliness. Discussions of boys' pocket collections indulgently celebrated a recognized quirk of boyhood. At the very least, the things boys noticed and picked up on their daily rambles documented a healthy venturesomeness, a lively interest in their surroundings.

It was harder to make the case that anything constructive could be made of the old gum wrappers and receipts that littered women's bags. Some women claimed that their purses contained whatever they might need for any emergency. The copious detritus collected in women's purses could be considered a way for women to carry a "home away from home." In a 1943 reflection in *The Atlantic Monthly*, wit Franklin Adams charged that women carry the equivalent of a roomful of things from a well-stocked apartment. "It seems to me," Adams mused, "that she can get along for days without going home." Admitting that his own schoolboy's pockets rattled as he walked, he hesitated to cast the first "pebble." Even so, he proceeded to publish an inventory of his "handbag confidant."

Psychologists questioned women's need to carry around their homes with them, like hermit crabs, and several agreed that purse stuffing had deep psychological roots. It might be the sign of a "compulsive worrier," suggested Dr. Joyce Brothers, an advice columnist and TV personality who, starting in the mid-1950s, helped to legitimize and translate psychological concepts to a broad audience. Psychological language and interpretations abound and continue to be deployed. In a 1997 essay titled "Accessory in Crisis," Daniel Harris provocatively called the handbag an umbilical cord that ties women to their homes. He pointed out that women evince a kind of amnesia when asked what they carry and, when pressed to provide an accounting, are surprised by their findings. They are also just as likely as critics to call some of that accumulation junk. For Harris, this was proof that women's collecting is involuntary, motivated by a memory of her atavistic fear of leaving home. He charged that the handbag was a "crutch," a "surrogate" for the bathroom, a "caldron of spinsterly reservations, taboos, pruderies and fears."

Perhaps the situation is not so dire as all that. In 1957, another expert, in a purse exposé published in the *Los Angeles Times*, countered that the large handbag did not reflect some kind of deep-seated fear of leaving home for too long. Rather it signified "a very sensible adjustment to complex living." The fact that makeup had to be reapplied over the course of a day twinned with the pressure to appear consummately put together meant that the handbag was foremost a kind of traveling vanity table. After the flappers of the 1920s normalized the use of makeup, which was previously common only for prostitutes and actresses, women have felt no compunction about touching up their lipstick while conferring with a mirror or performing other private ablutions in public. In 1934, Dan Beard, one of the founding members of the Boy Scouts, opined in *Boy's Life* that "a boy without a knife is as bad as a canoe without paddles, a lumberman without an axe, or a girl without a compact."

Reinforcing makeup's hold, designers produced compacts that matched lipsticks, cigarette cases, and combs, the whole made to carry in important bags. The fashion press obligingly reported on these en suite offerings, elegantly packaged and satisfying to handle. That such artifacts might become objects of totemic importance was realized by Katherine Mansfield in a short story published in 1920 titled "The Escape." Spying the contents of his wife's purse open on her lap—powder puff, rouge stick, mirror, and a delicate vial that contained "tiny black pills, like seeds"—the estranged husband realizes that "in ancient Egypt, she would be buried with these things."

Like boys, women have tended to overvalue nonessentials, according to popular lore. Although many women consider lipstick an essential, journalists had fun imagining the supposed crises that involved not having the perfect shade of lipstick on hand. "Adolescent fears of running into a real hunk without any makeup on remains," wrote Glenna Whitely for the *Chicago Tribune* in 1985. And because women carry such trifles, women's attachment to their purses was and continues to be the stuff of legend: "In shipwreck and storm, fire and flood, a woman may leave her jewels behind, yet risk her life to go back for her pocketbook," *Vogue* noted in 1973. The insistent directive—*Leave your personal belongings behind!*—heard during things like fire drills, seems in part directed at this stereotype. Whitely, in her 1985 piece, profiled a Texas woman who managed to hang on to her handbag after her boat sank. She and her companions spent four hours in heaving fifteen-foot waves, eventually scaling an oil rig. With sheer delight Whitely points out the really "incredible" part of this story: that after that ordeal, the woman still had her bag and was able to produce a piece of paper and a pen with which to write a "Help!" note to stuff in a bottle. The note was not what ultimately saved them, but "most would agree," Whitely concludes, "it would take Moses to part a woman from her purse."

Some women do agree, and with increasing forthrightness since the late twentieth century, they have declined to be baited by insults about their powerful attachment to their purses. They counter that the purse holds more than nonessentials. "My whole life is in there!" is a common refrain, and one Valerie Steele, chief curator at the Museum at the Fashion Institute of Technology, considered in her 2005 book on the handbag. While a bag's design may reflect the owner's aspiration—chic, sporty, practical—its private interior is an extension of a woman's identity, Steele contended. It serves as a nerve center; an indication of a woman's many roles, not necessarily one of her anxieties; a reflection of her adaptability, not necessarily her penchant for stockpiling. In a positive light, the purse is largely recognized as having both practical and emotional salience.

EVEN IN A confessional age, when people volunteer almost anything and everything, the desire to get a glimpse of what William Dean Howells called the "daily doings and dreamings" of others has not diminished over the years, and both pocket and handbag remain a unique site for investigation. As with the urge to see Lincoln's pocket collection housed in the Library of Congress, people still hope to find a conduit to the unguarded person. Madonna managed to monetize that urge by auctioning off the contents of her own purse (a magnifying mirror,

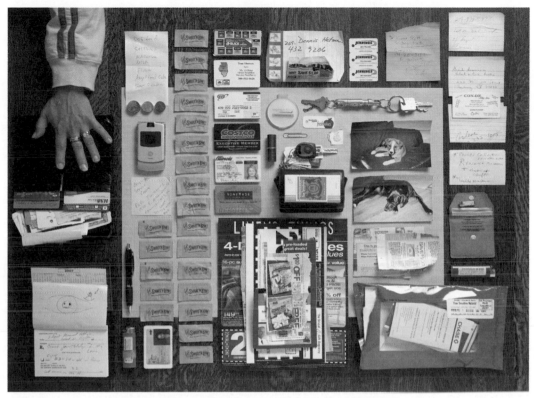

Figure 11. "21 Sweet'N Lows," by François Robert, part of the series *Contents*, 2010.

hair clips, skin blotting tissues, and lip gloss) at Cannes in 2007 to benefit AIDS research. During a sparkling gathering hosted by Sharon Stone, Madonna warned the audience not to underbid, reminding all who were present that that the lip gloss in the bag had touched her lips. Madonna created her own reliquary while very much alive.

The photographer François Robert proposed that the detritus of purses and pockets might serve as a medium of portraiture, that evidence of daily doings could be more revealing than one's face. In his series *Contents* (1978–2010), Robert depicts only the objects discovered in the pockets, handbags, and knapsacks of his subjects along with their outstretched hands (figures 11 and 12). The work is aligned with traditional portraiture in that subjects have long posed among their possessions. Whereas such objects tend to be carefully chosen, Robert's undertaking depended on the element of surprise. Told they

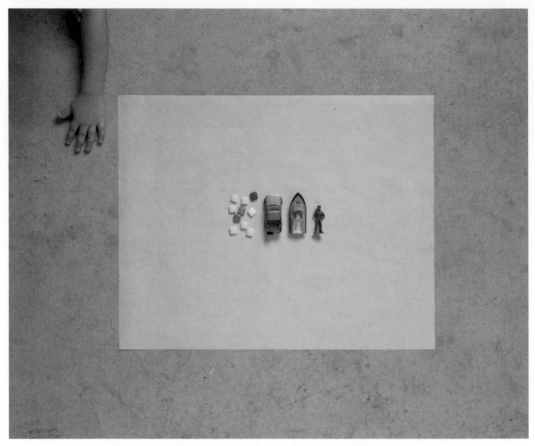

Figure 12. "Ten Chicklets," by François Robert, part of the series *Contents*, 2010.

were to participate in a fine arts project, none of his subjects—120 friends, relatives, and strangers ranging in age from four to seventy-five—were given any forewarning that they would be asked to reveal their personal belongings. Feeling vulnerable as she unpacked a canvas satchel, one participant considered editing her cache. This was an option Robert gave all his participants. But she ultimately left the material unedited, amazed that Robert "was able to, in such an abbreviated manner, catch somebody's entire life in that moment."

Robert organizes his subject's possessions by type, creating a composition from the everyday items with an eye to color and the patterns of graphic typefaces. He uses the same size sheet of paper in each the portrait as a backdrop or baseline, on top of which some collections spill out and some sit well within. In focusing viewers' attention so insistently on the contents themselves, viewers are left to wonder, for example, about those momentary compulsions to take an extra something *for the road* or *just in case*—and how purloined Sweet'N Lows might just add up after daily stops at the coffee shop (figure 11). Other than general age (figure 12), surprisingly little information about the person—for instance, their gender or occupation or status—is available in these still-lives-as-portraits; Robert strategically resists efforts to label the purse or pocket stuffers (and the few minimalists he photographed), disrupting the myths that have grown up around them. In doing so he reveals that all along, the notion that you are what you carry has required social types, enshrined in our imaginations, to support them. Tellingly, many of the negative or at least perplexing stereotypes concerning boys were eventually transferred to women. Like the nineteenth-century Robinson Crusoe–loving boys whose pockets were filled "with trash," women, too, according to this trope, cannot distinguish between the valuable and the worthless; they hoard and cannot throw anything way. Such characterizations have told us less about women as any kind of categorizable group than about how much modern culture values orderliness, on the one hand, and the assumptions it makes about who can or cannot be expected to achieve it, on the other.

One can always carry a smaller bag. Or avoid carrying one at all by engineering some kind of workaround in accordance with the times, like the recent practice of stuffing money and an ID in the back of a "souped-up" plastic cell phone case and placing that into one's waistband. Yet the handbag endures. And it remains something of a spectacle, an accoutrement of femininity. Women's handbags are still considered dangerous caldrons, and they come up whenever there is a need to account for some remarkable practice regarding women's care of their property. In a feature on "the good stories" of 2020, when recounting their favorite marriage proposals, the *New York Times* saw fit to note this detail: the future groom "hid the ring that day in a place that he said [his future bride] would never have looked for it: her handbag."

POCKETS The pocket theme dominates the Paris Collections, is structural, a part of the line. Above, Dior's calla-lily pockets, on beige with a linen look. Woodward & Lothrop; Marshall Field.

Figure 1. Christian Dior day suit, photograph by Arik Nepo, published in "The News in Paris," *Vogue*, March 15, 1949. With his "calla-lily pockets" Dior helped the "pocket theme" dominate the spring Paris collections in 1949.

CHAPTER 6

Pocket Play:
Designing for "Doubly Decorative Value"

Is it true, as Christian Dior claimed in 1954, that "men have pockets to keep things in, women for decoration"? If so, it is a phenomenon Dior actively helped to perpetuate. In the ten short years of his career before his early death in 1957, the fashion press often called out a dramatic pocket embellishment as "unmistakably Dior." Some Dior pockets were pointy and "whisked out beyond the shoulders" like wings in flight. His "kangaroo pockets" flopped high over the breasts rather disconcertingly, while his "calla-lily pockets" were petal shaped and rose up to the shoulders, jutting forward in a scrolling arch (figure 1). Whether set high under the slope of the clavicle or sharply angled along the hips, these gestural pockets helped stress some feature of the silhouette Dior hoped to accentuate. Very few, however, could carry much more than a pretty handkerchief.

In early twenty-first-century discussions of the gendered politics of pockets, Dior's witticism has made the rounds. Cited in articles and gallery-wall texts, it identifies differing design motives at work in men's and women's wear. The quip condenses what we sense to be generally true: that men's clothes are made for utility and women's for beauty. Dior's own work confirms that this was the case for women's wear in the 1950s, and a cursory survey of pocketing after the eighteenth century would have given him all the evidence needed to confirm that men's wear, in contrast, had not much bothered itself with decorative effects. Men's pockets have not jutted out spectacularly, drooped suggestively, or been made to mimic wings or calla lily petals. They have tended not to refer to other objects or involve jokes, mimicry, or trompe l'oeil. Resolutely straightforward, their form has followed their function.

Yet as with any pithy pronouncement, one does well to interrogate it. It is possible that Dior exaggerated the lack of whimsy in pockets that adorn clothing designed for men. Also possible: that Dior failed to acknowledge the cultural work that ornamental pockets can perform—that ornament can act as a vehicle through which to express aesthetic propositions and ideas. (Analogies and jokes, after all, challenge wearers and viewers to see things in a new way.) In fact pockets have participated in fashion's imaginative projects with increasing exuberance in the twentieth and twenty-first centuries, and this has been the case in women's wear, men's wear, and gender-agnostic clothing. As art historian Ann Hollander observed, sensible aspects of clothing are "no sooner put into use than put into play."

"POCKETS, POCKETS EVERYWHERE"

"POCKETS, POCKETS EVERYWHERE this spring," touted the caption for one of Erté's (Roman de Tirtoff's) first contributions to *Harper's Bazaar* in March 1915 (figure 2). Erté's illustrations of his own designs began to be published that year, and it seems only fitting that he introduced an element that fascinated him and on which he would continue to tinker for the next decade. Pockets had only rarely appeared on the surface of women's clothes in the eighteenth and nineteenth centuries,

Figure 2. Fashion designs and illustrations by Erté, published in *Harper's Bazaar*, 1915. "Pockets, pockets everywhere this spring" touted *Harper's Bazaar* in its coverage of the winter fashions from Paris.

but as the quantity of decorative lace and ribbons decreased with the transition to modern dress, pockets took up some of the decorative slack. Like the sudden emergence of budding flowers, the arrival of pockets in women's dresses, as the Erté caption suggests, delighted many. Perhaps because they were unprecedented and there was as yet no settled place for them, designers felt no obligations about form or position. As *Vogue* noted in 1916, they constituted "a *new* decorative element in design." Not surprisingly then patch pockets, sewn directly onto the outside of a garment rather than inserted at the side seam, were especially prevalent.

The fashion pages unapologetically stressed the visual interest of this new element, emphasizing the novelty of Erté's patch pockets in the shape of mittens: outlined in black and red leather with a furry trim, they enhanced a white leather jacket (center). Also featured was a halter with red leather patch pockets that stood out "like beacon lights" against a taupe-colored afternoon dress (top left). Pockets provided a key visual opportunity to showcase contrasting color or material, a way to repeat the activity at the collar or hem in a rhythmic counterpoint. "Novel pockets" served as punctuation marks, enlivening otherwise simple coats and dresses, making them "especially smart."

One of the few designers asked to illustrate his own work, Erté was also one of the few asked to provide occasional commentary. In several of his published letters to the editor of *Harper's Bazaar*, Erté cautioned that any ornament should have a purpose. He wrote that he "disliked intensely . . . frocks which are overburdened with useless ornamentation." And, in general, his many pockets seemed to be designed to function. He placed pockets accessible to the hand, ready for use. Such pockets had, as *Vogue* suggested in 1916, "doubly decorative value." For Erté, that double duty seemed more conceptual and less merely pretty: his formal manipulations allowed him to pursue a series of analogies, often reflecting in some way on containment. Some of these analogies are childlike in their concreteness—a pocket is like a mitten. Others are more abstract and concerned with how two-dimensional cloth could be manipulated into three-dimensional volumetric space. Over the years, Erté designed pockets folded like paper envelopes, woven like baskets, and knotted like traditional sewing bags. A favorite move was the simplest: turning up a panel from the coat, dress, sleeve, or scarf and securing it to form a large pocket. Some of Erté's pockets reference the long history of these containers as a previously detached accessory, including pockets suspended from belts and sashes, buttoned onto coats, and attached to halters to mimic aprons. In his yellow tennis sweater of 1920, Erté engineered a diagonal lattice netting at the elbows and hips alluding to the tennis net. At the hips, the netting was folded up into pockets to carry a mess of tennis balls (figure 3).

Ingenious as the pocket-net might be, the tennis outfit was more suited to "frivol away a summer afternoon" than to engaging in serious competition. A journalist for *Harper's Bazaar* reported seeing a player in Erté's tennis getup in Monte Carlo in August 1920, where Erté was then living. They also noted that the player had followed a suggestion by the designer to paint men's faces with varying expressions on the tennis balls, apparently to intensify the enjoyment of smashing them. In this seaside resort, a special order of leisure was possible. Not only could most women not afford his lyrical fantasies, but the basket pockets that adorned his "pretty garden frocks" were limited in application and hardly efficient for carrying roses. Erté's adventurous pocket forays nevertheless demonstrated just how adaptable a motif they proved, precisely because pockets could take on any form.

Figure 3. A tennis sweater, design and illustration by Erté, published in *Harper's Bazaar*, August 1920. The knitted sweater trails into diamond-shaped lattice at the elbows and hips, mimicking the tennis net, and loops up at the hips to form pockets that can hold tennis balls.

OTHER DESIGNERS TOOK up Erté's interest in making useful pockets in whimsical shapes, notably sportswear designers Claire McCardell and Bonnie Cashin, who crafted hold-everything pockets that recalled allied accessories like aprons and snap purses. It was Elsa Schiaparelli, however, who utilized the most diverse and improbable of sources throughout her career. Famously aligned with avant-garde artists, Schiaparelli used clothing as her medium for creating modern art. She discovered in clothing an unparalleled means in which to "make the fantastic real," as Salvador Dalí famously endeavored to do with his surrealist objects. Schiaparelli's designs confounded much of the couture-buying public. But her "apparent craziness," as she called it in her 1954 autobiography, *Shocking Life*, could be better described as a willingness to consider just what strange things clothes actually are, including the fact that garments specifically shaped to fit our bodies also comment on them and their erotic natures. Because of these fetishistic possibilities, clothes are always more than they appear.

Many of Schiaparelli's famous jokes, her punning, and what she called "fun and gags" have to do with pockets, including her lip-applique pockets on a 1937 day suit and her "bureau drawer" pockets in a 1936 collaboration with Dalí (figure 4). "Dalí was a constant caller," Schiaparelli recalled of their first collaboration. "We devised together

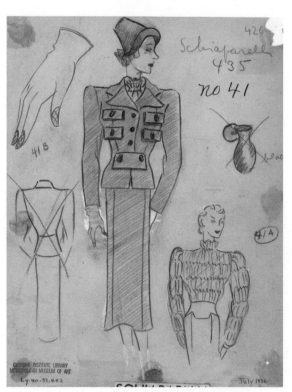

Figure 4. Fashion sketch from Bergdorf Goodman illustrating Elsa Schiaparelli's bureau-drawer suit, 1936.

the coat with many drawers from one of his famous pictures." For Dalí, that series of pictures worked out variations on a theme, a bureau transformed into a woman, what he called an "anthropomorphic cabinet." A committed, if not the most nuanced, reader of Freud, Dalí's drawers hang open in provocative ways. Drawers and pockets were one of those enclosing, hollow spaces Freud identified in his 1899 *The Interpretations of Dreams* as having clearly sexual analogues. When, also in 1936, Dalí desecrated the goddess of Love, the Venus de Milo, with drawers in a half-size plaster reproduction of the famous marble statue, the image was nothing if not salacious (figure 5).

The trompe l'oeil drawers that embellished Schiaparelli's day suit, in contrast, were firmly shut. Several of the bureau drawers had no pocket attachment, but a few were made into true, functional

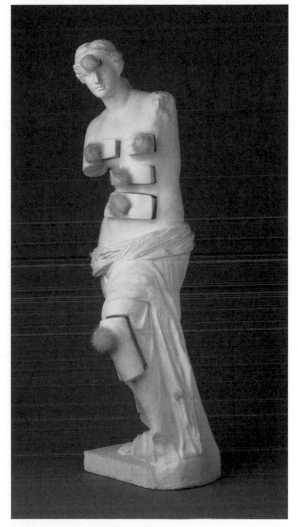

Figure 5. *Venus de Milo with Drawers,* by Salvador Dalí, 1936.

pockets, a feint that acknowledges the kinship between these interior places. Rather than exploring some personal psychosexual anxiety, as did Dalí, Schiaparelli was involved in a punning interpretation of a familiar artifact, exploring a human propensity to see bodily analogues in the domestic landscape. (A chest, we say, stands on legs and may have a tall back.) Schiaparelli's placement and sizing of her suit's drawers, however, allude to other fleshy parts. Offering two-, five-, and eight-pocket-drawer versions of the suit that slyly accentuate the breasts and belly, Schiaparelli created a "chest of drawers" rearranged, hinting at and yet resisting identification.

Completing the bureau illusion, Schiaparelli outfitted her drawer-pockets with a variety of drawer handles, employing plastic crystal doorknobs, black plastic rings, and hanging pull tabs. As she noted in her autobiography, Schiaparelli worked closely with talented jewelers, sculptors, and artisans who used "the most incredible things" to make her closures. "Not one [button] looked like what a button was supposed to look like," she reflected. Crafted from plastic, wood, or metal, they were shaped to resemble crawling insects, peanuts, chains, locks, clips, spent bullet casings, and lollipops. While Schiaparelli stayed close to her sources in this instance (drawers and doors), Dalí turned to mink-tufted pom-poms to act as drawer pulls in his Venus sculpture. These differing choices suggest that for all the productive spark of collaboration, these individual partners still pursued their own paths. Dalí's drawer pulls seductively invited touch. Schiaparelli's pull tabs, witty and slightly alarming on second glance, offered one of those invitations an observer knows not to follow up on. Of all the options, the hanging pull tab, so close to the nipple, seems to have been a little too racy for the retailer Bergdorf Goodman: the sketch of the model shows that a buyer crossed it out (figure 4).

Did Schiaparelli tame Dalí's work into a conservative suit that any woman could wear, as some critics have maintained? She clearly backed away from the overtly sexual. But one could also say that she had other motives, and that she intended to allow the wearer to keep hold of her secrets. As Gaston Bachelard observed in his 1954 book, *The Poetics of Space*, drawers and the locks and keys with which we secure them have resonances other than the sexual ones psychoanalysts have so "monotonously" attributed to them. Chests and drawers are hiding places, "hybrid objects" important to imaginative life that satisfy our need for privacy and mystery. Significantly, a drawer is a "space that is not open to just anybody." No chest or drawer exists that cannot be ransacked, however, and so rather than attempt to "frighten" the trespasser with ornate latches and bolts, "it is preferable to mislead him," mused Bachelard. In her bureau-drawer suit, only the wearer has privileged access to intimate space. Only the wearer knew which pockets were real and which were red herrings. Attentive to women's imaginative lives, Schiaparelli offered imaginative work that did not tame the suit so much as place the wearer in control.

AT THE TIME, the suit itself was something over which women hoped to gain some control. Much of the drama in women's wear over the course of the twentieth century involved appropriating the forms and symbolic authority of men's wear. Influenced by Schiaparelli (a "cunning carpenter of clothes," as Janet Flanner observed in the *New Yorker* in 1932), sleeker suits in a wider range of materials steadily replaced dresses for chic urban living. These suits were still almost universally worn with skirts, which would seem to confirm their femininity, but they nevertheless looked modern and severe. It is not surprising that ambivalence over women's encroachment into men's wear, and their parallel quest for increasing power and status, occasionally played out on the surface of coats and suits tailored to fit women's bodies. At the same time, pockets—and the manner in which they were manipulated at breast and hip—registered and animated those cross-gender tensions.

Breast pockets continued to be the site of provocative work for Schiaparelli, not all of it restrained. A wool evening coat from 1938–39, for example, decorated with six patch pockets, is startling in its directness (figure 6). The silk patch pockets are a vibrant pink, a color Schiaparelli called "bright, impossible, impudent, becoming, life-giving." They are made in the shape of eighteenth-century Sèvres porcelain vases, rococo objects par excellence, and they frame the breasts in confrontational ways. Outlined in gold embroidery, and sprinkled with white ceramic flowers, a specialty of the Sèvres manufactory, the center of each of the six vessels includes a sequined motif in a darker pink-mauve. From afar, the dark mauve sequins recall nothing so much as nipples standing out

Figure 6. Elsa Schiaparelli evening coat with pockets in the shape of eighteenth-century Sèvres porcelain vessels, winter 1938–39. Black wool with pink silk, gold embroidery, sequins, and porcelain flowers.

"like beacon lights," ridiculous in their repetition. Did an observer know where to look? "Who is left to feel uncomfortable," asks Robyn Gibson in reflecting on this coat, "the woman who has selected to wear the garment or the observer whose attention is fixed?"

By so insistently calling attention to the breasts, Schiaparelli broke the rules of propriety in elite dressing. Her design does not highlight the breasts in a usual way by strategically showing some cleavage. Rather it enlists elaborate decoration to question that very expectation. Using the decorative for subversive ends is hard to do, however. Sparkling sequins, texture, and vivid color tend to be associated with frivolous endeavors in art and culture, and that frivolousness threatens to undermine the wearer.

This worry preoccupied Schiaparelli's near contemporary and some-time rival, Coco Chanel, who hated that women's clothing so often served as jokes or entertainment. Insisting on "a dignity that was invulnerable," historians Caroline Evans and Minna Thornton explain, Chanel espoused an antidecorative uniform. When Chanel made her comeback collection in 1954 at the age of seventy, just as Schiaparelli was closing up her couture house, she produced the easy fitting suits for which she is now remembered (figure 7). References to the body are downplayed in these suits, which have been called "the nearest thing to a man's two- or three-buttoned suit in the twentieth century."

In a series of interviews marking her return, Chanel offered a primer on what she considered good design. She likened tailoring a well-fitted suit to making a watch, arguing that the designer needed to be attentive to the smallest of details of the suit's inner mechanism. A dress must "function" for the wearer, she declared. "Place the pockets accurately for use," she railed. "Never a button without a button-hole." Unlike the robust pockets of American sportswear designers, Chanel's pockets never really invited much more than "a key, a lighter, whatever," as *Vogue* off-handedly observed. Still, they worked. Chanel had no patience for pockets that turned into something else entirely or for designers who "leave [women] a fake, or at most a tiny little joker."

Figure 7. Coco Chanel suit of 1959. Chanel's decorative touches were minimal: her tweedy jackets were lined with complimentary checks and, when rolled up at the sleeve, formed contrasting cuffs that matched the edgings of the patch pockets. © The Museum at FIT.

Chanel suspected that the jokes and fake pockets that adorned women's suits and dresses served to amuse and belittle. When *Vogue* admired a 1952 resort dress with trompe l'oeil pockets—at that time selling like "the Paris-equivalent of hot cakes"—an editor praised it with the typical frothy carelessness that so enraged Chanel (figure 8). Heralding a new screen-printing technology, *Vogue* noted that the collar, pockets, and buttons of the dress were "all absolute frauds," not meant to deceive anyone. This roundup of tailored elements was "there only by the grace of the printing process, and they're there, frankly, for entertainment." The dress celebrated the idea that deception is central to women's fashion, not, as Schiaparelli would have it, to show up women's predicament in a patriarchy but to reaffirm something about the status quo. Much of the entertainment apparently involved witnessing the transformation of dress into suit with the knowledge that such a transformation would never be complete.

Figure 8. "The Trompe-L'Oeil Resort Dress," photograph by Norman Parkinson, published in *Vogue*, December 1, 1952. The dress was originally produced by the French firm Hèrmes and Herbert Sondheim, who ran a dressmaking business that produced affordable versions of Parisian high-end fashion, arranged to copy the dress for major US department stores.

Beyond endorsing fraudulent pockets in sometimes disparaging tones, fashion journalists often failed to explain all the jokes designers traded among themselves as they commented on each other's design work via quotation and parody. After Chanel's death in 1970, a period of tentative suiting followed as increasing numbers of women entered the workforce. Struggling over what to wear to the office, women initially followed the advice of image consultants

308

Figure 9. Franco Moschino suit with upside-down breast pockets, photograph by Walter Chin for the editorial "Suitable Plaids," *Vogue*, August 1, 1989.

like John T. Molloy, whose 1977 *Dress for Success* counseled women to look as unthreatening as possible. As *Vogue* noted, this questionable advice resulted in "horrifying," drab compromises punctuated by "flop-doodle little girl bow ties" that failed to make any statement at all. More confident power suits emerged by the mid-1980s that were brash, stylish, and highly desirable. Customers paid thousands of dollars and suffered long waiting lists for "a Chanel" tarted up, some judged, by the company's new design director, Karl Lagerfeld. Lagerfeld took all the recognizable elements of the tweedy Chanel suit, including its pairs of patch pockets with contrasting piping and double C monogrammed gold buttons, and revised them for elite clients clambering after legitimizing brands.

In his attacks on these iconic Chanel suits of the 1980s, the Italian designer Franco Moschino revived Chanel's old rival, Schiaparelli. Pillorying fashionable excess, Moschino crafted a look-alike Chanel suit and, signaling his admiration for Schiaparelli's punning and word-play, embroidered the words "Waist of Money" where Chanel's gold chain belt would have been. In other work, Moschino continued his campaign against the house, crafting miniature four-inch Chanel jackets and using them as patch pockets to adorn a Chanel-like suit. On another tweedy plaid, he matched collar, cuff, and pocket details in scalloped black felt, mimicking a matchy-matchy Chanel move, but turned the breast pockets upside down (figure 9). The model holds a Chanel-like quilted bag with gold chain tightly around her hand. She presumably doesn't need a working pocket. *Vogue* merely noted that the suit had a "dignified sense of humor."

What Vogue meant by "dignified sense of humor" is not clear. Moschino was suggesting that Lagerfeld's revisions were closer to pastiche, and that rather than breathing new life into a revered house, Lagerfeld had ignored first principles. (Lagerfeld did not seem as concerned as Coco Chanel was with allowing women to "be more important than [their] clothes.") With his upside-down pockets, Moschino may have made his point, although perhaps at the expense of the wearer. Who, after all, would want a suit with an upside-down pocket? In considering pocket play, one must also consider whom the joke is on.

In the same year that Moschino turned his patch pockets upside down, Patrick Kelly tossed them onto a pin-striped suit at quirky angles (figure 10). Inspired by the work of Schiaparelli, Kelly injected wit and playfulness into his work. He explained, "I want my clothes to make you smile" and fashion to be accessible at "real prices." Kelly was the first American and the first Black designer to have been inducted into the prestigious Chambre Syndicate du Prèt-a-Porter, the official governing body of the French ready-to-wear industry. He staged his inaugural show as a member of this group in the courtyard of the Louvre, where he paid homage to the *Mona Lisa*, and he posed as her in a number of different incarnations in the invitation to the show (figure 11). The pin-striped suit is an ensemble fit for one of those characters, "Las Vegas Lisa," a gambler who flashes a card from her hand, in the suit of hearts.

Figure 10. Patrick Kelly suit with randomly placed pockets, from *Mona's Bet* group, Spring/Summer 1989.

Figure 11. Invitation to Patrick Kelly's Spring/Summer 1989 show, featuring Kelly as Mona Lisa, draped in a shawl festooned with buttons, his favorite decorative device.

The pin-striped, Las Vegas Lisa suit was part of a group of several works featuring decorative dice, collectively titled *Mona's Bet*. Alluding to the random roll of dice, the scattered pockets helped Kelly take on the formal, masculine uniform. Not only was his intervention more causal in cotton twill, but the stripes came in playful colors, bright yellow and red, and did not align. It is possible that Kelly also included autobiographical references here. Paris, not the United States, took a "bet" on Kelly's artistry, supporting his business with its imprimatur. But there were also jokes aplenty for wearer and viewer to appreciate, including the cheater's pocket placed high at the shoulder blades. If the wearer wrapped her right arm over her left shoulder, she could just about reach it. With its willful randomness and knowing cheats, Kelly's suit reflected broadly on the chancy nature of pocketing in female versions of the tailored suit. While employing fun and gags may not have been a strategy everyone agreed with, including Chanel and allied modernists, Kelly continued a long tradition in women's wear that marshaled seemingly useless ornamentation to make useful points.

POCKETS IN MEN'S WEAR: SUITABLE FOR THE OCCASION

"A FUNDAMENTALLY CONSERVATIVE affair," as a writer for *Esquire* mused in 1955, men's fashions had not hosted playful or trompe l'oeil pockets. A settled form of centuries' standing and the neutral standard to which professional women aspired, men's suits seemed to offer nothing to joke about. Useful, working pockets, the same writer added somewhat defensively, are "one of the few exclusive prerogatives of apparel left to us by the ladies." The piece suggests that men had made peace with conservatism. Yet the 1950s was marked by attempts to integrate a more romantic, elemental, or "rugged masculinity" into everyday dress.

If much of the drama in women's wear has involved the appropriation of the authority of men's wear, the drama in men's wear has focused

Figure 12. Portrait of Frank Tengle near Moundville, Hale County, Alabama, by Walker Evans, published in James Agee's *Let Us Now Praise Famous Men*, 1936.

on shedding a little of that authority's stuffiness. Here, too, pockets play a notable role. Sticking to tradition, men's wear pockets have been restricted in form. Designers have not shaped them into baskets or lilies. Men's wear pockets have not hinted at the body below, nor have they reflected on privacy or chance. But in the "punctuation of pockets" (as well as buttons, vents, and notches) "the literal meaning" of men's clothing "hangs," according to the *Esquire* journalist. The exterior patch pocket, in particular, has served as a critical inflection point, one indicative of the "transition between business and pleasure."

Patch pockets originated in workwear. Whether placed on sturdy aprons or, beginning in the nineteenth century, on trousers and overalls, they were frankly visible. Bright topstitching famously outlines the back patch pockets of Levi's blue jeans, for example. This reinforcement, combined with metal rivets, for which Jacob Davis received a patent in 1873, signaled the durability of workwear. "Made expressly for miners, mechanics, engineers and labor-men," Levi's "waist-overalls" (the original term for blue jeans) and "bib-overalls" were so strong, the Levi Strauss and Co. leather label proclaimed, that two horses pulling in opposite directions could not tear them apart.

Documenting the lives of tenant farmers during the height of the Great Depression, James Agee devoted a romantic tribute to bib overalls in his 1941 book, *Let Us Now Praise Famous Men*, with photographic illustrations by Walker Evans (figure 12). Reflecting on the typical clothing he witnessed, Agee judged overalls to be unique in that they were "native to this country." The stitching of overalls especially intrigued Agee. He wrote that "the complexed seams of utilitarian pockets," bright white against dark indigo, looked like a "blueprint." This map, with its "complex and slanted structure, on the chest, of the pockets shaped for pencils, rulers, and watches," indexed the acts of marking and measuring critical to the productivity of American rural areas. Made conspicuous by their outlines, patch pockets signaled competence and a kind of handiness and ingenuity that Agee hoped to revalorize with his book.

In addition to farmers and aritsans, hunters and soldiers (professions that required some of the same skills and tools) have also historically worn clothing adorned with exterior patch pockets. Soldiers were at first notably adverse to any functional components that disrupted their flashy uniforms, however. Since the seventeenth century, the militaries of Europe and North America had gone to war in full dress, patterning their uniforms after the contours of the fashionable suit. As soldiers were known to be emboldened by bold looks, heightening pomp tended to override practical concerns. Soldiers in volunteer armies have to *want* to wear their uniforms, noted one modernizer of the British military forces in utter exasperation in 1889, as he witnessed his men strutting about in tightly tailored coats that prevented them from "completing a satisfactory day's work during war."

A change of heart was in part catalyzed by a new model, the mid-nineteenth-century safari suit, hunting gear worn by officers of the British East India Company. In their leisure hours, as officers sought risk and adventure hunting tigers and elephants, they came to appreciate the effectiveness of practical gear. Safari suits utilized a two-over-two pocket architecture, placing exterior patch pockets at chest and hips. These were often volumetric bellows pockets constructed with a fat pleat in the middle that expanded, like the tool that furnishes a blast of air, to hold bulky contents. Leather-lined, these pockets held small powder flasks for gunpowder, other ammunition, and necessities. Practical yet attractive to some, hunting suits like these offered the military a way to reconcile functionality with dash. The bellows-pocketed jacket, the now familiar battle dress of modern khaki armies, marked the military's somewhat belated recognition that civilian hunting gear was a far more relevant design reference than the formal suit (figure 13).

The visibly practical bellows pocket continued to accrue meaning. Scrambling to mobilize in the first years of World War II, the US military tweaked khaki tunics further, producing the first service uniforms that were neither tailored nor closely conforming to chest and waist (figure 14). The cotton windbreaker-like M1943 combat outfit (its name indicating the year it was developed) cinched with a drawstring at the waist and had substantial bellows pockets at chest and hips as well as newly devised cargo pockets on the trousers. The uniform seemed well tuned for a different conflict: unlike the static trench warfare of World War I, World War II was a mobile war. Troop commanders

Figure 13. World War I enlisted soldier's tailored woolen tunic, with cigarette holder discovered in pocket, 1914–18.

witnessing tests of the new uniforms reported that "the discovery that men could fight out of their jacket and trouser pockets" was the most important feature of the new battle uniform. General Dwight D. Eisenhower despised the loose fit of these uniforms, fearing it was impossible to look "neat and snappy" in them. Yet the relentlessly heroic images of uniformed American soldiers reproduced in newspapers and film reels shifted the public's perceptions. What appeared slouchy and unappealing to Eisenhower eventually gained a broad appeal.

CIVILIAN LEISURE WEAR would eventually incorporate all the pocketing of these uniforms. From workwear to military uniforms and sportswear, obvious pocketing engendered a whole host of appealing associations, "a map of a working man" whose competence, fortitude, determination, and derring-do were evident. In the casual revolution that followed World War II, designers ransacked this range of active

Figure 14. 79th Infantry Division soldiers wearing cotton M1943 field jackets after an October 1944 battle. Left to right; Pfc. Arthur Henry Muth, Sgt. Carmine Robert Sileo, and Sgt. Kelly C. Lasalle.

men's wear, borrowing emblems like pockets to build in a casual aesthetic. In 1949, *Apparel Arts* correctly foresaw that the informal trend was "not just a fad." Noting American men's "natural casualness" and their insistence on comfort, this trade magazine for men's wear manufacturers and retailers proposed that with some clever adjustments, men could be "AT EASE" no matter the context. The fashion pages promised the reader he could even be more like himself "at the opera."

Initial offerings of informal clothes were most successful in coating. Belted and pocketed leisure jackets, in silk or suede for film industry moguls and sturdier leathers and tweeds for suburban dads, became staple wardrobe items. Previously a woolen overcoat would have sufficed. Outerwear is "everywhere," insisted *GQ* in 1955, noting that the sportsman and spectator sportsman of every type could now wear leisure jackets meant to accompany him "on the by-ways," "at the stadium," and in his "own backyard." Exterior patch pockets were embellished with "sporting stitching." The pointed flaps of the bellows pockets had "style significance." The fashion press winked at all those pockets, which were not strictly necessary but buoyed up "ever hopeful" weekend warriors.

Such leisure wear offerings demonstrated expanded choice, but rules about dress were slow to change in the professional world. Anxiety around being correct still plagued men, and the context in which clothes were worn still mattered. Accordingly, the men's wear fashion press took it upon itself to help men navigate sartorial decisions, sounding more like etiquette manuals than purveyors of fashion choices. As *GQ* put it in 1964, "clothes should be suitable for the occasion," reminding readers that this or that component "is for sportswear, bud, not the office." Getting it wrong opened the wearer up to the threat of ridicule, and men remained on a "tightrope" when facing decisions about their clothes.

Yet men's desire to don something equally at home in town and country, in urban canyons and the great outdoors, meant that experiments continued. The casual aesthetic moved to suiting when Yves Saint Laurent appropriated the safari suit for his unisex collection of 1968. By this time, safari suits carried a hint of rebellion, as they had become

Figure 15. Safari suits worn for casual outings, photograph by Steinbicker / Houghton, published in "Suited for the Non-Occasion," *GQ*, February 1972. Note the trompe-l'oeil belt and front panel (mimicking a wrap dress) and the apparently real pocket (indicated by the handkerchief) on the woman's knit dress.

associated with anti-colonial revolt in Africa when some nationalist leaders chose to don them rather than the three-piece suits of their former colonizers. The fashion press, however, tended to emphasize their versatility. They were recommended for "peaceful outings" like Sunday brunch or gallery openings (figure 15). The "assertive touches" contributed by extremely generous flapped pockets toned down the suit part of the equation. Wearing a leisure suit, one could look elegant yet unstudied, ready for every "non-occasion."

Leisure suits ran their course after a few years, but flamboyant pocket detailing emerged elsewhere, especially in the avowedly casual spectrum. Western regional wear, for example, adopted shirt and jacket pockets that might be rounded like crescent half-moons or pointed like

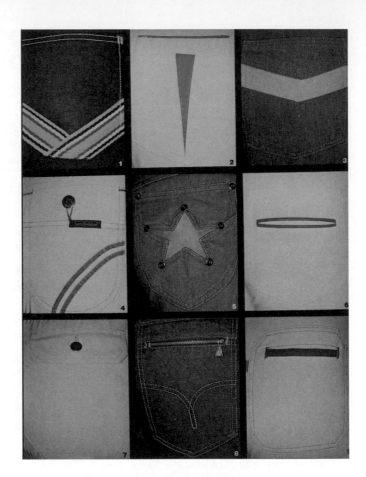

Figure 16. A collage of back pockets, photograph by John Peden, appearing in "Jeaneology: A Tribute to Fashion's Hot Pants," *GQ*, April 1977.

chevrons to suggest the broncobuster cowboys at the rodeo. Pockets were outlined in fringed leather for a Billy the Kid look. Surprisingly expressive detailing began to grace the back pockets of blue jeans as other firms began to compete with Levi's once the patent for the five-pocketed jean expired in the 1920s. The classic Levi's 501 jeans were "devoid of gimmicks," but, *GQ* wondered in 1977, could a good thing be made even better? All sorts of brands got into the act, throwing out curves, rainbow shapes, stars, and chevrons in bold leather piping (figure 16). Here was "styling with an extra zip," signaling the transformation of jeans into fashion.

Rejecting designer brands, hippies enlivened thrift store finds with personal flourishes, and pockets became the site of elaborate embroidery and vivid patchwork. Hoping to exploit this countercultural trend, retailers began adding patches on jeans, skirts, jackets, and vests to imbue them with folkloric notes. One 1973 jacket from the New York boutique Pinky and Dianne is made up entirely of square patches likely sourced from several pairs of jeans, some turned inside-out and others right-side-out (figure 17). In a witty move, the jacket's breast pockets are repurposed from the former back patch pockets of a pair of Lee jeans, a portion of Lee's "Lazy-S" stitch logo still visible. The patch pockets at the breast sit slightly lower than they normally would, calling attention to their oddness. Accompanying the play on inside-out and right-side-out is another play on back to front. This breaking the rules about where pockets belong was about as subversive as men's wear got. As the Pinky and Dianne man's jacket demonstrates, pocket jokes have tended to be more understated in men's wear than in women's wear—they involve transposing pocket types associated with one context to another and enjoying the resulting dislocation.

Experimentation with recontextualization would continue, a strategy linked to postmodern designers like Rei Kawakubo, Vivienne Westwood, and Jean Paul Gaultier, who expanded on the appropriations of the counterculture. In a 1990 suit, for example, Gaultier took a range of slash and patch pockets from the military and sport continuum and placed them in a gridlike composition in two vertical rows along the torso

Figure 17. Pinky and Dianne man's jacket, made from repurposed denim, 1973. © The Museum at FIT.

Figure 18. Suit coat with pockets, by Jean Paul Gaultier, 1990. © The Museum at FIT.

of an otherwise formal suit (figure 18). These pockets included functional hardware and aggressive zippering with pull tabs that matched the suiting fabric. Gaultier did not attempt to imagine a less formal alternative to the suit. Rather, he very deliberately retained a single finished buttonhole on the left lapel, recalling Saville Row traditions. (Such buttonholes once allowed the wearer to pull up and secure the lapels for warmth but have since become vestigial.) Gaultier reminds viewers that the many-pocketed suit had never actually attained that vaunted state of perfection so often attributed to it. As men before him had complained, how could you retain a slim silhouette if you filled your pockets with lots of gear? In calling on the bellows pocket, however, Gaultier did more than propose an innocent solution to the carrying-capacity problem. He dismantled the longstanding distinction between business and leisure, questioning just what made a garment "suitable for the occasion."

CARGO POCKETS: EMBLEM OF THE 1990S

A MORE WIDESPREAD example of decorative, baroque pocketing than the avant-garde interventions of Gaultier occurred with cargo-pocketed trousers. Cargo pockets for mainstream use evolved when the old partners workwear, military wear, and sportswear met subcultural style in the late 1970s to create an "urban-survival uniform" that relied on a new recruit. Pants with bellows pockets on the legs had not made too much of an impression in civilian dress initially, but counterculture's interest in military surplus drew new attention to them. Young punk rockers in the 1970s created drop-dead ensembles sure to disturb a conservative mainstream, and wearing cargo pants helped them do it. Designers were quick to co-opt this style, recognizing that trousers could stand to be a little more expressive. Why stop at the back pockets of blue jeans? "Fashion pocket treatments today aren't restricted to front and rear hip areas, but are placed anywhere there's room or reason," GQ enthused in 1973.

What *GQ* called survival wear looked postindustrial to some observers. It constituted workwear for people who weren't really at work but also highlighted obviously functional design details, including "enough pockets, sealed with Velcro closures or zippers, to store a week's rations." Ensembles featured hooded overshirts, anoraks, or parka tops paired with blowsy cargo-pocketed pants and accessorized with leg warmers, high-top sneakers, or more adventurous boots. Pierre Cardin's interpretation of survival wear in 1977 included a down-filled coat with D-ring closures (a military invention), a kangaroo-pocketed cable knit hoodie sweater, "combat inspired" trousers with cargo pockets, and hiking boots made by the firm Wolverine. The accompanying copy suggested that distinctions between what's right for town and for hiking trips were more than ever before actively being tested. "You may be facing more traffic jams than log jams," but such old distinctions about context or appropriateness seemed no longer operative.

Cargo pants were rediscovered in the 1990s by another generation of youth scouring inexpensive surplus, Gen X skaters and rappers, who crafted new quasi-uniforms that conferred power in a world that often ignored them. These fashion re-innovators integrated khaki, cargo-pocketed combat pants with sleeveless puffer jackets, plain white T-shirts, and old school Adidas trainers, transforming 1970s survival wear into something different. New streetwear labels launched to meet the needs of this generation, producing a pared-down style that was anti-fashion in its aesthetics. Skater and streetwear brands like Supreme along with designers concerned with utility (Moreno Ferrari at CP Company, Paul Harvey at Stone Island, and Massimo Osti) included a wide range of cargoes. As hip-hop and streetwear became more mainstream, the multi-pocketed cargo pant became an emblem of the 1990s.

Vogue explained the genesis of cargoes to readers in 1994: "taking their cue from urban street style, designers are rolling up their sleeves and crafting clothes inspired by field hands' overalls, workmen's uniforms, and other utilitarian classics." "Everyone wants to look active," explained *Women's Wear Daily* as it charted the trend in 1998, also noting that women sporting hip-hugging, drawstring, midriff-baring cargo pants were as keen to wear them as those who purchased less body-conscious ones at mid-market sports retailers. The speed with which cargoes were adopted by everyone from designers to mass-market retailers and spread from men's wear to women's wear clearly indicates that streetwear and utility brands were channeling something appealing. Cargoes evidently provided something that sweatpants and yoga leggings did not, perhaps enhancing humdrum chores with a little extra sense of purpose.

Cargoes' military origins were widely acknowledged. As Annette LaFleur, director of the Design, Pattern and Prototype Team of the US Army, mused, soldiers are the "ultimate athletes." "Why wouldn't the general public want to have utility and functional clothing?" she asked. Civilian designers reflected on the craft involved in military attire

Figure 19. Two examples of cargo pockets, each loaded with three grenades, tested at Camp Lee, Virginia, from November 1942 until July 1943. The photographs demonstrate some of the design challenges, including that when loaded with three hand grenades (their intended purpose), pockets strained under the weight and tended to swing heavily; soldiers reported that they could hamper fast movement and cause leg abrasions.

longingly, because having to think about combat readiness required a certain mindset or skill, a meticulous engineering attuned to bodies in motion that had atrophied in their own discipline (figure 19). Often some new detailing was the result of careful research in military archives. Certain flaps and button placements on cargo pockets, for example, can be traced to Canadian Artic Patrol gear or Danish Airforce trousers.

Some of most useful solutions came from uniforms designed for paratroopers, who, after being flown into enemy territory, had to drop from the sky carrying not only loaded weapons but everything they needed to survive. According to World War II reminiscences, para troopers were called the "red devils with baggy pants" by German prisoners of war. Designers working in consultation with airborne troops placed cargo pockets lower on the thigh to make them more accessible to soldier's strapped into a harness. They also included extra narrow cargo pockets closer to the ankle to store knives to cut away entangled parachute strings. Last-minute modifications made by soldiers, such as the straps they used to secure the contents of their heavy pockets, were evident in contemporary photographs, and designers like Helmut Lang, who produced many iterations of cargo pants, apparently referenced them.

Even as designers strived for authenticity in detailing, critics doubted their motives, and the style as reinterpreted on the runway was dubbed "utility chic." For a London-based journalist, James Sherwood, the fad revealed problems of context: the combat pocket looked "inappropriate on the Versace runway," he observed, a bit aghast that Donatella Versace had transplanted the cargo pocket onto a pink crystal-encrusted couture gown for her debut couture collection in 1998. Sherwood likened this translation to a masquerade, akin to Marie Antoinette's dressing up as a poor milkmaid at her getaway, Petit Trianon, wearing a gauzy, white shift as she played at country life to avoid the strictures of court and court dress. *What were women doing playing war games?* was the question at issue for some critics, which

Figure 20. Dolce and Gabbana pocketed vest trimmed in fur, cropped pants, and charm bracelet, photograph by Peter Lindbergh, published in *Harper's Bazaar*, November 2002.

reflects the fact that Britain didn't allow women in combat roles until 2016 and the United States, 2015. But that query neglects a very long history of such borrowings and the very real longings that prompted them. Women have historically adopted military looks during military conflicts, demonstrating a sympathetic, vicarious involvement.

In one 2002 fashion editorial surveying urban uniforms, *Harper's Bazaar* pictured models along a busy shopping street wearing "the new street-chic style," which, as they pointed out, "fuses utility basics with all out glamour" (figure 20). Reflected in the large plate-glass display windows that give a shopping street its particular feel, one model dreamily gazes as she walks, in no particular hurry. Here was a streetscape in which you might need a "distinguished uniform," because you were sure to be seen. The model is outfitted in a combat vest and matching cargo pants, a "pocket-laden" jigsaw alternately secured with buckled leather straps and snaps, with a zippered waist marking off the silhouette. This Dolce and Gabbana ensemble manages to go from "rugged to refined" with the addition of fur trimming and spiked heels. The vest alone cost $12,430. Was she a female urban warrior? At the very least she was streetwise (as in, *Don't mess with me*), if not combat ready.

Richard Martin, curator of the Costume Institute at the Metropolitan Museum of Art, put the decade's concerns into larger context in a 1995 exhibition. He titled the show *Swords into Ploughshares* after a pointed question from the fashion journalist Suzy Menkes suggested that some of fashion's borrowings, like Nazi jackboots and Sam Browne belts, crossed a line. "Is fashion playing dangerous and callous war games or fulfilling Isiah's vision of crafting fertile ploughshares from sharp swords?" she asked. The biblical parable suggests that military objects may be rendered harmless in their transition to civilian life, and that in fact such transformation is necessary for peace. Whether donning aggressive, threatening garb has a similar pacifying effect is less clear. Despite the harrowing accounts that veterans have produced to disabuse civil society of the romance of war, war remains a seemingly irresistible reference point in fashion.

Cargoes' popularity showed no signs of abating until, by the early 2000s, observers had to concede that in their diffusion, they had lost something of their original cachet. Many were worn loose and saggy, and the unfashionably unkempt loved them too. The disenchantment with cargoes, however, did not spell their demise. By 2010, the fashion press observed that cargoes were back and had received important upgrades. Some designers moved the pockets to the front of the pants to preserve "that jean like silhouette." Directives were now more insistent: "Don't stuff the pockets full of gear. You want to preserve the new, slimmer lines of these pants." Anyone and everyone could wear them, and anyone, more to the point, could attempt to trademark some new version, as Roz Chast cheekily observed in a *New Yorker* cartoon. Her "New Grandma® cargo pants" house everything from knitting to a last will and testament and come conveniently "pre-loaded" (figure 21). Cargo pants have joined the five-pocket jean and khakis as a casual staple, and their pockets are considered a "heritage utility feature," as *Women's Wear Daily* noted in 2016, a signature element that can be strategically detached and "deployed" anywhere to make "a fashion statement."

Figure 21. *Introducing . . . New Grandma® Cargo Pants*, by Roz Chast, from the *New Yorker*, 2021.

And what do those fashion statements look like? The tales pockets tell have surprising salience in a dressed-down age that has come to doubt fashion's relevance. Utilitarian pockets (and not just those on trousers) have at times helped legitimize elite runway fashion. They now complement old-style glamour and finish, as when Virgil Abloh used generously sized, military-flapped patch pockets to adorn a safari-like suit for Louis Vuitton in an "impossible and impudent" color, reminiscent of Schiaparelli's signature shocking pink (figure 22). Pocket embellishment is above suspicion, providing a sort of anti-fashion virtue signaling. This wearer, such emphatic pockets seem to proclaim, is ready for anything. For the designer Marine Serre, who merges couture with sportswear for an "eco-futurist" outlook, pockets are part of the gambit in a new era of urban-survival uniforms (figure 23).

While avowedly focused on function, fantasy is not far behind. If tactical overpreparation is the point, that point is made visible by enabling wearers to present themselves as perfectly geared-up cyborgs or "black-ops bike couriers" moving from one difficult task to another. Inevitably, such daydreams are easy to mock. Was it not overkill, this wearing of pseudo-tactical gear in relatively sheltered situations? Did one really need "Gore-Tex gaiters and lugged soles and emergency flashlights for getting in and out of taxis"? asked Russell Smith in his 2007 *Men's Style: The Thinking Man's Guide to Dress*. Perhaps not. Or perhaps so. Pockets demonstrate how much designers strive to place wearers at the center of the dramas in which they participate. Through pockets, designers signal that their clothes address some of the real psychological tolls encountered in the modern, industrialized world, a world buffeted by threats, in which challenges, social and environmental, can arise unexpectedly (or have long been simmering).

Figure 22. Suit designed by Virgil Abloh for Louis Vuitton men's wear, Fall 2020. Abloh subtly interrupts the symmetry of the military-style suit by including exterior patch pockets at the chest only, forgoing those usually placed at the hips (only the flaps remain at the hips).

Figure 23. Marine Serre dress, Spring 2019 ready-to-wear. Flapped cargo pockets (some with zips and cloth patches) adhere to a khaki gown like barnacles, suggesting that natural growth is at the root of pocket proliferation.

EVEN WHEN THEY do not stray far from their sources in military or workwear, patch pockets can assume roles that "transcend their function," as *Women's Wear Daily* concluded in a review of recent men's wear collections. This kind observation, echoed elsewhere, both acknowledges and refutes Dior's contention that "men have pockets to keep things in, women for decoration." While it would be unfair to suggest that in 1954 Dior should have foreseen men's wear's future expressiveness (including vis-à-vis pocketing), he clearly ignored the foundational work of the women's wear designers who both preceded him and were his peers, designers who crafted pockets that forthrightly addressed the sexual politics of pockets.

Since about 1900, as fashion came into its own as a design discipline, art form, and profession, these interventions have been as diverse as the human imaginations at work on them. Just as suffragists issued their demands for pockets, complaining that they too often "come and go," designers began to offer an astonishing output. The features of this output can be traced to a range of aesthetic interests and ideological points of view and have resulted in everything from the understated, well-considered pockets of Chanel to the zany abundance of Marine Serre. Pockets continue to be the subject of "fun and gags" of all sorts. Designers approach them in ways that are breezy or irreverent: "Look ma, no hands!" was the name of a raincoat with an attached carry-all bag that Cashin designed in 1973. Other designers cannot help but reflect on pockets' intimate placement, and delight in using pockets to highlight the contour at breast and hip and buttock, as when, in a 1993 collection, John Paul Gaultier applied free-standing cargo-pockets at the seat, which bounced as the wearer walked. The more one stuffed those back pockets, the cheekier the bounce.

Some of the most incisive jokes refer to what is now a long history of pocket fakes and feints, including Miuccia Prada's transparent raincoat from 2002 (figure 24). While the coat nods to Schiaparelli's early experiments in transparency (such as her 1935 cape made of cellulose-based plastic), Prada tailors her coat, exposing well-executed seams finished in black silk binding. From afar, those seams recall the lines of a lively pen and ink fashion sketch or the inked cells of classic two-dimensional animation (the drawings placed on celluloid sheets), as if the designer is openly trying to secure our belief in the coat's insubstantiality. Yet working snaps secure Prada's coat, while working pockets allow the model to stand resolutely, her hands firmly planted. Prada's bluff is a tour de force; she makes a look-alike fake that diagrams its own construction.

Such diagrams and blueprints have not coincided with consistent pocketing in women's clothes, however. What a pocket looks like offers no simple index of enfranchisement. Fashion play may even have ensured that there would be no smiple or single fix to the "pocket problem," especially as ideas move back and forth from rarefied conceptual design to

Figure 24. Miuccia Prada raincoat, Autumn–Winter 2002–3, photograph by David Sims. Of all the functional parts highlighted in this transparent coat, it is pockets that require the most evident engineering. Prada reveals the surprisingly large area it takes to make a working pocket that will at once lie flat while hanging in such a way (at a slight slant) to allow the hands to settle comfortably about the hips.

mass-market offerings, where manufacturers hoping to make a buck may not make the effort to include the working side of some new pocket arrangement. Yet no matter how apparently whimsical in appearance, pockets can be understood to be responding in some way to their own fraught history of incorporation as well as to a series of inventive past contributions. That novel pocket might just be performing some decorative "double duty."

Figure 1. Simone d'Aillencourt, in a dress by Trigere, by Richard Avedon, Cape Canaveral, Florida, November 13, 1959.

CHAPTER 7

Pocket Utopias:
Dreaming of a Pocketless World

As long as there have been designers who insist on pocketing, there have been those who just as insistently decline to pocket. Appreciating simple, abstract shapes, designers create everything from severe, minimalist wraps to snug, body-hugging sheaths that have no apparent place for pockets. While some have questioned the gendered politics of such offerings (most, although not all, of this fare is marketed to women), it is also possible to categorize the distinction between pro- and anti-pocket camps in another way—not through gender but through attitude—and to see a debate played out over the surface of clothes between the worriers and the optimists, depending on one's point of view.

Modernist designers might not use the word *optimistic* to describe the pocketless look, but such a commitment to reduction evolved in the twentieth century out of a confident embrace of technological advancement. In their mimicry of smooth, machined surfaces, these garments proclaimed an alliance with progress and the future. Commenting on the spare A-line dresses of the 1960s space age, fashion editors and photographers enthusiastically underlined this "relatedness." When Richard Avedon photographed at Cape Canaveral for *Harper's Bazaar*, he linked the "ordered perfection" of a simple shift to "the galactic beauty" of the rockets, towers, launch pads, and telemetry antennas that served as a dramatic backdrop (figure 1). The magazine contended that the launch site of the Air Force Missile Test Center was the "perfect context" in which to show off modernist fashion: the dress and the armature of space exploration appeared "united in a similar austere concept of functional design."

As the fashion pages depicted modern dresses' synergy with speeding rockets, they also touted the idea that one could travel light. Noting the "bareness" of all the ensembles showcased for the 1960 spring season, *Harper's* wrote approvingly that "fashion no longer burdens us with weight and coverage." Statements like these are easy to write off as chatty editorial commentary, but they do reveal a fashion aspiration. In her perfectly spare charcoal knit, the model in Avedon's photo seems as unfettered as the Atlas missile, poised to take off at any moment. Pockets would not only disturb the clean lines of the dress but very likely cause an unacceptable drag.

Such a disavowal of pockets highlights another aspect of the optimism inherent in futurist design, although one that was rarely recognized. What people choose to wear is based on the context in which it will be worn. Context specificity goes beyond the requirement that one should dress appropriately for the day's activities (that one should not show up for a job interview in one's pajamas). It also reflects the person's beliefs about the environments in which they find themselves day to day. Under what conditions would a person need neither a handbag nor a single pocket? That such conditions might exist was the rather radical proposition.

FUTURE FASHIONS IN H. G. WELLS'S UTOPIAN FICTIONS

TO THOSE VISIONARIES concerned with imagining brave new worlds in the early years of the twentieth century, determining how a person might be outfitted for them was of critical interest. The costumers responsible for *Just Imagine* (1930), Hollywood's first major science-fiction film, for example, recognized that dress was as important as architecture in suggesting the mood of a technologically advanced future. They took care to make the suit of the future appear as sleek and functional as the designed environment, and Fox's advertising highlighted the link: "New York gone futuristic . . . a towering tangle of pinnacles, viaducts and bridges . . . and what fashions in dress!" Applying the rationale of reduction and subtraction with rigor, the costumers paid special attention to men's dress, eliminating anything that might disrupt the smooth surface of the three-piece suit: collar, lapel, cuffs, and, most provocatively, pockets and pocket flaps. As the hero zips around the city with ease in his personal airplane (his flight and everyday suit are one and the same), he demonstrates the integration and seamlessness of modern life.

But it was H. G. Wells's vision for future dress that would be far more influential. For Wells, the man who is said to have "invented" the future, dress was a part of the "re-equipment of everyday life" that he discussed in his many utopian fables that outlined more perfect worlds made possible by technology and effective planning. One gets the sense that Wells looked forward to a radical change of clothes, that he did not want to make small tweaks to existing forms by eliminating things like collars and lapels in men's suits. Wells took seriously the idea that clothing might be demonstrably different in a more harmonious world, a world rationally planned and effortlessly navigable.

Wells's ideas were made visible to large audiences when his speculative future history *The Shape of Things to Come* was adapted into a 1936 science-fiction film. In it, he offered his influential contribution to futurist dress: a blueprint for simplicity of line and revelation of the body that resonated in later sci-fi costuming, from *Star Trek* to *Star Wars* (figure 2). Wells was an active contributor to the film version, titled *Things to Come*, but the collaboration between writer and filmmaker was a difficult one, and while Wells enjoyed unusual autonomy—

Figure 2. *Three Costume Designs*, by John Armstrong, for *Things to Come* (1936), directed William Cameron Menzies. The job of translating Wells's ideas into concrete form ultimately fell to British painter and set designer John Armstrong, who seems to have paid close attention to Wells's written descriptions and instructions, including that future dress should be unisex and comprise simple tunics worn with shorts.

Wells wrote the treatment and several screen adaptations, and then appeared on the set every day as consultant—he did not always agree with the vision of the future that the filmmakers, set designers, cinematographers, and costumers had in mind. The film's exasperated producer, Alexander Korda, complained the that Wells "fussed over the costumes," making "minute changes" in every area he hoped might "represent his vision of the future accurately."

Meanwhile, Wells's dissatisfaction with the filmmaking process grew so great that Wells wrote and circulated a memo addressed to everyone concerned, which he later released for publication. In the memo, Wells hoped to delineate a set of guidelines to mark out a future style—a style difficult to describe exactly but whose most salient feature was that it should be "unobtrusive." "For God's sake," Wells encouraged the designers, "let yourselves go." But "being inventive and original," he cautioned, "is not being extravagant and silly." Notable for its irritable tone, Wells's open memo revealed his upset over competing visions of the aesthetics and direction of future dress that, at their root, revealed competing visions of the future. Would a future overtaken by technology and machines be inhumane and dreary or—as Wells envisioned—equitable and peaceful? Did your clothes need to prepare you for "audacity and risk," as some believed, or would a simple tunic do the job?

Wells's rationale for these costumes is mostly forgotten, but it is useful to consider the principles Wells set forth for future dress at a time when science fiction sought to influence fashion. Doing so helps elucidate an otherwise perplexing conundrum: while sleek modernist style mimics the functional look of the streamlined machine, it does not offer much practical convenience for the wearer.

Practical convenience, however, was very much on Wells's mind. In a series of interviews that led up to the release of *Things to Come*, Wells described his predictions more thoroughly, insisting that he was not just guessing about dress made possible by advanced technology. He had given a lot of thought to why we dress as we do, he explained, and had decided that much of the protection derived from thick suits with "innumerable pockets" that held the "impedimenta" of existence would no longer be needed. Future citizens would not require "buckles and gadgets to hold themselves together," he added with increasing agitation, worried that the set and costume designers for the film had not understood his intentions and were instead relying on notions sourced from comics and pulpy science-fiction fantasy (figure 3). Future fashions, Wells believed, would not need to be protective. In a more thoughtfully designed world not governed by "walls, fences, locks, [and] bars," dress would be "less inspired by defenses and reservation." He argued passionately that in the future "we will have freer, simpler, more beautiful clothes."

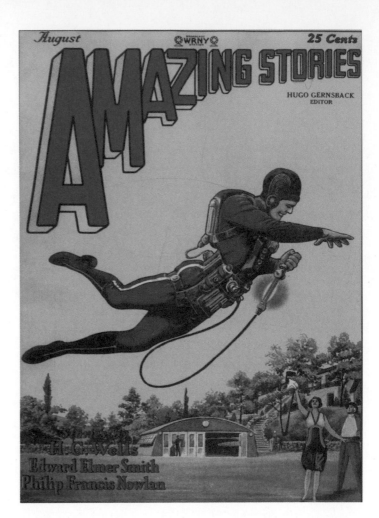

Figure 3. Cover illustration of a "Flying Man," by Frank R. Paul, published in *Amazing Stories*, August 1928. Before Superman's appearance in 1938, the Flying Man of early science fiction and comic books encounters the world with a flight pack firmly affixed to his torso and thighs and protective headwear.

Wells foresaw a world of wireless devices that would make this easygoing freedom possible, one remarkably akin to our own digital age, in which certain tools would be miniaturized and placed onto clothing (figure 4). He conceded that "men and women of the future will carry the equivalents of the purse, pocketbook, fountain pen, watch, &c., &c., of today." Even though humans would not manage to rid themselves of these companion devices, they would never again need to travel around "with pockets full of coins paying on every slight occasion." For money, he envisioned a kind of E-ZPass system akin to digital banking services accessed on a mobile phone. Tools, including "portable radio telephones," flashlights, and notebooks, would be carried on the person in a shrunken state, attached to the padding at the shoulder or on a bracelet worn on the wrist. Of utmost importance to Wells, these devices would not be "obtrusive." The person of the future should wear "dignified" garb, he insisted, and not look like "a padded lunatic or an armored gladiator."

Wells associated the psychological desire to be "rigged up like a telephone pole" with an overpreparation that had historic roots in the deprivations of the Great Depression, a calamity in which everyone, except for an elite minority, went "short." Bereft of even basic necessities, people guarded what they did have with anxious watchfulness. In Wells's vision, a socialist state would amply provide for each citizen, and such support would free people from the impulse to hoard. One of the paradoxical results of abundance "is the abolition of encumbrance," he wrote. Wells quite literally imagined someone taking off for a trip without packing a suitcase or umbrella. Clothing would be disposable and laundry obsolete; the department store would replace closets. Anything the future citizen needed "he [would] find on his way."

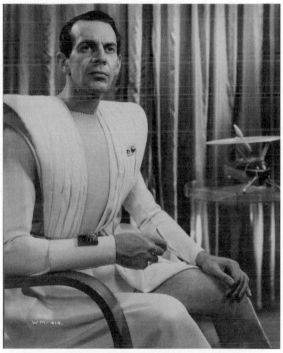

Figure 4. Studio portrait of Raymond Massey as John Cabal in *Things to Come* (1936). Note the "radio-telephone arrangement" on the chest and the bracelet, which accessed an "identification disk," purse, pocketbook, fountain pen, watch, notebook, and flashlight.

Futuristic dress as envisioned by Wells did not affect fashion in any broad way in the late 1930s as it would during the Space Age in the 1960s. But Wells's ideas did transform dress depicted in speculative fiction and fantasy. In June 1938, when Jerry Siegel and Joe Shuster introduced the comic book hero

Figure 5. Donald Deskey's forecast for future dress, photograph by Anton Bruehl, published in *Vogue*'s 1939 New York World's Fair edition, February 1, 1939.

Superman, he could fly without a flight pack, harness, or oxygen tanks. As onlookers famously remarked when they saw this mysterious figure streaking through the sky unaided: "Is it a bird? Is it a plane? No, it's Superman!" Wells evidently won the argument regarding the necessity for defensive garb; even into the present day, your average superhero looks like a "naked spacefarer sheathed in a silvery pseudoskin," as novelist Michael Chabon so aptly described the uniform.

Wells's ideas about the future were also taken up enthusiastically (if not quite accurately) at New York's 1939 World's Fair, the first international exhibition to use the future as an organizational theme. Corporate exhibitors showcased their most promising developments, from self-driving cars to dishwashers and air conditioners, to convince hesitant Americans recovering from the Depression of the benefits of modernization—to tantalize them, explicitly borrowing Wells's words, with "the shape of things to come."

Part of the sell involved showing off what future fashion would look like, too, so fair organizers approached *Vogue* and invited the magazine to devote an issue to the sartorial possibilities for the "Future of Dress." Fearing that such an endeavor would lead fashion designers to create costume rather than fashion, *Vogue* editor Edna Wolman Chase hedged, proposing instead that leading industrial designers do the job. With scant knowledge of textiles (at this early stage in the profession, industrial designers were known for cleaning up the outer housing of mechanical devices, producing "streamlined versions" of ships, trains, and numerous household appliances), nine designers nevertheless gamely submitted their fashion predictions for the year 2000.

Vogue led with the contribution of Donald Deskey, who stuck close to the principles Wells had outlined (figure 5). Deskey explained that the "Woman of the Future" would live in a perfect air-conditioned universe (air-conditioning had just been invented, and many were excited to experience so-called perfect weather), travel by "stratospheric plane," work only a few hours a day, and enjoy perfect health. Such a life of ease required only "a little drapery," and thus he proposed simple mix-and-match units made of flowing chiffon. Deskey further rationalized how the future shaped his thinking: women's makeup would be "permanent"; money would be obsolete, "for life will be on a credit basis"; and the door key would be made redundant by the "automatic lock." The "completely emancipated" woman of the future, in this view, would never need to carry makeup, money, or keys in either a bag or pocket. But she might not avail herself of this perk; Deskey concluded the interview with a casually misogynistic remark about women's legendary attachment to their purses: "being a woman, she will probably carry a reticule [a handbag] anyway."

In the utopian imagination of Wells and Deskey, the spare silhouette showcased the benefits of "comprehensive design." Simple and "unobtrusive" dress was proof of the efficacy of well-designed future environments. Confidence about walking out the door without provision or accommodation would arise because responsibility will have moved from garment to planned environment, from person to place. Wells and Deskey expected that people would be able to delegate responsibility to objects and systems that surrounded them. In the future, Wells confidently proclaimed, "we [will] wear less clothing than our ancestors, partly because of our healthier condition, partly because we do not like to hide lovely bodies, but mainly because in the past men wrapped themselves up against every contingency."

LACK OF ANY functional components like pockets in 1960s futuristic fashions went mostly unremarked. The same is true of the next iteration of austere dress that surfaced during the 1990s, when minimalist fashion took hold. Critics focused on aesthetics, praising designers like Miuccia Prada, Calvin Klein, Jil Sander, and Helmut Lang for their asceticism and restraint. When Sander was interviewed for *Harper's Bazaar* at the height of the minimalist trend, she admitted dreaming about living in a monk's cell with its beautiful proportions, clean edges, and "nothing else." As she explained, "What you see in my work is really more a lifestyle concept. Perhaps even a fanatical attempt to improve people. I really hate vulgar, glitzy stuff."

This strain of perfectionism sees pure surface as a kind of moral duty, a way of making sure that women do not look "like Christmas trees." However well garments in this style resist the decorative impulse, however, they also embrace divestment. Although this motive goes unacknowledged, a desire to shed excess baggage (to walk out the door without carrying anything at all) has been visible all along in a consistent lack of pockets. In pared down designs, the person announces their unconcern, their belief that nothing is required and that nothing will go wrong.

Figure 6. A minimalist dress by CO Collections, Spring–Summer 2020.

The minimalism of the 1990s is periodically revived, and for some designers it is a preferred mode. On occasion, a fashion stylist or blogger will make oblique reference to its functional drawbacks. In tips for pulling off 1990s minimalism, one writer noted that you'll need a "bigger bag!" Some fashion brands have taken to accessorizing slip dresses with major rucksacks and backpacks (figure 6), but on the catwalk, many models are not so accoutered. In this they make a particularly explicit status claim. Without a place to stash a cell phone, these dresses, whether they are form fitting or diaphanous, suggest that wearers do not actually need anything, that they have outsourced their support and security to an army of invisible retainers. Other people stand by to carry the keys and make the appointments. These lucky wearers have managed to emancipate themselves from burdensome stuff. As much as a minimalist garment says, *I am modern and free*, it also says, *I do not need to accessorize myself for a world through which I move confidently.*

THE ASPIRATION TO travel light, even empty-handed, has been articulated ever more explicitly in a newer wave of science-fiction-meets-fashion synergy: the field of wearables. Wearable technology refers to any electronic device that can be worn as an accessory, embedded in clothing, or implanted in a person's body. One can now strap a computer around their wrist, a solution Wells foresaw and that Apple computer accomplished with its version of a smartwatch. The inclusion of networking and communication devices in experimental cloth via shape-changing polymers, e-textiles, and nanoscale electronics has further accelerated technologists' desire to diminish or erase the boundary between people and the tools and devices they carry. As today's designers consider the far-out possibilities of engineered textiles, the question of pockets—will we need them or won't we—seems especially timely.

The stakes of this debate do not seem all that clear at first. Is there any demonstrable difference between portable and wearable tools? The technology theorist Steve Mann (one of MIT's so-called cyborgs in the 1990s) thinks not. He contended that "wearable computing has been around since the beginning of time" and that eyeglasses and wristwatches as well as slide rules and pocket calculators could be counted as wearables. These tools augment the wearer, performing computations and increasing visual acuity. Others do not agree. The goal should not be miniaturization but integration, according to Stefano Marzano, CEO of Philips Design from 1991–2011 (a branch of Koninklijke Philips electronics). Concurring with Wells, Marzano argued that humans "don't want to be bogged down by material encumbrances." Those encumbrances include the pocket calculator that the technologist once so proudly stuffed in his breast pocket, a sign of both his obliviousness to good fashion sense and his commitment to a radically rational view of the world.

While a preponderance of the research in wearables has focused on military and health applications (and still does), Philips began serious exploration of wearable electronics for a general consumer market with a series of proposals that they documented in a book, tellingly titled *The New Nomads*. The design group echoed the language of earlier technological utopias when they said that technology should unambiguously benefit humankind, and that wearables might promote "omnipresence, omnipotence and omniscience—the ability to be everywhere, to do everything and to know everything." "What people really want," Marzano surmised in a 1999 speech,

> is to be free of any attachments. We don't want to bother with tools at all. We don't want to fly in an aircraft, we want to fly like a bird. We don't want to sit in a car in a traffic jam, we want to be beamed around by the transporter in *Star Trek*.

To meet this grandiose objective Marzano proposed that Philips Design move beyond miniaturization to "progressive integration."

The nomads Philips focused on were tech-savvy young people, from athletes interested in measuring their heart rates to anxious parents hoping to reign in their youngsters' wandering inclinations via tracking devices. Prominently featured were "nomadic workers" who needed to remain connected while in airports, coffee bars, and other transient places. The New Nomads' business suit, a "digital suit for professionals," featured an embroidered keypad woven into the sleeve that would allow the wearer to interact with their networked devices.

Only one of these prototypes, a jacket produced through a collaboration between Philips and Levi Strauss called the Levi's ICD+, made it to the market in 2000–2001. This jacket, with specially designed pockets to hold Philips electronic devices, received an inordinate amount of press but sold poorly. Some major problems had not yet been worked out, including that a variety of these "smart pockets" seemed dumb as ever, having been consigned to holding or hiding quite a bit of the early infrastructure of wearables: battery packs, audio speakers, and cables. As a number of critics pointed out, there were plenty of other less expensive garments on the market with specialized compartments to hold electronic devices. Assessing the failure of the New Nomads garments to succeed even with their target group, Philips admitted that "energy sources must be embedded in textile structures. Carrying batteries in pockets is not a robust solution."

In one of the New Nomads garments designed by Philips for "enhanced body care and adornment," the Feels Good, pockets were included for a familiar, if contested, use. The cream gown was made of a synthetic fabric with woven panels of conductive thread down the back and sleeves. It had a device located in a pocket that initiated electrostatic charges that ran through the conductive threads, creating a tingling sensation designed to relax the wearer. Biometric sensors in the gown monitored the wearer's degree of relaxation and adjusted the charge levels automatically. To illustrate the serenity to be gained from the Feels Good, Philips pictured a monastic figure wearing rubber Teva sandals and reverently holding a bowl of a frothing incense, suggesting some kind of mystical encounter with his garb. Would anyone say, *Take your hands out of the Feels Good!* Perhaps not, but the secreted hand controling pleasurable tingles recalls the charges that initiated the taboo against reaching into one's pockets.

A number of artists and designers working outside consumer product design have critiqued the project of embedding everyday clothing with sensors and monitors that aid in various sorts of data collection while claiming to provide therapeutic benefits. They have produced often preposterous working and nonworking objects for publication or museum display. How much energy do wearables consume, and is this technology really effective? are among the questions Joanna Berzowska poses in her speculative 2010 garment, "Sticky," from a group of works titled *Captain Electric and Battery Boy* (figures 7 and 8). The hooded leather dress is meant to evoke a 1930s superhero; rather than using an external power source, it is self-powered. The garment's sleeves are tethered to what Berzowska calls "shell" structures on the hips and chest; as the wearer strains against them, inductive generators in the

Figure 7. "Sticky," by Joanna Berzowska, part of the series *Captain Electric and Battery Boy*, 2007–2010. The wearer generates power by pulling on the sleeves, which are attached to a belt (left). This activates the "luminescent pocket pebbles" (right), which heat up and glow, soothing the wearer and acting something like worry beads.

shells convert kinetic energy from the body into electric energy. The accumulated energy fuels the dress, powering luminescent pocket pebbles, concealed silicone forms that throb with bright blue LEDs. Soft, tactile, and warm, the glowing pebbles act as something like worry beads or the "sucking stones" that Molloy circulates between pockets in Samuel Beckett's eponymous experimental 1951 novel.

Berzowska does not reference Molloy, but this mid-century fictive character had devised among the lowest tech of methods with which to soothe himself. Even so, it is not perfect. Picking up sixteen stones along the seashore on a walk, Molloy encounters a problem of method: he only achieves "comparative peace of mind" when he is able to successfully undertake "a round," sucking one stone after the other in

Figure 8. Joanna Berzowska's luminescent pocket pebbles in the hip pocket of "Sticky," part of the series *Captain Electric and Battery Boy*, 2007–2010.

succession, without sucking the same stone twice. So he decides to use his trouser and coat pockets as a kind of accounting system to distinguish already-sucked stones from unsucked stones. Molloy arrives at his pocket-accounting solution after quite a bit of "wrestling and wrangling" with the problem; so, too, must the wearer of Berzowska's "Sticky" wrestle and wrangle. And that seems to be Berzowska's central aim. Amid all the self-congratulatory language that sees a place for technology to relieve everyday anxiety, she draws attention to its redundancy. If you had to power the technology yourself, you might alleviate all that nervous tension on your own.

WHAT WOULD A (technologically enhanced) smart pocket actually look like? One of the few wearables proposals to imagine a pocket that might take on new challenges came out of the short-lived i-Wear Project, run by Starlab research lab in collaboration with the Belgian men's wear designer Walter Van Beirendonck. In his Autumn/Winter 2000–2001 collection, "Dissections," Beirendonck proposed a prototype of six shirts worn on top of one another, each having a specific technological function. An energy-supply shirt powered the whole endeavor (it was the base shirt), while the others were optional; the wearer could add and subtract shirts as needed, like the "memory shirt" or the "motion-sensing shirt." The "storage shirt" contained pockets that could keep track of their contents. The proposal was only theoretical, but the idea that one would want to enlist such a complex system to perform such simple tasks indicates the ways technologists scramble to rationalize all this nifty innovation. Like so much technology thus far in the wearables realm, the "storage shirt" did not solve a pressing problem. At the same time, it denied the wearer the undeniable pleasure of discovery.

As of the early 2020s, retail designers have not only retained pockets but also kept their ambitions modest. After their work with Philips concluded, Levi Strauss next partnered with Google on a collaboration titled the Commuter x Jacquard by Google Trucker Jacket, the first so-called smart jean jacket, which sells commercially at relatively low cost. Envisioned for a small market segment of young, urban cyclists making their daily commutes, this jacket allows wearers to interact with their mobile phones without having to pull them out of a pocket. The technology saves that one step. A removable "snap tag" at the cuff—basically a transmitter or Bluetooth connector with a battery that holds a charge for several days—transmits data wirelessly between the wearer's sleeve and the wearer's phone. Via light and vibration, wearers are alerted to incoming calls and texts. Conductive yarn sewn into the left cuff of the sleeve is programmed to recognize various gestures, allowing wearers to tap, swipe, or hold the sleeve to perform "common digital tasks" like blocking or answering calls, changing music tracks, or accessing navigation information delivered by voice. The flexible snap tag can be removed for washing, making the jacket a lot more practical.

The project name—Jacquard by Google—suggests something of Google's grand ambitions: the Jacquard loom, the card-based, programmable mechanical loom developed by Joseph-Marie Jacquard in 1804, is commonly referenced in histories of technology as among the earliest steps toward the migration of control from the human body to the machine. By spinning the computer's electrical conductivity into thread itself, the Levi's and Google collaboration seems to have taken computing full circle and, in the process, finally made technology unobtrusive. The engineer and design lead at Google, Ivan Poupyrev, was among the winners of the 2019 Cooper Hewitt National Design Awards. The project was cited for its "seamless blending of digital and physical interactivity in everyday objects and devices." Here were "breakthrough interaction technologies for people's future digital lives," wrote the national design museum. Customer reviews have been a bit more tempered. This is not a smart jacket but a "gifted and talented jacket," wrote a customer from New York City; while acknowledging that more functionality was sure to come, this reviewer noted that wearers were limited to three commands.

In interviews about the commuter trucker jacket, project members have admitted that initially there were tensions between the technologists, who wanted "to make the activated space on the denim as explicit as possible," and the apparel folks, who wanted that space be known only to the wearer. Ultimately, the team recognized that many potential customers associated wearables with unfashionable sci-fi gadgetry, and that the unsightly cables and batteries of early experiments were not too far removed from visions of mad scientists with glass bulbs and electrical wire sticking out of their heads. The apparel folks won the argument. "The technology should not be apparent at all," argued Paul Dillinger, VP of global product innovation at Levi's. According to him, wearables should surprise with their abilities, "like a magician's trick."

However much the smart jean jacket would seem to have fulfilled technologists' dream that the interface between person and machine could disappear, it did not achieve what they have identified as the ultimate dream: to not have to bother with external tools at all; to have the tools you need implanted into the body itself. But so far, the tools have not really gone anywhere. Like magicians, we perform all sorts of hand gestures, albeit without a nifty wand. And like magicians, we understand that the successful staging of tricks often involves hiding tools and props offstage, or at least out of spectators' view. One could say that, to date, wearables allow people to interact with the tools they keep offstage, safely tucked in their pockets.

Successful new technologies have a way of habituating wearers to their more frequent use. This is one of the ways technologists secure the futures they imagine. Google certainly did not ask whether anyone really needed to check in with the office on their way to work to remain competitive. Maybe the worker could just wait until they arrive? In seeking to challenge expectations of continuous reachability, what Sherry Turkle identifies as a culture of always "being on," some designers have recently begun offering their versions of disruption, designs that enable wearers to disconnect. In 2019, the New York City–based brand the Arrivals offered a winter parka with a chest pocket lined in a blend of polyester, copper, and nickel. Drawing on the techniques of a Faraday cage, an electromagnetic-field-proof mesh shield created in 1836 by British scientist Michael Faraday, the combination of materials blocks cellular and GPS signals on smartphones. "We live in a time where we are more connected to our devices than to the environments we inhabit," Jeff Johnson, cofounder of the Arrivals, explained. "We began conceptualizing solutions that would enable users to reconnect with the outdoors by disconnecting from everything else." As laudable as that objective might be, here again was an unnecessarily complicated and resources-heavy solution to a made-up problem. Could the wearer not just turn off her phone?

A protective pocket lined in copper could have more compelling uses, allowing protesters to elude surveillance by authoritarian states. One can imagine that protestors and dissidents might welcome the protection that an electromagnetic-field-proof shield could provide above and beyond simply turning off their phones. These examples demonstrate the threats posed by any garment or accessory that receives and transmits digital signals, and that is worn on or fitted ever closer to the body. It is not in everyone's interest that an embodied Internet replace the more concentrated, device-based system we have now.

But an embodied Internet may be coming sooner than we think. In 2018 futurist Amy Webb predicted the end of smartphones in the year 2031, a prediction she reconfirmed in 2022. "There will be fewer things done by one device like we have now." Apple concurred when it announced that it would replace iPhones with augmented reality contact lenses by the 2030s. Digital technology "will be close to us and worn all over us," Webb surmised. Her predictions make debates over whether tools are portable, wearable, or integrated seem moot. Yet at stake are much larger questions about the trade-offs we make when we delegate the control of our tools to others.

"IT'S GOT POCKETS!"

THE ASPIRATION FOR lack of encumbrance could be said to be the initial, and an enduring, design motive behind pocketing, one first evinced when tailors decided to stitch drawstring pocket-bags inside men's breeches in the sixteenth century. Whether people trust or desire the frictionless world promised by technology, and yearn for fewer impediments, remains to be seen. Will we want to retain pockets even after we've realized some version of a more seamless second skin?

While futurists divine signs of emerging trends, attempting to forecast enduring change, one key fact remains: wearers continue to value pockets. In focusing on the myriad apparatuses that "civilization demands" and chafing at the practical need to be equipped, technologists characterize their desire to be rid of things as a universal one. They imagine technology has all the answers, but to date, no one has invented a digital form of the handkerchief. Such assumptions miss much that is evidently true about human attachment to material objects, including that those relationships are not always purely instrumental and that they extend to things beyond the absolutely necessary. While not everyone needs something akin to Molloy's "sucking stones" to soothe some existential angst, the record shows that humans are incorrigible collectors of odds and ends, and that these odds and ends serve all sorts of functions.

Some of those functions are avowedly superstitious. Under threat, we acknowledge the efficaciousness of magical protection and hope that carrying some sort of charm, like "pockets full of posies" to ward off contagion, will give us a special pass to navigate dangerous environments safely. Designers remain attuned to people's not-so-secret desire for analog things that offer protection—or instill confidence or sustain momentum. During the virtual presentations of fashion collections in the 2021 pandemic year, for example, Walter Van Beirendonck, who had, twenty years earlier, proposed a tech-enhanced "storage pocket" that could keep track of its contents, offered just the opposite, a multi-pocket garment that evoked premodern beliefs. Each of the stiff patch pockets over chest, arms, and back looked something like a reliquary box, and each had inset mirrored panels that "serve as protection from evil forces," he explained, invoking clothing traditions from southern Europe to southeast Asia that have used small mirrors or reflective metals attached to clothing to reflect back the evil eye, confusing and misdirecting malevolent spirits (figure 9). As an aesthetic proposition, the bulky patch pockets bolstered up the silhouettes, offering the kinds of novel shapes that fashion requires. As an emotional proposition, the pockets addressed more elemental concerns.

Pocket posies and preservatives do not necessarily shield the wearer in the moment: in a haunting confrontation recorded on a cell phone during the first days of Putin's war in Ukraine in February 2022, a woman from Henichesk, Ukraine, demands that a Russian soldier take her proffered gift of seeds and put them in his pocket, "so when you die here, sunflowers will grow from the spot." The woman offered the soldier seeds intended neither to preserve nor to protect him, but like any complicated gift, they did offer something in return: from the pockets of his military fatigues, the seeds, she prophesized, would eventually be returned to the ground he and his army had lately trampled. They would germinate in soil fertilized by his corpse, offering a kind of atonement. Only then, she explained to him, would "some good" come from his presence.

Figure 9. Walter Van Beirendonck, Spring–Summer, 2021. When fashion collections were halted during 2020, Beirendonck produced a collection that could be presented on small-scale dolls.

THAT NO ONE wants to give up on pockets just yet is suggested by women's as yet unfulfilled pocket aspirations. Why would women give up something that they are only now starting to acquire? The joyful exclamation, *It's got pockets!* still occurs with frequency, often preceding the decision to purchase a new garment. The comment can also be made after receiving a compliment, with a conspiratorial wink: *Yup, I like this dress,* and *it's got pockets.* Observing one of his friends put her hands in the pockets of a new dress and make "the requisite twirl," programmer and entrepreneur Jim Sabo exclaimed, "I'm gonna buy 'dresseswithpockets. com' and get rich." After some initial hesitancy, and some continuing encouragement, Sabo did, launching his website in February 2019. Rather than begin his own line of well-pocketed offerings, Sabo decided to become a kind of pocket aggregator and started scraping all the metadata from other clothing sites, including construction details often invisible to individual consumers. In highlighting the pockets already available, his site provides a service to his customers while making a small commission via the links Dresseswithpockets.com makes to others. Sabo's business has grown. Trans women love the site, he notes, as they are in the rare position of having experienced both sides of the pocket divide. "My ultimate goal for the site is to fade into irrelevancy," he contends.

A few brands forthrightly make the case that *it's got pockets!* integral to their advertising campaigns (although not necessarily with any consistency). Enjoy our "pocket empowered" dresses, the female-owned and -run sportswear brand Title Nine has invited consumers, using the ironic tone of social media vernacular to position their wares: "Here at T-9 we're big on pockets, so you won't find a dress we sell without 'em. Pockets that let us ditch the purse, live more freely, and carry our own damn stuff." Others have added what amounts to an *It's got pockets!* icon in the informational details and features list that accompanies any online garment description. A maker of skinny jeans includes a cute little sketch of a back pocket, showing it full of tools safely hooked via pocket clip.

Will such icons become more commonplace? Or will pockets become so standardized in clothing designed for women that such assurances will no longer be necessary? At the moment, pockets remain the burden of the wearer to ensure, and even female superheroes face uncertainty. "OK, it has a lot of pockets!" acknowledges Yelena Belova in a recent installment in the spiraling Marvel Cinematic Universe, 2021's *Black Widow*, when she admits that she has purchased a utility vest online and made some of her own pocket additions. The vest is the first piece of clothing she has ever purchased herself (this kind of self-determination is difficult when you've participated since childhood in a state-led assassination squad). "The point is, I've never had control over my own life before, and now I do. I want to *do* things," she explains. Yelena wears the vest *over* her Avengers superhero suit,

"Oh, my God—it's got pockets!"

Figure 10. *Oh, my God—it's got pockets!*, by Sharon Levy, published in the *New Yorker*, January 20, 2020.

which looks more like a sleek boiler suit than the unitard-and-tights costume of old, and in doing so makes an unprecedented critique of superhero attire. If even superheroes cannot sally forth perfectly free of any accommodation, what does that say about the rest of us?

UNASSUMING IN AND of themselves, it is pockets' capacity to carry other things, and to stay literally at our sides, that makes them remarkable. Pockets and their contents constitute a sort of microcosm, a representation of our "other selves," as one "philosopher of pockets" remarked. Admittedly much of what is evident from exploring these little worlds is evident in some form elsewhere. One doesn't need to peer into pockets to understand that people rather like to conceal incriminating bits, or to identify specific pocket poses to recognize that how we wear our clothes is just as important as what we wear. Nor does it take the uneven distribution of pockets in gendered attire to register that all sorts of traditions support the patriarchy. Disputes around concealment, deportment, and power nevertheless gain a vivid specificity when analyzed via the medium of pockets.

The centuries' long tailoring tradition furthermore reveals that we are held together with some industry and determination. Something of an engineering puzzle, pockets (like our clothes) have right and wrong sides. Inquiring too much about their unsightly "rough seems," in the words of Thomas Carlyle, threatens to undercut the commanding outer "edifice" of the person. Perhaps this is the reason human jealousy over marsupials' capacities continues unabated. "It's got pockets!" observe the hikers on encountering the abominable snowman in Sharon Levy's 2020 *New Yorker* cartoon, less startled by the apparition of the mysterious beast than by its pocket endowment (figure 10). Such envious surprise is one reason to think we will not give up pockets any time soon. With pockets at our sides, we preserve some confidence that we can meet, or at least parry, any contingency.

Notes

Introduction

2 **"notorious blunder"** *London Journal*, Sept. 4, 1725, quoted in J. Paul Hunter, "Gulliver's Travels and the Novel," in *The Genres of Gulliver's Travels*, ed. Frederick N. Smith (Delaware: Univ. of Delaware, 1990), 68. Hunter recovered this contemporary joke and used it to examine Jonathan Swift's attack on the emerging novel and the "false realism of Defoe." Defoe's critics called the novel the "most palpable lie from Beginning to End," and the novel's continuity problem helped prove it.

3 **Defoe engineered** For generations of writers of subsequent castaway tales betrayed by this authorial deus ex machina, from Jean Jacques Rousseau (*Emile*) to Johann David Wyss (*Swiss Family Robinson*) to the producers of the reality TV show *Naked and Afraid*, the question would become how few tools did one need to survive.

3 **"the famous Passage"** Hunter, "Gulliver's Travels," 68.

3 **"feeblest of bipeds"** Thomas Carlyle, *Sartor Resartus*, ed. Rodger L. Tarr (Berkeley: Univ. of California Press, 2000), 31.

4 **marsupial mammals** Ibid., 50.

4 **tools that allow** Ibid., 50.

4 **"oblong pouch"** George Barrington, *The History of New South Wales* (London: Printed for M. Jones, [1802] 1810), 432. The first European printed image of the kangaroo that featured her pouch appeared in a book attributed to an infamous gentleman pickpocket, George Barrington. Banished for his crimes to the penal colony of New South Wales, the "prince of pickpockets" soon embraced reform, and the histories of the colony attributed to him did much to incite curiosity. See Ronald Younger, *Kangaroo: Images through the Ages* (Sydney: Hawthorn, 1988).

4 **"A man without"** William Livingstone Alden, *Domestic Explosives and other Sixth Column Fancies* (New York: Lovell, Adam, Wesson, 1877), 50.

5 **"pocket . . . are peeping"** Sally Sketch, *An Alphabetical Arrangement of Animals for Young Naturalists* (London: Harris & Son, 1821).

5 **journey to "get one"** Emmy Payne, *Katy No Pocket* (Boston: Houghton Mifflin, 1944).

5 **seems to be "ALL pockets"** Ibid.

5 **His gift will allow** His gift will also allow Katy to perform professional work. When she gets back home to the forest, she supplies daycare services, pocketing a range of forest creatures in her workman's apron.

6 **"locate to lust"** Howard Nemerov, "Pockets," in *The Western Approaches* (Chicago: Univ. of Chicago Press, 1975), 39.

8 **"layers upon layers"** Bernard Rudofsky, *Are Clothes Modern? An Essay on Contemporary Apparel* (Chicago: Paul Theobald, 1947), 124.

8 **"pocket equality"** "Give Woman Equality in Pockets," *Baltimore Sun*, Feb. 23, 1894, 4.

9 **"Got a ship in your pocket?"** William Golding, *Lord of the Flies* (New York: Penguin, [1954] 2006), 111.

9 **anticipate human need** Elaine Scarry, *The Body in Pain: The Making and Unmaking of the World* (New York: Oxford Univ. Press, 1985). In her consideration of the nature of design, Elaine Scarry argues that even anonymous, mass-produced objects represent "objectified human compassion," in part because the artifactual world both "projects" and "reciprocates the live body." Scarry contends that artifacts people imagine and create help "to alter the human being in his or her full array of capacities and needs" (288, 324).

Chapter 1: Pocket Origins

11 **"of being a knight"** Mark Twain, *Notebooks*, quoted in Henry Nash Smith, *Mark Twain's Fable of Progress* (New Brunswick, NJ: Rutgers Univ. Press, 1964), 41.

11 **"No pockets in"** Ibid.

11 **"underhand blow"** Mark Twain, *Connecticut Yankee in King Arthur's Court*, vol. 9 of *The Works of Mark Twain*, ed. Bernard L Stein (Berkeley: Univ. of California Press, 1979), 144.

11 **first time-travel** Philip Klass, "An Innocent in Time: Mark Twain in King Arthur's Court," *Extrapolation* 16, no. 1 (Dec. 1974): 23.

12 **"holy grailing"** Twain, *Connecticut Yankee*, 116.

12 **"Hang a man"** Ibid., 119.

12 **"scandalous"** Ibid.

12 **"iron dudes"** Ibid.

12 **in his library** According to Alan Gribben's *Mark Twain's Library: A Reconstruction* (Boston: G. K. Hall, 1980) Twain owned, for example, Paul Lacroix's 1874 *Manners, Customs, and Dress During the Middle Ages, and During the Renaissance Period.*

12 **Earl Tupper** Alison Clarke, *Tupperware: The Promise of Plastic in 1950s America* (Washington, DC: Smithsonian Institution Press, 1999).

13 **Books that promise** See, for example, Harry Oliver, *Bubble Gum and Hula Hoops: The Origins of Objects in Our Everyday Lives* (2010); Trevor Homer, *The Book of Origins* (2007); Joel Levy, *Really Useful: The Origins of Everyday Things* (2002); Charles Panati, *Panati's Extraordinary Origins of Everyday Things* (1987).

13 **buttons with corresponding buttonholes** Mary Stella Newton, *Fashion in the Age of the Black Prince* (Woodbridge, Suffolk, UK: Boydell Press, 1980), 15–18. Decorative buttons date to prehistory and to the Indus Valley, circa 2000 BCE, but the use of button and coordinating buttonhole arose with the advent of fitted clothes in medieval Europe.

13 **utilized in draped clothing** See Dorothy K. Burnham, *Cut My Cote* (Toronto: Royal Ontario Museum, 1973), 3.

13 **the chuba robe of Tibet** M. Ahmed and S. Vickery, "Dress of the Exile: Tibetan," in J. Dhamija, ed., *Berg Encyclopedia of World Dress and Fashion: South Asia and Southeast Asia* (Oxford: Bloomsbury Academic, 2010), 194–200.

14 **Roman *sinus*** F. P. Leverett, ed., s.v. "sinus," *A New and Copius Lexicon of the Latin Language* (Boston, 1850). "The Romans made use of this fold in the toga as a pocket, in which they carried letters, purses, daggers, &c; and hence, Augustus used to cause the sinus of person's approaching him to be searched."

14 **"God of Love . . . nothing without elegance"** Frances Horgan, trans. and ed., *The Romance of the Rose*, Oxford World's Classics (Oxford: Oxford Univ. Press, 1999), 33.

14 **Purses served** Claire Wilcox, *Bags* (London: V & A Publications, 1999), chap. 1.

14 **In 1342, Giovanni Villani** Newton, *Fashion*, 6–7.

15 **admires the beautiful Alison's girdle** Gale R. Owen-Crocker, "Sensuality and Sexuality," in *Encyclopedia of Medieval Dress and Textiles*, http://dx.doi.org/10.1163/2213-2139_emdt_SIM_000751 (accessed January 17, 2018).

16 ***Pocket* is a borrowing** *Oxford English Dictionary*, vol. 2, P–Z (Oxford: Oxford Univ. Press, 1987), s.v. "pocket, n. and adj."; *Middle English Dictionary* (Ann Arbor: Univ. of Michigan Press, 1956–), s.v. "pocket."

16 **a pocket lined in wax** Geoffrey Chaucer, *The Canon's Yeoman's Prologue and Tale*, in *Selected Tales from Chaucer*, ed. Maurice Hussey (Cambridge: Cambridge Univ. Press, [1965] 2016), 85.

16 **"staunch the flux . . . grievance"** William Copland, *A Boke of the Properties of Herbes Called an Herball* (London: Wyllyam Copland for Iohn Wyght [1552?]; Ann Arbor: Text Creation Partnership, 2011), http://name.umdl.umich.edu/A03040.0001.001.

16 **carried about one's person** François Boucher, *20,000 Years of Fashion* (New York: Harry N. Abrams, 1966), 433.

16 **A henpecked husband** Walter L. Strauss, *German Masters of the Sixteenth Century: Erhard Schoen, Niklas Stoer* (New York: Abaris Books, 1984), 336.

16 **Cloth was far more expensive** Sarah Grace Heller, *A Cultural History of Dress and Fashion in the Medieval Age* (London: Bloomsbury Academic, 2017), 50–51.

16 **complex constructions** Naomi Tarrant, *The Development of Costume* (London: Routledge, 1994), 44–48.

17 **Norse Greenland grave sites** Else Østegärd, *Woven into the Earth: Textiles from Norse Greenland* (Aarhus: Aarhus Univ. Press, 2004).

17 **The slits were carefully finished** Ibid., 94–95, 179–80.

18 **compromised a garment's reuse** See Desiree G. Koslin and Janet E. Snyder, eds., *Encountering Medieval Textiles and Dress: Objects, Texts, Images* (New York: Palgrave Macmillan, 2002). The information in this paragraph is derived from personal communication with Desiree Koslin, February 15, 2007.

18 **trousers have an ancient lineage** Naomi Tarrant, Mayake Wagner, et al. "The invention of twill tapestry points to Central Asia: Archaeological record of multiple textile techniques used to make the woollen outfit of a ca. 3000-year-old horse rider from Turfan, China," *Archaeological Research in Asia* 29 (March 2022).

18 **development of plate armor** See Oldie Blanc's discussion of the pourpoint, a doublet that was first worn under armor and that was adopted in civilian wear. Blanc, "From Battlefield to Court: The Invention of Fashion in the Fourteenth Century," in Koslin and Snyder, *Encountering Medieval Textiles*, 163.

20 **"fight for the breeches"** Laura Gowing, *Domestic Dangers: Women, Words, and Sex in Early Modern London* (Oxford: Clarendon Press; Oxford: Oxford Univ. Press, 1996), 83.

20 **"breeches as big"** U. Fulwell, *Like Will to Like* (1568), quoted in C. Willett Cunnington and Phillis Cunnington, *Handbook of Costume in the Sixteenth Century* (London: Faber and Faber, 1954), 121.

20 **could attempt to flaunt it** Philip Stubbes, *Anatomie of Abuses* (1583), quoted in Aileen Ribeiro, *Dress and Morality* (New York: Holmes & Meier, 1988), 68.

21 **"monstrous and outrageous"** Quoted in Wilfred Hooper, "The Tudor Sumptuary Laws," *The English Historical Review* 30, no. 119 (July 1915): 439.

21 **A 1562 edict** Ibid. Hosiers and tailors were also required to enter into bonds of forty pounds each to observe these provisions, and those who resisted were threatened with fines and imprisonment.

22 **"good for none"** Richard Edwards, *Damon and Pithias*, in *The Oxford Anthology of Tudor Drama*, ed. Greg Walker (Oxford: Oxford Univ. Press, 2014), 376.

22 **"other folk's, stuff"** Ibid.

22 **city gates checked** Hooper, "Tudor Sumptuary Laws," 443.

22 **"monstrous hose"** Ibid., 441.

22 **"where they may aptly"** Ibid.

22 **Thomas Bradshaw** Ibid.

22 **"his breeches contrary to the Law"** John Bulwer, *Anthropometamorphosis: The Man Transformed or the Artificial Changeling* (London: William Hunt, 1653), 541–42. Bulwer cited the anecdote (and then lifted it word for word) from Lucas Gracian Dantisco's *Galateo Espagnol, or The Spanish Gallant*, an English translation of Dantisco's 1590 adaptation of Della Casa's *Galateo*.

23 **"other things of use"** Quoted in Janet Arnold, *Patterns of Fashion: The Cut and Construction of Clothes for Men and Women, ca. 1560–1620* (London: Macmillan; New York: Drama Book, 1985), 76–77.

23 **"strewn" with his belongings** Ibid.

23 **"no safer a store-house"** Ibid.

23 **"a straight prison"** Ibid.

23 **"alter the furniture"** Ibid.

23 **Svante Sture** Ibid., 59.

24 **"Oh that I had the Dutchman's Hose"** Jean MacIntyre, *Costumes and Scripts in the Elizabethan Theatres* (Edmonton: Univ. of Alberta Press, 1992), 132.

24 **"carried the moon"** William Shakespeare, *Cymbeline*, act 3, scene 1, line 47.

25 **codpiece, an emblem** William Fisher, *Materializing Gender in Early Modern English Literature and Culture* (Cambridge: Cambridge Univ. Press, 2006), 68–69. While modern historians have suggested that the accessory was intended to indicate a "permanent state of erection," Fisher points out that many were "distinctly non-phallic" and linked, as their name suggested, to the scrotum/testicles and related ideas about procreation and lineage.

25 **stuffing of the codpiece "stands out"** Carolyn Dinshaw and David Wallace, *The Cambridge Companion to Medieval Women's Writing* (Cambridge: Cambridge Univ. Press, 2003), 72–73.

25 **"a new man of fashion"** Henry Medwall, *Fulgens and Lucres*, I.734–5, in *The Plays of Henry Medwall*, ed. Alan H. Nelson (Cambridge: D.S. Brewer, 1980).

25 **"unknit . . . made way"** Quoted in Fisher, *Materializing Gender*, 59.

27 **codpiece as a container** The portrait makes clear that codpieces were sometimes used to contain things. The codpiece was baglike, and the connection between the form (if not the function) was noted when codpieces were in fashion. For example, in the 1460 Towneley cycle of mystery plays, one character refers to a "kodpese like a pokett." *Middle English Dictionary* (Ann Arbor: Univ. of Michigan Press, 1956–), s.v. "codpiece."

27 **"too much express"** Bulwer, *Anthropometamorphosis*, 540.

27 **"so sweet a closet . . . uncivil"** Quoted in Rebecca Unsworth, "Hands Deep in History: Pockets in Men and Women's Dress in Western Europe, ca. 1480–1630," *Costume* 51 no. 2 (2017): 160.

27 **rationalize their century-long use** Fisher, *Materializing Gender*, 78.

27 **tailor's manuals** Arnold, *Patterns of Fashion*, 3.

27 **"for [two] leather pockettes"** Quoted in Cunnington and Cunnington, *Handbook of English Costume*, 122.

27 **trunk hose that remain** Arnold, *Patterns of Fashion*, 59, 63, 75, 87, 89, 91.

28 **wardrobe accounts of Elizabeth I** Unsworth, "Hands Deep in History," 156.

29 **"pocket dags . . . carried privily"** Paul L. Hughes and James F. Larkin, eds., *Tudor Royal Proclamations*, 2 vols. (New Haven, CT: Yale Univ. Press, 1969), 2:398–99.

29 **dramatic wake-up call** On January 16, 1549, a jealous Thomas Seymour (allegedly hoping to take over as regent to Edward VI, a position held by his brother) entered the king's private apartments to discuss some matter using a key he had secured. Thomas Seymour's entry awoke Edward's dog, whose barking startled Seymour, who reached for his gun and shot the dog. Things did not go well thereafter for Thomas Seymour. He was tried for treason, and although two of the three judges cleared him, he was executed as a traitor. See Lois G. Schwoerer's description of the event in *Gun Culture in Early Modern England* (Charlottesville: Univ. of Virginia Press, 2016), 61.

30 **wheel-lock pistol** Bert S. Hall, *Weapons and Warfare in Renaissance Europe* (Baltimore, MD: Johns Hopkins Univ. Press, 1997), 190.

30 **loaded ahead of time** Lisa Jardine, *The Awful End of Prince William the Silent: The First Assassination of a Head of State with a Handgun* (New York: Harper Perennial, 2007), 77–85.

30 **appreciated for its ease** Schwoerer, *Gun Culture*, 3.

31 **Sir Martin Frobisher** The portrait was completed after the semi-disastrous second of Frobisher's three voyages to the New World, where he neither managed to discover the fabled Northwest passage to Asia nor accomplished much else to satisfy his investors' expectations. Frobisher's posture, his depiction of himself as an uncompromising sea dog, could be considered something of a promotional stunt. See James McDermott, *Martin Frobisher: Elizabethan Privateer* (New Haven: Yale Univ. Press, 2001).

31 **"clogged" with gold and silver** Philip Stubbes, *The Anatomie of Abuses* (London: John Kingston for Richard Iones, 1583), 62.

31 **"greatest gallant . . . longest blade"** John Stow, *Annales, or a General Chronicle of England* (London: Richardi Meighen, 1631), 869.

31 **state began to limit** Schwoerer, *Gun Culture*, 60.

31 **incomes lower than one hundred pounds** Ibid., 46, 61.

31 **minuscule law-enforcement** Joyce Lee Malcolm, *To Keep and Bear Arms: The Origins of an Anglo-American Right* (Cambridge, MA: Harvard Univ. Press, 1994), 2.

31 **"a time of peace"** Paul L. Hughes and James F. Larkin, eds., *Tudor Royal Proclamations*, 2 vols. (New Haven: Yale Univ. Press, 1969), 2:398–99.

31 **A 1579 regulation** Ibid., 2:442–45

32 **banned the pocket dag** Schwoerer, *Gun Culture*, 97.

32 **A 1564 ordinance of Henri III** Two nineteenth-century sources of dress history claimed that French rulers tried to ban pockets. In locating the ordinances at issue, I see only reference to keeping the pockets a small size, apparently so as to make them incapable of carrying twelve-inch-long guns. See James Robinson Planché, *A Cyclopaedia of Costume or Dictionary of Dress* (New York: J.W. Bouton, 1877), 84.

33 **"pistol pockets"** "Anti Hip-Pocket Bill: South Carolina's Newest Plan for Reducing the Number of Murders," *Boston Daily Globe*, Jan. 6, 1898.

33 **"odious . . . polluted with blood"** England and Wales, Sovereign (1603–1625: James I), *A Proclamation against the Use of Pocket-Dags* (London: Robert Barker, 1613).

33 **"knightly and honorable . . . daggers"** James I, King of England, *Basilikon doron, or, King James's Instructions to His Dearest Sonne, Henry the Prince* (London: Simon Stafford for Thomas Salisbury, 1604; Ann Arbor: Text Creation Partnership, 2011), 113, https://quod.lib.umich.edu/e/eebo2/A04230.0001.001/1:7?rgn=div1;view=fulltext.

33 **"Out with . . . your pocket-dagger"** John Fletcher and Philip Massinger, *The Custom of the Country*, in *The Dramatic Works in the Beaumont and Fletcher Cannon*, vol. 8, ed. Fredson Bwers (Cambridge: Cambridge Univ. Press, 1992), 672.

33 **"murder men"** Ibid.

33 **first successful assassination** See Jardine, *Awful End*. Sir Francis Walsingham reported that the assassin approached William "as if he had some letter to impart" (52).

34 **Hogenberg's graphic depiction** Andrew Pettegree, *The Invention of News: How the World Came to Know Itself* (New Haven, CT: Yale Univ. Press, 2014), 88–93.

34 **Commentators kept coming back** Ibid., 54, 58.

35 **Pieter Bruegel's 1568 painting** Todd M. Richardson, *Pieter Bruegel the Elder: Art Discourse in the Sixteenth-Century Netherlands* (Farnham, Surrey: Ashgate, 2011), 151.

35 **"plunge into the water . . . into your Storage"** John Dunton, *An Hue and Cry after Conscience, or, The Pilgrims Progress by Candlelight in Search after Honesty and Plain-dealing Represented under the Similitude of a Dream* (London: Printed for John Dunton, 1685; Ann Arbor: Text Creation Partnership, 2011), 132–34, http://name.umdl.umich.edu/A36902.0001.001. The diver describes the education afforded young aspirants to the "Trade," replete with a school and instructor to declaim theory and practice. The practicum included hanging a pair of breeches upon a line fastened cross the room; the young aspirants able to disentangle the purse without disturbing a bell (hung from the pocket's entrance) were well on their way.

35 **"holds himself . . . disdain"** Robert Greene, *The Second Part of Conny-Catching . . .* (London: Iohn Wolfe for William Wright, 1591; Ann Arbor: Text Creation Partnership, 2011), http://name.umdl.umich.edu/A02141.0001.001.

35 **"Nimble handed"** Ibid.

36 **"dives . . . new swept"** Peter Aretine, *Strange News from Bartholomew-Fair, or, the Wandering-Whore Discovered Her Cabinet Unlockt . . .* (London: Printed for Theodorus Microcosmus, 1661; Ann Arbor: Text Creation Partnership, 2011), 4, http://name.umdl.umich.edu/A61777.0001.001.

36 **calls their "antecedent" artifact** George Basalla, *Evolution of Technology* (Cambridge: Cambridge Univ. Press, 1988), vii.

36 **"are never pure"** Ibid., viii.

36 **"a grand and vast"** Ibid., 209.

36 **their proximity belies** Ibid.

37 **"to pocket up"** *Oxford English Dictionary*, vol. 2, P–Z (Oxford: Oxford Univ. Press, 1987), s.v. "pocket," extended uses. First and earliest "extended" use of the word *pocket* is to "pocket up" a wrong. "To take or accept (an affront, etc.) without showing resentment; to submit to, endure meekly; to swallow."

37 **"crouch and bow"** Anthony Stafford, *Stafford's Niobe: Or His age of Teares* (London: Humfrey Lownes, 1611; Ann Arbor: Text Creation Partnership, 2011), 104, http://name.umdl.umich.edu/A12821.0001.001.

37 **"smooth front"** Ibid.

37 **"lick the feet"** Ibid.

37 **"must pocket up"** Ibid.

38 **counseled readers not to draw out a letter** Giovanni Della Casa, *Il Galateo*, trans. Konrad Eisenbichler and Kenneth R. Bartlett (Toronto: Centre for Reformation and Renaissance Studies, [1558] 1986), 11.

39 **"speak . . . lie"** William Shakespeare, *The Tempest*, act 2, scene 1, line 63.

40 **"good clothes . . . torn pockets"** Thomas Dekker, *A Tragi-comedy: Called,*
Match Mee in London (London, 1631; Ann Arbor: Text Creation Partnership,
2011), 55, https://quod.lib.umich.edu/e/eebo/A20088.0001.001/1:4.4?rgn=div
2;view=fulltext.

40 **"still are poring on"** Joseph Hall, *Virgidemiarum*, 2 vols. (1599;
Ann Arbor: Text Creation Partnership, 2011), book 4, satire 6, line 8,
https://quod.lib.umich.edu/e/eebo/A71324.0001.001/1:3.7?rgn=div2;view
=fulltext;q1=Virgidemiarum.

40 **A revival** A number of portraits of male figures in Italy, France, Germany,
and Britain from between 1560 and 1564 depict this O-ring purse, and
several include handkerchiefs. See, for example, Alessandro Allori, *Portrait*
of Tommaso De' Bardi (1560); Hans Eworth, *Portrait of Thomas Howard,*
4th Duke of Norfolk (1563); Pieter Pourbus, *Portrait of Pierre Dominicle*
(1558).

40 **"plain country fellow"** Quoted in Jane Ashelford, *Dress in the Age of*
Elizabeth (London: Batsford, 1988), 114. Greene warned that this outfit
marked the countryman as easy prey for the conman or thief.

41 **and not without contention** Sonja Kudei, "The Problem with Man-Bag and
Other Man Words," *The Atlantic*, April 10, 2014. https://www.theatlantic.com
/health/archive/2014/04/the-problem-with-man-bag-and-other-man-words/359830/.

41 **"luxe murse market"** Christian Allaire, "I Test-Drove the 'Murse,' Summer's
Surprising Breakout Trend," *Vogue*, July 4, 2019.

Chapter 2: Pocket Proliferation

44 **"vex the world"** Jonathan Swift, letter to Alexander Pope, Sept. 29, 1725,
in *Gulliver's Travels*, ed., Albert J. Rivero (New York: W. W. Norton,
[1726] 2002), 261.

44 **"simple and plain . . . union"** Swift, *Gulliver's Travels*, 25.

44 **measure and "compute"** Ibid., 237.

44 **"a God he worships"** Ibid., 29.

44 **Gulliver has approached the venture** Ibid., 28–31.

45 **Swift decisively lampoons** At the end of the book, Gulliver defends his
project and tries to dispel any "objections" to his travels, including the charge
of colonization. He notes that "those Countries which I have described, do
not appear to have any Desire of being Conquered, and enslaved, murdered or
driven out by Colonies, nor abound in Gold, Silver, Sugar or Tobacco" (Swift,
Gulliver's Travels, 249).

45 **"united by a fraternity"** Barbara Burman and Ariane Fennetaux, *The Pocket:*
A Hidden History of Women's Lives, 1660–1900 (New Haven, CT: Yale Univ.
Press, 2019), 26.

45 **The structure of the three-piece suit** Several authors discuss King Charles II's introduction of the suit. See Diana de Marly, "King Charles II's Own Fashion: The Theatrical Origins of the English Vest," *Journal of the Warbug and Courtald Institutes* 37 (1974): 378–82; David Kuchta, *The Three-Piece Suit and Modern Masculinity: England, 1550–1850* (Berkeley: Univ. of California Press, 2002); Aileen Ribeiro, *Fashion and Fiction: Dress in Art and Literature in Stuart England* (New Haven: Yale Univ. Press, 2005), 224–38.

45 **Such breaks do not occur often** Ann Hollander, *Sex and Suits* (New York: Knopf, 1994) 15.

46 **reached absurd extremes** Ribeiro, *Fashion and Fiction*, 202.

46 **as if they'd "plundered"** John Evelyn, *Tyrannus, or The Mode*, ed. J. L. Nevinson (Oxford: Published for the Luttrell Society by B. Blackwell, 1951), 11.

47 **"a new fashion"** Quoted in Ribeiro, *Fashion and Fiction*, 230.

47 **pinpoint the date** Ibid.

47 **stately, reserved, and "manlike"** Quoted in Kuchta, *Three-Piece Suit*, 90; Ribeiro, *Fashion and Fiction*, 232.

47 **"for a comely vest"** Quoted in Kuchta, *Three-Piece Suit*, 83; Ribeiro, *Fashion and Fiction*, 230.

48 **Versions of kaftans** Charlotte Jirousek, "The Kaftan and its Origins," in *Berg Encyclopedia of World Dress and Fashion: Central and Southwest Asia* (Oxford: Berg, 2010), 134.

48 **"the most graceful"** Quoted in Kuchta, *Three-Piece Suit*, 121.

49 **two sets of vertical pockets** Avril Hart and Susan North, *Historical Fashion in Detail: The 17th and 18th Centuries* (London: V & A Publications, 1998), 96.

49 **Sixteenth- and seventeenth-century kaftans** J. M. Rogers and R. M. Ward, *Süleyman the Magnificent* (Secaucus, NJ: Wellfleet Press, 1988), 166.

50 **The suit was among** Beverly Lemire and Giorgio Riello, eds., *Dressing Global Bodies: The Political Power of Dress in World History* (Abingdon, Oxon: Routledge, 2020), 44.

50 **Churyo Morishima decoded** Jan van Bremen and Akitoshi Shimizu, *Anthropology and Colonialism in Asia and Oceana* (Richmond, Surrey: Curzon, 1999), 53.

50 **"there are parts"** Lemire and Riello, *Dressing Global Bodies*, 44.

50 **"the [Dutch] dress system"** Ibid., 45.

51 **outlined with metallic braiding** Hollander, *Sex and Suits*, 65

52 **"various scallop of the pocket"** Richard Steele, *The Guardian*, no. 149, Sept. 1, 1713.

53 **The blue silk taffeta lining** Hart and North, *Historic Fashion in Detail*, 98.

53 **striped, checked, and speckled** Claudia B. Kidwell and Margaret C. Christman, *Suiting Everyone: The Democratization of Clothing in America* (Washington, DC: Published for the National Museum of History and Technology by the Smithsonian Institution Press, 1975), 23.

55 **"gray cloth coat"** *Virginia Gazette* (Williamsburg), April 2, 1767, available at Freedom on the Move, https://www2.vcdh.virginia.edu/gos/search/related Ad.php?adFile=sg67.xml&adId=v1767041552.

55 **ready-made clothes** Whether "the usual slave clothing" had pockets was of interest to Works Progress Administration interviewers in the 1930s. Charles L. Perdue Jr., Thomas E. Barden, and Robert K. Phillips, eds. *Weevils in the Wheat: Interviews with Virginia Ex-slaves* (Charlottesville: Univ. Press of Virginia, 1976), 374. See appendix 6, question 265.

56 **not guaranteed** One runaway advertisement distinguishes the two jackets that David carried with him near Williamsburg, Virginia: "He carried with him a brown coloured Kersey Jacket, [and] a blue and white Virginia cloth One with coarse Osnabrug Pockets." *Virginia Gazette* (Williamsburg), November 5, 1772, available at the Geography of Slavery, http://www2.vcdh .virginia.edu/saxon/servlet/SaxonServlet?source=/xml_docs/slavery/ads/rg72 xml&style=/xml_docs/slavery/ads/display_ad.xsl&ad=v1772110772.

56 **Nathaniel Burwell hired** Linda Baumgarten, *What Clothes Reveal: The Language of Clothing in Colonial and Federal America* (Williamsburg, VA: Colonial Williamsburg Foundation, in association with Yale Univ. Press, 2002), 135.

56 **"chose to have"** Quoted in Phillip Morgan, *Slave Counterpoint: Black Culture in the Eighteenth-Century Chesapeake and Lowcountry* (Chapel Hill: Univ. of North Carolina Press, 1998), 129.

56 **"first pants had no pockets"** Lydia Parris, *Slave Songs of the Georgia Sea Islands* (Georgia: Univ. of Georgia Press, [1942] 1990), 131 n4.

56 **confusion about social roles** Kidwell and Christman, *Suiting Everyone*, 19.

57 **manipulate appearances** David Waldstreicher, "Reading the Runaways: Self-Fashioning, Print Culture, and Confidence in Slavery in the Eighteenth-Century Mid-Atlantic," in "African and American Atlantic Worlds," special issue, *William and Mary Quarterly* 56, no. 2 (Apr. 1999): 243–72.

57 **Stepney from North Carolina** *City Gazette* (Charleston, SC), Aug. 8, 1794, available at Freedom on the Move, https://fotm.link/cYzxWrCQBWFV WwcUbXzKhR. The addition of a velvet cape (the short cape added to the shoulders) followed the style of great coats and was a more expensive article of dress.

57 **"knowledge of hair dressing"** Shane White and Graham White argue that hair was a critical arena of self-expression for enslaved Americans. Some men in eighteenth-century America "styled their own hair to resemble the wigs worn by members of the dominant caste." They did so, the authors argue, not to imitate but to parody. Shane White and Graham White, *Stylin': African American Expressive Culture from Its Beginnings to the Zoot Suit* (Ithaca, NY: Cornell Univ. Press, 1998), see chap. 3.

57 **But a runaway hoping** Waldstreicher, "Reading the Runaways," 256. Waldstreicher notes that it was difficult to determine who was a slave, who a freeman, who a servant, and who a runaway "precisely because the markers of clothing and skill were themselves commodified, and because runaways expertly played the market, these ethnic markers, though relied upon, were often unreliable as guides to the status of persons. So was race, if race means skin color" (257).

57 **a runaway named Edom** *Virginia Gazette* (Williamsburg), Jan. 10, 1771, available at the Geography of Slavery, http://www2.vcdh.virginia.edu/saxon /servlet/SaxonServlet?source=/xml_docs/slavery/ads/rg71.xml&style=/xml _docs/slavery/ads/display_ad.xsl&ad=v1771010636.

57 **"dyed his cotton jacket"** Confusingly, the word *cotton* was used to describe a poor-quality wool in the eighteenth century.

57 **Another runaway, Dick** *Virginia Gazette* (Williamsburg), Mar. 5, 1772, available at the Geography of Slavery, https://www2.vcdh.virginia.edu/saxon /servlet/SaxonServlet?source=/xml_docs/slavery/ads/rg72.xml&style=/xml _docs/slavery/ads/display_ad.xsl&ad=v1772030702. And another example: an enslaved person named London, having been in South Carolina for three months, ran away in the winter of 1772 from St. John's Parish with three others who were clothed alike in jackets and breeches of cheap white woolens that their enslaver, Daniel Ravenel, had provided. Although Ravenel did not indicate specifically if the alteration was of his own making, it seems likely, for London alone "had a jacket dyed with hickory bark, with red pockets." *South-Carolina Gazette and Country Journal* (Charleston), Feb. 25, 1772, quoted in Baumgarten, *What Clothes Reveal*, 135.

58 **Accordion-shape compartments** See, for example, a French court suit dated to 1778–85 at the Costume Institute, Metropolitan Museum of Art, Fletcher Fund, 1961, C.I.61.14.2a–c.

58 **useful for documents** One advertiser noted the function of large great coat pockets: "He took with him the following clothes, viz. a great coat of French twilled striped cloth with pockets of the same, and pocket flaps at the side, made for the convenience of carrying papers." *Virginia Gazette* or *American Advertiser* (Richmond), Apr. 16, 1785, available at the Geography of Slavery, http://www2.vcdh.virginia.edu/saxon/servlet/SaxonServlet?source=/xml_docs /slavery/ads/vg1785.xml&style=/xml_docs/slavery/ads/display_ad.xsl&ad =v1785040016.

58 **To "fob" is "to cheat"** *Oxford English Dictionary*, vol. 1, A–O (Oxford: Oxford Univ. Press, 1987), s.v. "fob, v. 1." If the fob pocket was originally a secret pocket, it may have been connected with this sense.

58 **"private pocket"** Trial of Timothy Robinson (t17290827-58), Aug. 1729, Old Bailey Proceedings Online, https://www.oldbaileyonline.org version 8.0, accessed July 15, 2022), August 1729.

59 **"I have a pocket sextant"** Quoted in Silvio Bedini, *Jefferson and Science* (Chapel Hill: Univ. of North Carolina Press, 2002), 16.

59 **"walking calculator"** Ibid., 16, 35.

60 **permanent records at home** Thomas Jefferson Foundation, "I Rise with the Sun," A Day in the Life of Thomas Jefferson, https://www.monticello.org/thomas-jefferson/a-day-in-the-life-of-jefferson/i-rise-with-the-sun/ (accessed Oct. 3, 2022).

60 **A set of playing cards** Each of the playing cards in the set is illustrated with a picture of an instrument used in the fields of surveying, navigation, mining, engineering, astronomy, and so on, and a description (the backs of the cards are plain). "Nine of Spades: Pocket Cases," Rare Book Division, New York Public Library Digital Collections, 1702, https://digitalcollections.nypl.org/items/510d47dd-cdea-a3d9-e040-e00a18064a99.

61 **"the Careless, the Scornful"** Quoted in Madeline Siefke Estill, "Colonial New England Silver Snuff, Tobacco, and Patch Boxes: Indices of Gentility," in *New England Silver and Silversmithing, 1620–1815*, ed. Jeannine Falion and Gerald R. Ward (Boston: Colonial Society of Massachusetts, 2008), 54–55.

61 **Seaman's Protection Certificates** Douglas L. Stein, "Seamen's Protection Certificate," Mystic Seaport Museum, 1992, https://research.mysticseaport.org/item/l006405/l006405-c041/.

61 **to carry freeman's papers** Alicia Olushola Ajay, "Bondage by Paper: Devices of Slaveholding Ingenuity," in *The Black Experience in Design: Identity, Expression and Reflection*, ed. Anne H. Berry, Kareem Collie, Penina Acayo Laker, Lesley-Ann Noel, Jennifer Rittner, Kelly Walters (New York: Allworth Press, 2022), 219.

62 **"rigged out in sailor style"** Frederick Douglass, *Life and Times of Frederick Douglass* (Boston: De Wolfe, Fiske & Co., 1892), 247.

62 **"drew from my deep"** Ibid. As Douglass explains, "My means of escape were provided for me by the very men who were making laws to hold and bind me more securely in slavery." Ajay observes that "Douglass assumes the role of a freed man by performing the retrieval of the document" (Ajay, "Bondage by Paper," 219).

62 **Joseph Trammell** "The Paradox of Liberty: Joseph Trammel's Freedom Papers," March 7, 2017, National Museum of African American History and Culture, https://nmaahc.si.edu/explore/stories/joseph-trammells-freedom-papers.

62 **with the reassuring weight and feel** Ajay, "Bondage by Paper," 225. Ajay writes that "Free Negro Bonds—the paper itself, often handled with care and close to the body so as to have easy access to it all the time—became part of one's identity, marking one's transference from being property to having property."

63 **"supply the want . . . fight"** *The Soldier's Pocket Bible* (London: G.B. for G.C., 1644), title page; "Soldier's Bible," in *Puritans and Puritanism in Europe and America*, vol. 1, ed. Francis J. Bremmer and Tom Webster (Santa Barbara, CA: ABC-CLIO, 2005), 584

63 **his pocket Shakespeare** Harriet Preble, letter to Anica Preble Barlow, Aug. 10, 1817, in *Memoir of the Life of Harriet Preble: Containing Portions of her Correspondence, Journal and Other Writings, Literary and Religious* (New York: G.P. Putnam's Sons, 1856), 409. "As we were driving home, he drew out his favorite Shakespeare from his pocket, and read aloud to us all the way."

64 **"contrawise . . . What thoughtlessness"** Laurence Sterne, *A Sentimental Journey through France and Italy by Yorick* (London: Macdonald, [1768] 1975), 93–94.

65 **"purchase [his] life"** Swift, *Gulliver's Travels*, 189.

65 **"when I am at home"** Ibid., 213.

65 **precision instruments** As Clifford Siskin and William Warner write of the Enlightenment, "knowing required tooling." Siskin and Warner, "This Is Enlightenment: An Invitation in the Form of an Argument," in *This Is Enlightenment*, ed. Clifford Siskin and William Warner (Chicago: Univ. of Chicago Press, 2009), 5.

65 **Women's dress remained** The development of the one-piece mantua in the late seventeenth century, however, did simplify construction, and during this period, female mantua-makers took over the production of women's clothes from male tailors.

66 **"at home anywhere"** Daniel Defoe, *Moll Flanders*, ed. Edward H. Kelly (New York: W. W. Norton, [1722] 1973), 139. "But I knew that with money in the pocket one is at home anywhere."

66 **history of women's tie-on pockets** For an in-depth analysis of women's tie-on pockets, see Barbara Burman and Ariane Fennetaux, *The Pocket: A Hidden History of Women's Lives, 1660–1900* (New Haven, CT: Yale Univ. Press, 2019).

66 **categorized as underwear** Ibid., 40.

66 **"Clothes that I had of Mrs D . . . New"** Sally Bronsdson, clothing list, 1794–1800, Winterthur Library: Joseph Downs Collection of Manuscripts and Printed Ephemera, Doc 1136.

69 **organizational compartments** Burman and Fennetaux, *Pocket*, 116.

69 **Women often carried** Ibid., 67–69, 79.

69 **Revolutionary War diarist** Eliza Yonge Wilkinson, *Letters of Eliza Wilkinson, during the Invasion and Possession of Charleston, S.C., by the British in the Revolutionary War* (New York: S. Colman, 1839), 40. "If you must see what's in my pocket, I'll show you myself," Wilkinson's mother insisted.

69 **a "dark closet"** Jedediah Oldbuck, "Lament for an Extinct Article of Female Dress," *The Artist; A Monthly Lady's Book*, Nov. 1842, 124.

70 **"no bottom to them"** Quoted in Burman and Fennetaux, *The Pocket*, 114.

70 **significant bit of privacy** Ibid., 21, 187–97.

70 **"half as deep as she is high"** Samuel Richardson, *Clarissa, or the History of a Young Lady*, vol. 4 (London: Printed for S. Richardson, [1749] 1750), 44.

70 **"ballast-bags . . . full sail"** Ibid.

70 **Tales told by inanimate witnesses** Christopher Flint, "Speaking Objects: The Circulation of Stories in Eighteenth-Century Prose Fiction," *PMLA* 113, no. 2 (Mar. 1998): 212–26.

70 **"looseness of her soul"** As related by Itself, *The Adventures of a Black Coat* (Edinburgh: Printed for and sold by Alex. M'Caslan, 1750), 69. *The Adventures* is told from the point of view of an object narrator, a threadbare black coat rented out for special occasions. So-called object narratives date to the early eighteenth century in Britain and usually involve currency but also include other articles of daily life. The object-narrators make fun of the humans who use and circulate these objects.

70 **"a select number"** Ibid., 71.

70 **riding habits** See Aileen Ribeiro, "Dashing Amazons: The Development of Women's Riding Dress, c. 1500–1900," in *Defining Dress: Dress as Object, Meaning, and Identity*, ed. Amy de la Haye and Elizabeth Wilson (Manchester: Manchester Univ. Press; New York: St. Martin's Press, 1999), 10–29.

71 **"long Coat buttoned down"** Randle Holme, *Academie or Store House of Armory and Blazon* (Chester: Printed for the author, 1688; Ann Arbor: Text Creation Partnership, 2011), bk. 3, chap. 3, 95, http://name.umdl.umich .edu/A44230.0001.001.

71 **"amphibious . . . hermaphroditical"** Addison, *Spectator*, no. 435, July 19, 1712, in *The Spectator*, by Joseph Addison and Richard Steele, ed. Donald F. Bond, 5 vols. (Oxford: Clarendon Press, 1965), 4:27.

71 **"cockaded her hat"** Ibid.

71 **"female cavaliers . . . masculine assurance"** Ibid.

71 **"boldly lug out . . . officer like air"** "Remarks on the Rage of the Ladies for the Military Dress," *Gentleman's Magazine*, vol. 51 (London: J. Nichols, 1781), 58.

71 **pinned to their dress** Alexis McCrossen, *Marking Modern Times: A History of Clocks, Watches and Other Timekeepers in American Life* (Chicago: Univ. of Chicago Press, 2013), 85.

71 **"female delicacy"** "Remarks," 58.

71 *en tenue Amazone* Arnold, "Dashing Amazons," 16.

72 **"plunder our sexes'"** Richard Steele, *The Spectator*, Friday, June 29, 1711, No. 104, quoted in Ibid.

73 **finely woven handkerchief** Fashion also decreed handkerchief display, specifying "how much the handkerchief should hang out of the Right Pocket." Quoted in Ribeiro, *Fashion and Fiction*, 262.

73 **"breeches parts"** See Pat Rogers, "The Breeches Part," in *Sexuality in Eighteenth-Century Britain*, ed. Paul-Gabriel Boucé (Manchester: Manchester Univ. Press; Totowa, NJ: Barnes & Noble Books, 1982).

73 **Female warriors** See Diane Dugaw, *Warrior Women and Popular Balladry, 1650–1850* (Cambridge: Cambridge Univ. Press, 1989).

73 **"a thousand little Privileges"** Quoted in Ribeiro, *Fashion and Fiction*, 266.

74 **"jacket, trowsers"** Harriet Jacobs [Linda Brent], *Incidents in the Life of a Slave Girl*, ed. L. Maria Child (Boston, 1861), 169.

74 **a sailor's "ricketty" walk** Ibid., 170.

74 **"passed several people . . . his arm"** Ibid., 170, 172.

74 **interior breast coat pocket** Aileen Ribeiro, *Dress in Eighteenth-Century Europe, 1715–1789* (New Haven: Yale Univ. Press, 2002), 211.

74 **"the man's pockets remain alike"** Charlotte Perkins Gilman, "Why These Clothes?," *Independent* 58 (Jan. 26, 1905): 468–69.

74 **men's garment industry** Michael Zakim, *Ready-made Democracy: A History of Men's Dress in the American Republic, 1760–1860* (Chicago: Univ. of Chicago Press, 2003).

75 **David Clapp** Linzy Brekke-Aloise, "'A Very Pretty Business': Fashion and Consumer Culture in Antebellum American Prints," *Winterthur Portfolio* 48 (Summer–Autumn 2014), 206. Brooks Brothers did not begin as a purveyor of fine suits to the propertied classes but selling low-priced ready-mades at the wharves of the East River in New York City.

75 **"pocket monopoly"** William Livingstone Alden, *Domestic Explosives and other Sixth Column Fancies* (New York: Lovell, Adam, Wesson, 1877), 49.

75 **Carlyle's still widely remarked upon** Carlyle's *Sartor Resartus* was frequently alluded to throughout the nineteenth century, and certainly during any discussion of pockets. See, for example, an essay on pockets by Julian Hawthorne (son of Nathaniel Hawthorne), "Pochiasty," *Christian Union* 32, no. 12 (1885): 6.

75 **"essential to civilization"** Alden, *Domestic Explosives*, 48.

77 "Emulous . . . virtually pockets" Ibid., 49.

77 "Comparative anatomists . . . extraneous" Ibid.

77 "women are not designed" Ibid., 48.

77 "certificate of empire" "A Boy's Pockets," *Harper's Bazaar* 27, no. 13 (Mar. 31, 1894), 257.

77 "I have only praise" Quoted in Christopher Breward, *The Suit: Form, Function and Style* (London: Reaktion Books, 2016), 8.

77 "primeval dress . . . self reliant" Ibid.

Chapter 3: Pocket Attitudes

79 "an *indelicate* fashion" Kitty Delicate [Joseph Dennie?], letter to the editor, in "Original Papers," *Port-Folio*, Mar. 27, 1802, 89.

80 "take your hands out" Cornelia Holroyd Bradley Richards, *At Home and Abroad* (New York: Evans and Brittan, 1858), 40.

80 "revolters against propriety" Quoted in Ed Folsom, "Appearing in Print: Illustrations of the Self in *Leaves of Grass*," in *Cambridge Companion to Whitman*, ed. Ezra Greenspan (Cambridge: Cambridge Univ. Press, 1995), 136.

80 "mock . . . dominant culture" Elizabeth Wilson, *Adorned in Dreams: Fashion and Modernity* (New Brunswick, NJ: Rutgers Univ. Press, 2003), 10.

80 this particular "bad habit" Richards, *At Home*, 40.

81 "Put not your hands" John Russell, "Boke of Nurture," in *Babbes Book*, ed. Frederick James Furnivall (New York: Greenwood Press, [1868] 1969), 21. Furnivall's modern English translation substitutes "do not scratch yourself" for Russell's more descriptive wording.

81 grew almost paranoid See Harry Berger, *Absence of Grace: Sprezzatura and Suspicion in Two Renaissance Courtesy Books* (Stanford, CA: Stanford Univ. Press, 2000). Berger argues that Della Casa's advice is so overblown that it in fact satirizes the conduct book genre.

81 "pleasing . . . unappealing" Giovanni Della Casa, *Galateo* (Toronto: Centre for Reformation and Renaissance Studies, [1558] 1986), 4–5.

81 "brings to mind . . . disgusting" Ibid., 5.

81 "It is an indecent habit" Ibid.

81 more evidently rude In his slightly earlier conduct book directed at younger boys, Erasmus advised that it was not "seemly to stand or sit with one hand resting on the groin, although to some people such a posture seems elegant and to give a soldierly bearing." Desiderius Erasmus, "On Good Manners for Boys" ("De civilitate morum puerilium"), in *Collected Works of Erasmus: Literary and Educational Writings*, vol. 3, ed. J. K. Sowards, trans. Brian McGregor (Toronto: Univ. of Toronto Press, 1985), 277.

81 **even hand washing** Della Casa, *Galateo*, 5.

82 **"But what do your hands *do*"** Jean Racine, *The Litigants*, trans. Mr. Ozell (London: Printed for Jonas Brown, 1715), act 3, scene 1, 30.

82 **the hand's projected path** In a later section, Della Casa insists that servants should not "place their hands on any part of the body which is kept covered, *nor even appear to do so*, as do some careless servants who hold them inside their shirt or keep them behind their backs hidden under their clothes" (*Galateo*, 9; emphasis added).

82 **"vulgar Boys . . . thrust"** *The Polite Academy: Or School of Behaviour for Young Gentlemen and Ladies* (London: Printed for R. Baldwin and B. Collins, in Salisbury, [1758] 1765), 37.

82 **Civilized boys** Norbert Elias, *The Civilizing Process*, trans. Edmund Jephcott (Oxford: Blackwell, [1939] 1994). Elias demonstrated that rules having to do with behaviors linked to the body's intimate functions tend to drop out of the discourse on etiquette after the sixteenth and seventeenth centuries—Elias's primary evidence that a rising sense of shame about the body governed everyday social behavior in the modern state.

82 **"ungenteel . . . class of people"** "Original Papers," Mar. 27, 1802, 89.

82 **"the fleeting topics and manners"** "Original Papers, No. 1," *Port-Folio*, Jan. 16, 1802, 1.

82 **"rude rustik"** François Nivelon, *The Rudiments of Genteel Behavior* (London: Paul Holberton, [1737] 2003), introduction.

83 **Dennie disregarded all** Charges and countercharges regarding "outrageous attacks . . . made upon our sex" filled the pages of the "American Lounger." Although Dennie invited "many an ingenious female" to pen letters for his series, Dennie admitted that he felt free to invent them himself: "Should I be occasionally detected in addressing letters to myself, I may plead the example of preceding writers." "The American Lounger, No. 1," *Port–Folio*, Jan. 1, 1803, 1.

83 **"formed himself upon"** "Original Papers, No. 1," Jan. 16, 1802, 1.

84 **hand-in-waistcoat pose** Arline Meyer, "Re-dressing Classical Statuary: The Eighteenth-Century 'Hand-in-Waistcoat' Portrait," *Art Bulletin* 77, no. 1 (Mar. 1995), 53.

85 **"yet easy and without Affectation"** Nivelon, "Standing," in *Rudiments of Genteel Behavior*.

85 **painters seized on** Meyer, "Re-dressing Classical Statuary," 49, 61.

85 **"the fashionable world"** Joseph Addison, *Spectator*, no. 119, July 17, 1711, in Joseph Addison and Richard Steele, *The Spectator*, ed. Donald F. Bond, 5 vols. (Oxford: Clarendon Press, 1965), 1:489.

85 **"fellow Powder'd"** Tom Brown, *Letters from the Dead to the Living* (London: Printed for Sam Brisco, [1702] 1720), 144.

85 **"[walk] in a French air"** George Farquhar, *The Beaux Strategem*, ed. H. Macaulay Fitzgibbon (London: J. M. Dent, [1707] 1898), 43.

85 **"carries his hands in his pockets"** Ibid.

86 **points his toe** Diane Donald, *The Age of Caricature: Satirical Prints in the Reign of George III* (New Haven: Yale Univ. Press, 1996), 80.

86 **the macaroni's loose breeches** Peter McNeil, "'That Doubtful Gender': Macaroni Dress and Male Sexualities," *Fashion Theory* 3, no. 4 (1995): 425.

87 **"It is but too common"** "On Fashionable Practices," *The Lady's Miscellany; or, the Weekly Visitor* 11, no. 5 (May 26, 1810), 75–76.

88 **"beaux of Philadelphia . . . fine persons"** Ann Lively, *Philadelphia Repository and Weekly Register* 3, no. 21 (May 21, 1803), 166.

88 **"seize hold of . . . buttoning again"** "On Fashionable Practices," 76.

88 **"lady of modesty"** Ibid.

89 **"gropes his breeches"** Della Casa, *Galateo: Or, a Treatise on Politeness and Delicacy of Manners. Addressed to a Young Nobleman*, ed. Richard Graves (London: Printed for J. Dodsley, in Pall-Mall, 1774), ix, xxi. Graves quotes Samuel Johnson's 1738 poem "London."

89 **flagrant expressions of bad behavior** Erin Mackie, *Rakes, Highwaymen, and Pirates: The Making of the Modern Gentleman in the Eighteenth Century* (Baltimore, MD: Johns Hopkins Univ. Press, 2009), 2.

91 **"not dazzled" by anyone** Earl of Chesterfield, *The Letters of Phillip Dormer Stanhope, 4the Earl of Chesterfield*, ed. Bonamy Dobré (London: Eyre & Spottiswoode, 1932). London, May 31, O. S. 1748, 3:1151.

91 **"trembled" in the presence** Ibid.

91 **a kind of social "annihilation"** Ibid.

91 **"extremely engaging . . . behavior"** Ibid., London, June 21, O. S. 1748, 3:1170.

91 **"loosen your garters . . . couch"** Chesterfield, *Letters*, Greenwich, June 13, O. S. 1751, 23, 4:1752.

91 **"proprietor . . . prisoner"** Ibid., London, September 27, O. S. 1749, 4:1408.

91 **"slouch is the word"** George Coleman, *The Heir at Law, a Comedy in Five Acts* (London: Printed for Longman, Hurst, Rees and Orms, Paternoster Row, 1808), 42.

91 **dandies and fops** Ellen Moers, *The Dandy: Brummell to Beerbohm* (Lincoln: Univ. of Nebraska Press, [1960] 1978).

92 **"lounging lazily along . . . dandy"** Coleman, *Heir at Law*, 42.

92 **"That's the fashion"** Ibid.

92 **"airs . . . pretenders"** James Fenimore Cooper, "On American Deportment," in *The American Democrat: or, Hints on the Social and Civic Relations of the United States of America* (Cooperstown: H & E Phinney, 1838), 155.

92 **"an American code"** A Gentleman, *The Perfect Gentleman; or, Etiquette and Eloquence* (New York: Dick & Fitzgerald, 1860), title page.

92 **undemonstrative sobriety** Fred Kasson, *Rudeness and Civility: Manners in Nineteenth-Century Urban America* (New York: Hill and Wang, 1990), 121.

92 **"negligent guises"** *The Canons of Good Breeding* (Philadelphia: Lee and Blanchard, 1839), 14.

93 **"regulate his hands"** "The Family Journal," *New Monthly Magazine and Literary Journal*, vol. 9 (London: Henry Colburn, 1825), 166.

94 **dock loafer to the literary loafer** Michael Zakim, "The Business Clerk as Social Revolutionary; or, A Labor History of the Nonproducing Classes," *Journal of the Early Republic* 26, no. 4 (Winter 2006): 563.

94 **"loitering out"** Charles Dickens, *American Notes* (New York: Appleton, 1868), 79.

95 **"glorious . . . go-to-hell-impudence"** "Hireling Scribblers—Tom Nichols and the Charleston News," *Subterranean* 4, no. 29 (Dec. 12, 1846), 2.

95 **"I lean and loafe"** Walt Whitman, *Leaves of Grass* (Brooklyn, NY, 1855), 13, available at the Walt Whitman Archive, ed. Matt Cohen, Ed Folsom, and Kenneth M. Price, https://whitmanarchive.org/published/LG/1855/poems/1.

95 **Whitman also demonstrated** See Folsom, "Appearing in Print."

95 **One hot July day** Roger Asselineau, *The Evolution of Walt Whitman* (Iowa City: Univ. of Iowa Press, 1999) 44. According to his brother George, Whitman sometimes showed up to help, and other times "he would lay abed late, and after getting up would write a few hours if he took the notion—perhaps would go off the rest of the day. We were all at work—all except Walt" (44).

95 **"I'm dying"** Horace Traubel, *With Walt Whitman in Camden*, 4 vols. (New York: Mitchell Kennerley; Philadelphia: Univ. of Pennsylvania Press, 1914–1915, 1953), 2:502.

96 **"It is natural"** Ibid., 3:13.

96 **the street figure** Ibid., 2:412.

96 **"disorderly, fleshy and sensual"** Whitman, "Song of Myself," *Leaves of Grass*, 29.

96 **"lazily into his pocket"** Quoted in James K. Wallace, "Whitman and *Life Illustrated*: A Forgotten 1855 Review of *Leaves*," *Walt Whitman Review* 17 (Dec. 1971): 137.

97 **"saying defiantly"** Traubel, *With Walt Whitman*, 4:150.

97 **"The man is the true"** Quoted in Folsom, "Appearing in Print," 137.

97 **"War was waged"** Traubel, *With Walt Whitman*, 2:503.

97 **"unpromising frontispiece"** Quoted in Ted Genoways, "'One Goodshaped and Wellhung Man': Accentuated Sexuality and the Uncertain Authorship of the Frontispiece to the 1855 Edition of *Leaves of Grass*," in *Leaves of Grass: The Sesquicentennial Essays*, ed. Susan Belasco, Ed Folsom, and Kenneth M. Price (Lincoln: Univ. of Nebraska Press, 2007), 87.

98 **"one good shaped"** Genoways, "'One Goodshaped,'" 87–123.

98 **"to find a new unthought-of nonchalance"** Walt Whitman, "One Hour to Madness and Joy," in *Leaves of Grass* (New York: W. E. Chapin, 1867), 112–13, available at the Walt Whitman Archive, ed. Matt Cohen, Ed Folsom and Kenneth M. Price, https://whitmanarchive.org/published/LG/1867/poems/10.

99 **"in the unconscious . . . gentleman"** Robert de Valcourt, *The Illustrated Manners Book: A Manual of Good Behavior and Polite Accomplishments* (New York: Leland, Clay, 1854), 54.

99 **impertinent and unruly** Claire Perry, *Young America: Childhood in Nineteenth Century Art and Culture* (New Haven: Yale Univ. Press, 2006), 12. The figure of the "country boy" appeared in portraiture, illustration, advertisements, and products.

99 **"[drop] disguise and ceremony"** [Walt Whitman], "Walt Whitman and His Poems," *United States Review* 5 (Sept. 1855): 205–12, available at the Walt Whitman Archive, ed. Matt Cohen, Ed Folsom, and Kenneth M. Price, https://whitmanarchive.org/criticism/reviews/lg1855/anc.00176.html .

100 **"honest, easy and spontaneous"** Traubel, *With Walt Whitman*, 3:13.

100 **"abandon . . . careless grandeur"** Valcourt, *Illustrated Manners Book*, 463. The "unfortunate gentleman" who saunters along with hand in pocket wearing "shabby genteel clothes" deserves the reader's "most earnest reprobation," Valcourt warned.

100 **"nature's aristocrat"** Eliza Cook, "The Active and the Idle Man," in *Eliza Cook's Journal*, vol. 7 (London: Charles Cook, 1852), 126.

100 **"trick of putting"** "Trouser Pockets," *The Saturday Review of Politics, Literature, Science, and Art*, Mar. 8, 1879.

100 **"carried his arms stiffly"** Katherine Mullin, *James Joyce, Sexuality and Social Purity* (Cambridge: Cambridge Univ. Press, 2003), 101.

100 **"strode . . . glided"** Emily Post, *Etiquette in Society, in Business, in Politics and at Home* (New York: Funk Wagnalls, 1922), 261.

101 **"obnoxious habit"** "The Frock Coat Toilet," *Philadelphia Inquirer*, Jan. 7, 1900.

101 **"slangy nonchalance"** "From the New York Press: Hands in Pockets," *Kansas City Star*, Sept. 1, 1903, 2.

102 **"strut down the avenue"** "No Bar Now to Women's Emancipation," *New York Tribune*, Mar. 11, 1913.

102　**"made to be carried"** Jonathan Bonner, *Front Pockets* (Providence, RI: Museum of Art, Rhode Island School of Design, 2001).

104　**more "imagistic"** David McNeil, *Gesture and Thought* (Chicago: Univ. of Chicago Press, 2005), 15.

104　**"bolstered up"** "Tales of Fashionable Life," *Select Reviews, and Spirit of the Foreign Magazines* 2 (Dec. 1809): 373. Sitting this way, the figure's "secret and inordinate arrogance" is on full display, according to the narrator.

104　**tend to ignore** Adam Kendon, *Gesture: Visible Action as Utterance* (Cambridge: Cambridge Univ. Press, 2004), 10–12.

104　**the hand is contained** Mark Johnson, *The Body in the Mind: The Bodily Basis of Meaning, Imagination and Reason* (Chicago: Univ. of Chicago Press, 1987). According to Johnson, "we look for common structure in our many experiences of being *in* something." Our bodies, he notes, are experienced as containers into which we put food and water; our surroundings include containers that shelter us (such as clothing, vehicles, rooms, and houses); and we place all sorts of objects into containers (such as cups and bags). "Our encounter with containment and boundedness is one of the most pervasive features of our bodily experience," he writes (21). And it is our bodily experiences, Johnson argues, that "organizes our more abstract thinking" as we "project patterns from one domain of experience in order to structure another domain of another kind" (xiv). We comprehend the physical consequences of containment—such as that an object in a box is inaccessible—and transfer it to other registers, including emotional ones.

105　**"sphere of indifference"** Georg Simmel, *The Sociology of Georg Simmel*, ed. and trans. Kurt H. Wolff (Glencoe, IL: Free Press, 1950), 413, 416.

105　**how one holds oneself** Pierre Bourdieu, *The Logic of Practice*, trans. Richard Nice (Stanford, CA: Stanford Univ. Press, 1990), 69. Signs of deference enacted through "forms of respect" are the "most natural manifestations of respect for the established order," Bourdieu argues.

105　**wore the height of fashion** Kate Irvin and Laurie Anne Brewer, *Artist, Rebel, Dandy: Men of Fashion* (New Haven, CT: Yale Univ. Press in association with Museum of Art, Rhode Island School of Design, 2013), 68.

105　**Lester Young** Joel Dinerstein, *The Origins of Cool in Postwar America* (Chicago: Univ. of Chicago Press, 2017), 37–40, 43, 50.

106　**"cool figures . . . aristocrats"** Joel Dinerstein and Frank H. Goodyear III, *American Cool* (Washington, DC: National Portrait Gallery, 2014), 10.

Chapter 4: Pocket Sexism

109　**Ammi Phillips** *Ammi Phillips: Portrait Painter, 1888–1865* (New York: C.N. Potter for the Museum of American Folk Art, 1969), 12.

109　**"badge of servitude"** Helen Dare, "Now Dragging the Pocket into Female Emancipation Problem," *San Francisco Chronicle*, Apr. 16, 1913, 7.

109 **high-waisted dress** Claire Wilcox, *Bags* (London: V & A Publications, 1999), 49.

110 **Greek goddesses** Harold Koda, *Goddess: The Classical Mode* (New York: Metropolitan Museum of Art; New Haven: Yale Univ. Press, 2003), 58.

110 **lost their place** Barbara Burman and Ariane Fennetaux, *The Pocket: The Hidden History of Women's Lives, 1660–1900* (New Haven: Yale Univ. Press, 2019). In their book, Burman and Fennetaux note that some women adapted their tie-on pockets in this period, crafting narrower ones in white. They emphasize that tie-on pockets lasted through the nineteenth century.

110 **purses called reticules** Vanda Foster, *Bags and Purses* (New York: Drama Book Publishers, 1982), 33.

110 **"walked with their"** "Letters from London," *Atheneum; or, Spirit of the English Magazines* 1, no. 7 (July 1, 1817), 467.

110 **"great interest . . . pocket question"** The article was reprinted as "The Wardrobe of the Nations" in *Rhode-Island American and Providence Gazette*, May 9, 1828, and the *Ladies Garland* (Harper's Ferry, Virginia), April 5, 1828, 1.

110 **"silliness . . . without pockets"** "Female Dress," *Weekly Visitor; or, Ladies Miscellany* 4, no. 52 (Oct. 25, 1806), 409.

111 **Desperate for a customer** Ibid.

111 **classified as undergarments** Burman and Fennetaux, *Pocket*, 40.

112 **referred to it as a "ridicule"** Foster, *Bags*, 33.

112 **"old ladies"** Advertisement for a book "sufficiently portable to be carried in old ladies' pockets and young ladies work bags." *People's Friend & Daily Advertiser*, 1807.

112 **"honest" and useful** Jedediah Oldbuck, "Lament for an Extinct Article of Female Dress," *Artist; A Monthly Lady's Book*, Nov. 1842, 124.

112 **"Anti-Pocketist . . . such a thing"** Mabel Lloyd Ridgely, ed., *What Them Befell: The Ridgelys of Delaware and Their Circle in Colonial and Federal Times: Letters, 1751–1890* (Portland, ME: Anthoensen Press, 1949), 94.

113 **"in some innermost recess"** Edith E. Mecalf, "The Greatest Lack in the World—Pockets," *Congregationalist* 73, no. 42 (Oct. 19, 1893), 530.

113 **more difficult to locate than "paradise"** Mazy Whirl, "Society Notes," *Courier* (Lincoln, NE), Aug. 23, 1902, 4.

113 **salvaging material** "A Boy's Pockets," *Harper's Bazaar* 27, no. 13 (Mar. 31, 1894), 257.

114 **"practically inextricable"** T. W. H., "Women and Men: Concerning Pockets," *Harper's Bazaar* 26, no. 44 (1893), 902.

114 **"How can I possibly"** Ibid.

114 **"statistical inquiry"** Ibid.

114 **"world's use"** "The World's Use of Pockets," *New York Times*, Aug. 28, 1899, 7.

114 **"Men's Clothes Full of Them"** Ibid.

115 **"developed, increased"** Ibid.

115 **cross-dressing is a "nightmare"** Kenneth Grahame, *Wind in the Willows* (Oxford: Oxford Univ. Press, [1908] 2010), 86.

115 **"eternally situated"** Ibid., 87.

115 **"unequipped for the real contest"** Ibid.

115 **"many-pocketed . . . no-pocketed productions"** Ibid.

115 **"undoubtedly made"** "A New Agitation," *New York Times*, June 10, 1880, 4

116 **"equality in pockets"** "Give Woman Equality in Pockets," *Baltimore Sun*, Feb. 23, 1894, 4.

116 **"free as a lark"** "Fashions Against Suffrage: Elizabeth Cady Stanton's Opinion of Women Who Wear Gowns without Pockets," *New York Tribune*, June 14, 1899, 7.

116 **"unrecognized disabilities"** "Pockets and Purses," *Harper's Bazaar* 15, no. 42 (1882), 663.

116 **"greatest lack"** Mecalf, "Greatest Lack," 530.

116 **psychological "preparedness"** Charlotte Perkins Gilman, "If I Were A Man," *Physical Culture* (July 1914): 32.

116 **"leather apron . . . oilskin cloak"** Charlotte Perkins Gilman, *The Dress of Women: A Critical Introduction to the Symbolism and Sociology of Clothing*, ed. Michael R. Hill and Mary Jo Deegan (Westport, CT: Greenwood Press, 2002), 17–18.

116 **all-female utopia, *Herland*** Gilman serialized *The Dress of Women* in conjunction with *Herland* over several issues in the *Forerunner*, the monthly magazine she wrote and edited. Carol Farley Kessler, *Charlotte Perkins Gilman: Her Progress towards Utopia* (New York: Syracuse Univ. Press, 1995), 275.

116 **"fairly quilted"** Charlotte Perkins Gilman, *Herland* (New York: Pantheon Books, 1979), 36.

116 **"were most ingeniously arranged"** Ibid.

117 **"now dragging"** Dare, "Now Dragging," 7.

117 **"clamor . . . real grievance"** "Superiority in Their Pockets: Woman Discovers Wherein Man Is in Advance of the Gentler Sex," *Detroit Free Press*, Feb. 19, 1907, 7.

117 **"By-m-bye, no pockets"** Helen Campbell, "The Ethics of Pockets," *Boston Cooking-School Magazine* 12, no. 5 (Dec. 1907), 260.

118 **"fly in the face of nature"** Alice Duer Miller, "Why We Oppose Pockets for Women," in *Are Women People? A Book of Rhymes for Suffrage Times* (New York: George H. Doran, 1915), 44.

118 **If you could claim** Miller was not making this up: in 1901, anti-suffrage forces *had* actually attempted a pockets-are-men's-natural-right argument in their quarterly magazine, the *Anti-Suffragist*. "Man is a perfected marsupial. He is a creature of pockets. With him the necessity of a pouch simply develops one. This is the law of evolution. The first we read of him as a pocket-bearing animal he was on a level with the kangaroo. He then had a pouch fastened to his belt. Now look at him and compare him to woman. She has not evolved under the laws of nature, but under the sterner decrees of the dressmaker. What a difference between no pockets and a score of pockets!" Quoted in "Women and Pockets," *Chicago Daily Tribune*, Mar. 16, 1901, 6.

118 **Gail Laughlin** Maya Salam, "How Queer Women Powered the Suffrage Movement," *New York Times*, Aug. 19, 2020.

118 **"Only on rare occasions"** "Pockets in Evening Gown Her Fad," *St. Louis Star and Times*, July 18, 1919.

118 **realizing that such "creations"** Ibid.

118 **"Miss Laughlin declined"** Ibid.

119 **"vulgar clamor for rights"** Bettina Friedl, ed., *On to Victory: Propaganda Plays of the Woman Suffrage Movement* (Boston: Northeastern Univ. Press, 1987), 246.

119 **"speechifying . . . like a man"** "Mrs. Belmont in Suffragette Costume," *Nashville Tennessean and the Nashville American*, Oct. 8, 1910, 8.

119 **"pockets mean business . . . equipped for the street"** "No Bar Now to Women's Emancipation," *New-York Tribune*, Mar. 11, 1913.

119 **"Is anything so convincing"** "Taxation without Pockets: This, Not Lack of Representation, the Real Grievance of the Female Sex," *New-York Tribune*, Oct. 23, 1910, C5.

120 **"no fight"** "The Question of the Pocket," *Harper's Bazaar* 23, no. 50 (Dec. 13, 1890), 997. A contributor to the *New York Observer* argued that women preferred to hold their purses in their hands "in order that possession may always be assured by the sense of touch." He concluded that "woman herself furnishes a basis for the charge by her pocketless condition." "A Serious Defect," *New York Observer*, Dec. 27, 1894, 722.

120 **Dressmakers produced** Marla Miller, *The Needle's Eye: Women and Work in the Age of Revolution* (Amherst: Univ. of Massachusetts Press, 2006), see chap. 7.

121 **"manufactures excuses . . . bulge you out just awful!"** Elizabeth Cady Stanton, "The Pocket Problem," *Utica Sunday Journal*, May 26, 1895.

121 **Stanton nevertheless believed** Ibid.

121 **The company intended** Nancy Martha West, *Kodak and the Lens of Nostalgia* (Charlottesville: Univ. Press of Virginia, 2000), 121–29.

122 **"nice little jackets"** Theodore Dreiser, *Sister Carrie*, ed. Neda M. Westlake (New York: Penguin Books, 1994), 69.

122 **"in touch with modern needs"** "Fashion: What She Wears," *Vogue*, Oct. 2, 1909, 500.

122 **"yearned for a pocket . . . rejoice"** "The New Apron and Pocket Dresses: How Fashion's Most Useful Fancy Is Applied to Cool Summer Suits and Gorgeous Evening Robes," *Washington Post*, July 18, 1913, M6.

122 **"Where is the ready-made suit"** "Taxation without Pockets," C5.

123 **But manufacturers** Rebecca Arnold, *The American Look: Fashion, Sportswear and the Image of Women in 1930s and 1940s New York* (London: I. B. Tauris, 2009), 4.

123 **"women's clothes aren't made"** "Taxation without Pockets," C5.

123 **"Woman's dress is so"** "Pockets," *Independent*, Sept. 12, 1912, 629.

123 **"young knapsacks"** "Military Lines and Military Capes," *Women's Wear Daily*, Aug. 21, 1918, 3.

123 **"the result of"** "Vogue Points: Decorative Little Guideposts to Point the Traveler on the Right Road to Smart Spring Fashions," *Vogue* 47, no. 3 (Feb. 1, 1916), 36.

124 **"to harbor letters . . . without a reason"** "Fashion: First Fruits of the Paris Openings," *Vogue*, Mar. 15, 1915, 32.

124 **"and then, presto"** Virginia Yeaman, "Pockets for Women," *Vogue*, Sept. 1, 1918, 114.

124 **"pockets should follow"** Ibid.

124 **"cross as bears"** Ibid.

124 **"impersonal, severely logical"** Ibid.

124 **"average woman"** Ibid.

124 **"seems content to take the cash"** Ibid.

124 **the modern handbag** Wilcox, *Bags*, 73–74.

124 **Framed handbags were sturdy** Ibid.

125 **sign of independence** Fred Cheounne, ed., *Carried Away: All about Bags* (New York: Vendome Press, 2005), 21.

125 **"shameful handbag"** Dare, "Now Dragging," 7.

125 **Radclyffe Hall** Judith Halberstam, *Female Masculinity* (Durham, NC: Duke Univ. Press, 1998), 88.

125 **Women's Auxiliary Army Corps** The Women's Auxiliary Corps was created in 1942 to provide additional workers for to the US Army in administrative and support roles. By 1943 the term "auxiliary" was dropped; the members of the newly christened Women's Army Corps gained official standing, benefits, and pay. Eventually, 100,000 Wacs, 60,000 members of the army nursing service, and 1,000 WASPs (Women's Air Service Pilots) served in the army in World War II.

127 **make uniforms that "lasted"** Peggy LeBoutillier, "Women's Uniforms Are Made to Last," *New York Times*, Nov. 28, 1943. Such reports often

glorified textile science: the tensile strength of cloth was checked "by energetic machines," waterproofing assessed by "violent sprays," and cold-weather gear subjected to subfreezing temperatures.

127 **described the purse's adoption** Mattie Treadwell, *The Women's Army Corps* (Washington, DC: Center of Military History, United States Army, 1954), 36.

127 **rumors that Wacs** Ibid., 206.

127 **"quickly produced a rule"** Ibid., 37.

127 **recognizable as women** Intercepted letters home, sampled and recorded by the Office of Censorship, expressed intense negative feeling about the issue of women in the armed forces. "I would rather we never see each other for 20 years, than to have you join the Wacs," wrote one serviceman to his sweetheart. Servicemen threatened to initiate divorce or to withhold financial support, and discussed their anger and confusion. "I want to come home to the girl I remember," wrote another. Treadwell, *Women's Army Corps*, 212.

127 **enforce the rule** Ibid. This had happened with belts. The initial uniforms were belted, but because Wacs tended to pull them too tightly across the waist, the agencies in charge decided to simply omit the belt instead. Treadwell, *Women's Army Corps*, 157.

127 **long debates** To this day, US Army Green Service Uniforms (AGSU) for women and "smaller statured persons" retain a pocket flap at the chest without an attached pocket. The flap is used to hold medals and other insignia. The military otherwise goes to great lengths to minimize gendered distinctions in uniforms; as the army's website is careful to note, "an all-female Army Uniform Board determined that aside from some very minor fit type differences, the issue male and female AGSU are essentially the same." US Army, FAQ, Description of the Army Green Service Uniform, https://www.army.mil/uniforms/.

128 **"I've got the best idea!"** "Diana Vreeland Brainwaves!," *Vogue*, Apr. 1, 1984, 347. In this interview before the debut of her 1984 memoir, *DV*, *Vogue* called Vreeland the woman "who tried—and failed!—to eliminate handbags."

128 **"bloody old handbag . . . do with pockets"** Ibid.

128 **"like a man . . . rather chic"** Ibid.

128 **"there's nothing that limits"** Ibid.

128 **"hold-everything pockets"** "Cottons at Morro Castle," *Harper's Bazaar*, Jan. 1947, 100.

128 **"We're interested in"** "Headlines for the South," *Harper's Bazaar*, Jan. 1940, 43. Later that year, *Harper's* reported that "fashion still loves tremendous pockets. Months ago, Schiaparelli and Balenciaga in particular began to remind us that a pocket can be something more than a ladylike cache for an accidental handkerchief." "Pockets," *Harper's Bazaar*, July 1940, 76.

128 **"modern dress code"** Richard Martin, *American Ingenuity: Sportswear, 1930s–1970s* (New York: Metropolitan Museum of Art, 1998), 51.

129 **Responding to a challenge** Kohle Yohannan and Nancy Nolf, *Claire McCardell: Redefining Modernism* (New York: Harry N. Abrams, 1998), 67.

129 **"pot-and-pannish"** Capella, "Confidential Chat: Don't We Dress Up for Ourselves?," *Boston Globe*, Jan. 24, 1941.

129 **"visible, spacious"** Martin, *American Ingenuity*, 52.

129 **they "flaunted" them** Ibid.

130 **"I really have contempt"** Stephanie Lake, *Bonnie Cashin: Chic Is Where You Find It* (New York: Rizzoli, 2016), 198.

130 **"nomad by nature"** Ibid., 66.

131 **purse-pocket in 1950** Ibid., 43.

131 **"woman is without pockets"** Yeaman, "Pockets for Women," 114.

131 **"day shift"** "Dear Future, If You Have a Moment," *Harper's Bazaar*, Feb. 1958, 116.

131 **the computer's "Svengali"** Ibid.

131 **"flights of calculation"** Ibid.

133 **"large as pouches"** "Pockets for No Purpose Are Fashion's Newest Decoration," *Life*, Jan. 22, 1940, 32.

133 **"will wear pockets . . . expects"** Ibid.

133 **"social product"** Gilman, *Dress of Women*, 3.

134 **"their garments of emancipation"** "A Plea for the Bloomers: A Bicycle Costumer Talks of Women's Cycling Apparel," *New York Times*, Aug. 4, 1895.

134 **"Not all of them"** Ibid.

134 **"stowed away . . . speeches"** "Her Feminine Way," *Kansas City Daily Journal*, Apr. 8, 1896, 4.

134 **"plenty of pockets"** Quoted in Chelsea G. Summers, "The Politics of Pockets," *Vox*, Sept. 16, 2016.

134 **"women's pockets could carry"** Ibid.

134 **cost-cutting production manager** Yohannan and Nolf, *Claire McCardell*, 51.

134 **fake pockets** Adriana Gorea, Katya Roelse, and Martha L. Hall, *The Book of Pockets: A Practical Guide for Fashion Designers* (London: Bloomsbury Visual Arts, 2019), 174.

135 **After measuring pockets** Jan Diehm and Amber Thomas, "Someone Clever Once Said Women Were Not Allowed Pockets," *Pudding*, August 2018, https://pudding.cool/2018/08/pockets/.

136 **pocket size "political"** Ibid.

137 **Another inventive demonstration** In the nineteenth century, writers did carry out thought experiments imagining "the pocketless man" that began with some variation on the question, "Could he be a man without a pocket?" After answering in the negative, such accounts then often devolved, imagining

him incapacitated in various ways: "*reduced* in desperation to carrying a bag dangling by the string from his arm . . . his whole career would be crippled!" Mecalf, "Greatest Lack," 530.

137 **real-world experiment** BuzzFeed Motion Pictures, "Men Experience Pocketless Pants for the First Time: Men, Why Do You Think Ladies Get Excited over Pockets?" July 2017, https://www.buzzfeed.com/bfmp/videos/21406.

137 **"It's stressing me out . . . lose my things"** Ibid.

137 **"PLEASE PUT POCKETS"** Heather Kaczynski (@Hkaczynski), Apr. 20, 2018, www.twitter.com/Hkaczynski.

137 **Nurse Alison Chandra** Ed Mazza, "A Mom's Plea for One Simple Change to Girls' Clothing Goes Viral," *HuffPost*, Apr. 23, 2018, https://www.huffpost.com/entry/mom-wants-pockets-in-girls-pants_n _5add5c45e4b089e33c896afo.

138 **"Pockets are a small symptom"** Heather Marcoux, "Viral Plea for Girls' Pockets Reaches Reese Witherspoon," *Motherly*, May 6, 2018.

138 **"8¼ years old"** Hattie Gladwell, "Little Girl Writes Letter to Fat Face Asking for Bigger Pockets on Girls' Clothes," *Metro UK*, May 15, 2018.

138 **"stylish yet practical"** Ibid.

138 **"tough, durable, and ready for action"** Ibid.

138 **"Girls need"** Ibid.

138 **subsequent letters** Cathy Free, "First-Grader Wrote Old Navy Asking for Girls' Jeans to Have Pockets," *Washington Post*, April 9, 2021.

139 **1999 Supreme Court case** See Petition for Writ of Certiorari to the Supreme Court of Ohio for a discussion of *Mercier v. Ohio* and *Wyoming v. Houghton*, two cases that examine whether the Fourth Amendment requires probable cause for the search of purse worn or held by an automobile passenger, accessed at https://law.yale.edu/sites/default/files/documents/pdf /Clinics/Mercier_yale.pdf. A majority of states protect the woman's purse as part of her person; a minority of states hold that her purse can be searched with the car, including Ohio, Montana, and Wyoming. At issue is that pocketed men receive greater Fourth Amendment protections in this scenario than women carrying purses. The law "has consequences that are illogical, arbitrary and fundamentally inequitable," write the petition authors (15).

140 **"the unique, significantly heightened"** Ibid. The petition notes: "So far as societal expectations of privacy are concerned, a purse is quite different from other carriers such as knapsacks or briefcases that may contain personal items. Such carriers are usually not worn by passengers in a car; it is common experience that the driver of a car often will place passengers' briefcases, knapsacks, and other larger bags in the trunk or rear seat, but generally will not offer to place a woman's purse in the trunk, just as the driver will not ask a man if he would like to empty the contents of his pockets into the trunk" (15 n2).

140 **with other containers** Justice Scalia stated that "even a limited search of outer clothing" constitutes a severe intrusion upon personal security. But not so when the police examine an item of personal property—a "container" such as a purse, a briefcase, or a box.

141 **envisioned "domains"** Emily Dickinson, "Let Me Not Thirst," in *The Complete Poems of Emily Dickinson*, ed. Thomas H. Johnson (Cambridge: Harvard Univ. Press, [1945] 1983). "Let me not thirst with this Hock at my Lip, / Nor beg, with domains in my pocket—."

141 **"fossil bird-tracks"** Dan Chiasson, "Emily Dickinson's Singular Scrap Poetry," *New Yorker*, Nov. 27, 2016.

141 **rework or reject** Emily Dickinson, *The Gorgeous Nothings* (New York: Christine Burgin/New Directions, 2013), 1.

Chapter 5: Pocket Inventories

143 **"whole year's shakedown"** "Speaking of Pictures: One Year's Dungaree Debris," *Life*, Apr. 8, 1957, 21.

143 **"Like small boys"** Ibid.

143 **"dungaree debris"** Ibid.

143 **"major, identifiable objects"** Ibid.

144 **"a remarkable picture"** "Speaking of Pictures: A US Family of Four Eats 2½ Tons in One Year," *Life*, Sept. 9, 1946, 18.

144 **an experimental "yield"** Ibid., 21.

145 **Agatha Christie's *Pocket Full of Rye*** The contents of the businessman's pockets in Agatha Christie's 1953 *A Pocket Full of Rye* are one of her famous red herrings, placed there by the murderer to create a false lead—a link to a failing business adventure, Blackbird Mine, and an alternate suspect.

145 **Amateur sleuths** Spies have planted credible "pocket litter" as a way to support phony identities, as when British agents included a snapshot of a fictitious girlfriend along with fake documents in the pockets of a corpse that washed up during World War II's Operation Mincemeat. See Ben Macintyre, *Operation Mincemeat: How a Dead Man and a Bizarre Plan Fooled the Nazis and Assured an Allied Victory* (New York: Harmony Books, 2010).

145 **old axiom** The phrase "you are what you eat" derives from French scholar Jean Anthelme Brillat-Savarin's comment in his 1825 *The Physiology of Taste*: "Tell me what you eat; and I will tell you who you are." Brillat-Savarin linked national stereotypes to food consumption. Noting that food preferences tend to be culturally specific, he argued that different kinds of foods produced different kinds of people. The phrase carries with it classifying and moralizing overtones. Daniel, *Voracious Children: Who Eats Whom in Children's Literature* (New York: Routledge, 2006), 13.

145 **"defied reason . . . world"** "A Boy's Pocket," *New England Farmer; a Monthly Journal*, Nov. 1861, 536.

145 **"challenged the wonder"** Scott Way, "A Few Random Remarks about Pockets," *Puck*, Jan. 7, 1885, 294

145 ***"theoretically*, a boy's pocket"** "The Contents of a Boy's Pocket," *Every Saturday: A Journal of Choice Reading*, Aug. 6, 1870, 499.

145 **"strange" as it might be** "What Boy's Pockets Contain," *Maine Farmer*, Apr. 3, 1862, 4.

146 **"the variety and number"** "Contents of a Boy's Pocket," 499.

146 **live rat** Pyngle Layne, "What's in a Pocket?," *Home Journal*, May 17, 1851, 1.

146 **"caught our devil"** "What Boy's Pockets Contain," 4.

146 **"one eel skin"** Ibid.

148 **"load limit"** Robert Belknap, *The List: The Uses and Pleasures of Cataloging* (New Haven: Yale Univ. Press, 2004), 31. Seven years later, Mark Twain's inventory of Tom Sawyer's pockets managed to capture a sense of the disordered jumble with a succinct four items. The trope concerning the contents of boys' pockets had clearly been around before Twain utilized and perfected it. "A lump of chalk, an india rubber ball, three fish-hooks, and one of that kind of marbles known as a 'sure' nough crystal" crowd the pockets of Tom Sawyer. Mark Twain, *The Adventures of Tom Sawyer* (Hartford, CT: American Publishing [1884] 1892), 154.

148 **an effective anchor** Belknap, *List*, 18.

148 **something else meaningful** The pocketed items face what the philosopher Umberto Eco calls "contextual pressure," some kind of forced interaction due to limited space. Umberto Eco, *The Infinity of Lists* (New York: Rizzoli, 2009), 116.

148 **"queer contrivances . . . mechanical turn"** *Monroe City Democrat*, Feb. 24, 1916.

149 **"an accurate index"** Frank H. Cheley, "The Job of Being a Dad: What Is in Your Son's Pockets?," *Boston Daily Globe*, Nov. 20, 1923, 14.

149 **a mysterious "cipher"** Ibid.

149 **"trait . . . all boys"** "A Boy's Pockets," *Harper's Bazaar*, Mar. 31, 1894, 257.

149 **"never has pockets enough"** Ibid.

149 **"promiscuous taste . . . boy"** Ibid.

149 **age-graded schools** Steven Mintz, *Huck's Raft: A History of American Childhood* (Cambridge, MA: Belknap, 2006), 187.

150 **"what a boy"** William Dean Howells, *A Boy's Town* (New York: Harper & Brothers, 1890), 1.

150 **"good boys"** Mark Twain, *Mark Twain's Sketches, New & Old* (Hartford, CT: American Publishing, 1875), 56. Mark Twain's satire of the "good boy," a wooden character of antebellum fiction, always obeyed his mother, never told a lie, and was fond of his school lessons and "infatuated" with Sunday School (53).

150 **"natural boy . . . filled with trash"** "For the Children: A Lost Type," *Watchman*, Sept. 26, 1901, 22.

150 **could not "penetrate"** Howells, *Boy's Town*, 67. "It is a great pity that fathers and mothers cannot penetrate that world [of boys]; but they cannot, and it is only by accident that they can catch some glimpse of what goes on in it," wrote Howells.

150 **"should not be astonished"** "Contents of a Boy's Pocket," *Every Saturday*, 499.

150 **all the "trash"** "For the Children," 22.

150 **"keys that opened nothing"** Cheley, "Job of Being a Dad."

150 **"treasures of almost"** Twain, *Tom Sawyer*, 154.

150 **"inexplicable" to the adult** "The Diet of Boys," *New York Times*, Oct. 21, 1883, 8.

150 **"to a juvenile mud-turtle"** "Contents of a Boy's Pockets," *Every Saturday*.

150 **Apportioning value to things** Igor Kopytoff, "The Cultural Biography of Things: Commoditization as Process," in *The Social Life of Things*, ed. Arjun Appadurai (Cambridge: Cambridge Univ. Press, 1986). As the anthropologist Igor Kopytoff argues, one of the most important things cultures do is set up and perpetuate agreed upon categories. In a world of endless numbers of things, culture groups them and "marks [certain] things as having value" (64).

151 **"a dead rat . . . bottle glass"** Twain, *Tom Sawyer*, 35.

151 **"Diamonds have"** "Boys," *Democratic Enquirer*, Mar. 7, 1867.

151 **"nuts and acorns"** Howells, *Boy's Town*, 210. The boys resemble naturalists in Howells's account, albeit naturalists with violent urges. As they meander along their way, and can hear various birdsong, the boys reflect that, if only they had a gun with them, "they could have killed lots of things" (162).

151 **Evident in these** Bill Brown, *The Material Unconscious: American Amusement, Stephen Crane, and the Economics of Play* (Cambridge, MA: Harvard Univ. Press, 1996), 177.

151 **Counterfeit arrowheads** John C. Whittaker, *American Flintknappers: Stone Age Art in the Age of Computers* (Austin: Univ. of Texas Press, 2004), 39.

152 **"sure-enough . . . foundations"** Twain, *Tom Sawyer*, 50.

152 **"inconceivable grandeur"** Ibid.

152 **"Every fellow"** Advertisement for Remington, "Your Robinson Crusoe— A Remington Scout Knife Is Your 'Man Friday,'" *Boy's Life*, Feb. 1924, 31.

152 **"is to be pitied"** "Pockets," *Independent*, Sept. 12, 1912, 629.

152 **"You cannot make"** Ibid.

153 **"doing . . . teacher"** Ibid.

153 **"index" of his wealth** Henry William Gibson, *Boyology or Boy Analysis* (New York: Association Press, 1922), 141.

153 **"From time . . . newspaper paragraphist"** "A School Girl's Pocket," *Wilmington Daily Commercial*, May 6, 1876.

154 **"Lucy Locket, lost her pocket"** Iona Opie and Peter Opie, *The Oxford Dictionary of Nursery Rhymes* (Oxford: Oxford Univ. Press, 1951; 2nd ed., 1997), 279–80.

154 **The whole imbroglio** Ibid. Iona and Peter Opie note that various historical persons have been associated with Lucy Locket and Kitty Fisher, but none have been substantiated. That nineteenth-century commentators were well aware of the rhyme's provenance is evident in an 1856 discussion in the *Pittsfield Sun*, which explained that the nursery rhyme began "as a little song on a famous lady of easy virtue." "Yankee Doodle," *Pittsfield Sun*, Jan. 17, 1856.

154 **"My daughter has"** "A Boy's Pockets," *Harper's Bazaar*, 257.

154 **"first and greatest"** Sarah Sherwood, "The First Pocket," *Friend's Intelligencer*, May 5, 1894, 286.

154 **"there is no use"** Ibid. Laura Ingalls Wilder described excitedly filling her pockets with pebbles and her dismay when her pocket ripped at the seams and the pebbles fell out. She was frustrated because "nothing like that ever happened to [her sister] Mary. Mary was a good little girl who always kept her dress clean and neat and minded her manners. . . . Laura did not think it was fair." *Little House in the Big Woods* (New York: Harper & Row, [1932] 1971), 174.

155 **"on that day . . . me"** Ibid.

155 **"What else have you got"** Lewis Carroll, *Alice's Adventures in Wonderland* (New York: MacMillan, 1898), 34.

155 **"Only a thimble"** Ibid.

155 **the "elegant" thimble** Ibid.

155 **child sizes** Asa Briggs, *Victorian Things* (Harmondsworth, UK: Penguin, 1990), 209.

155 **"always have a piece"** Theresa Tidy, *Eighteen Maxims of Neatness and Order* (London: J. Hatchard and Son, Piccadilly, 1838), 25.

155 **The charitable ideal** Lynne Vallone, *Disciplines of Virtue: Girls' Culture in the Eighteenth and Nineteenth Centuries* (New Haven: Yale Univ. Press, 1995), 16–17. Acts of charity were an extension of the domestic ideal, considered part of women's domestic duty, and described extensively in children's didactic fiction.

155 **"the heroine of a moral storybook . . . tracts in her pocket"** Louisa May Alcott, *Little Women* (Boston: Roberts Brothers, 1880), 519.

156 **"only a struggling human girl"** Ibid.

156 **being good** Emily Hamilton-Honey, *Turning the Pages of American Girlhood: The Evolution of Girls' Series Fiction, 1865–1930* (Jefferson, NC: McFarland, 2013), 59–60.

157 **"sugar and spice"** Opie and Opie, *Oxford Dictionary of Nursery Rhymes*, 100–101.

157 **"right of search"** "Contents of a Boy's Pocket," *Every Saturday*.

157 **"to discover secrets"** Cheley, "Job of Being a Dad."

157 **"Do not undertake"** "Pockets," *Independent*, 629.

157 **nothing much to satirize** Satires about men stuffing their pockets return in the twentieth century. In his 1922 *Babbitt*, a critique of middle-class American conformity, Sinclair Lewis's narrator describes the scene when pink-faced George Babbitt in his BVD underwear decides to change the contents of his pockets from the brown suit to the gray as "a sensational event." Few of the objects could be said to be necessary, like the newspaper editorials "from which Babbitt got his opinions" and the "notes to be sure and do things which he did not intend to do," but Babbitt "was earnest about these objects. They were of eternal importance, like baseball or the Republican Party." Sinclair Lewis, *Babbitt* (New York: Harcourt Brace, 1922), 9.

158 **braided hair** Helen Sheumaker, *Love Entwined: The Curious History of Hairwork in America* (Philadelphia: Univ. of Pennsylvania Press, 2007), 50.

158 **"turned inside out"** Alexander Gardner, "A Harvest of Death," in *Gardner's Photographic Sketch Book of the War* (New York: Dover, [1865–66] 1959), plate 36.

158 **"pressing need of survivors"** Ibid.

158 **"unwritten law . . . dead"** James Madison Stone, *Personal Reflections of the Civil War: By One Who Took Part in It as a Private Soldier in the 21st Volunteer Regiment of Infantry from Massachusetts* (Boston, 1918), 143.

158 **"Our own dead"** Ibid.

158 **In 1937, the Library of Congress** Library of Congress, "Artifacts of Assassination," American Treasures, https://www.loc.gov/exhibits/treasures/tr11b.html.

158 **"Do Not Open"** Nardi Reeder Campion, "The Contents of Lincoln's Pockets, and What They Suggest About Him," *New York Times*, Mar. 29, 1986.

158 **sensational remnants of Lincoln's death** Such relics included the bed on which Lincoln died; the bloody cape that Mary Todd Lincoln wore; or hair samples purported to be from near the bullet's entry point. Richard Wightman Fox, *Lincoln's Body: A Cultural History* (New York: W. W. Norton, 2015), chap. 3.

159 **"should try to humanize . . . engulfed"** "Lincoln Carried His Insurance,"
New York Times, Feb. 13, 1976, 70.

159 **"was very much like the rest of us"** Ibid.

159 **"become like relics"** Library of Congress, "Artifacts of Assassination."

160 **most frequently ask to see** Ibid.

160 **"Huck Finn Era Gone"** "Huck Finn Era Gone, Boys' Pockets Show; Cash
and Bankbooks Crowd Out Eels, Gum," *New York Times*, May 13, 1950.

161 **"Talk about a boy's pocket!"** J. L. Harbour, "What Was In It," *Puck*,
July 7, 1905, 11.

161 **"a boy's pocket ain't"** Ibid. See also "Boy's Pockets Not in It with a Handbag,"
Sun, May 11, 1913, L7: "The time has come for those who think a boy's pocket
is a carryall to revise their previous opinions and take a look into a woman's
handbag."

161 **"the science of pocket equilibrium"** Alfred J. Waterhouse, "Women and
Pocket Equilibrium," *New York Times*, Mar. 22, 1903, SM5.

161 **"and scarcely realize"** Ibid.

161 **the reason she "jams"** Ibid.

162 **"there's nothing in it"** P. L. Travers, *Mary Poppins* (New York: Harcourt
Brace [1934] 1962), 10.

162 **Between a bottle of scent** Ibid., 11.

162 **"not exactly Buckingham Palace"** Bill Walsh, dir., *Mary Poppins*
(Burbank, CA: Walt Disney Productions, 1964).

163 **"as full of tricks"** "Beauty in the Bag," *Vogue*, May 15, 1935, 87.

163 **Absorbed and "busy"** Ibid., 86.

163 **"to throw light"** "An X-Ray Penetrates the Messy Interior of a Woman's
Handbag," *Life*, Nov. 6, 1939, 48–49.

164 **"penetrate . . . messy interior"** Ibid.

165 **lugged around "impediments"** Ibid.

165 **"a sort of psychiatrist's effect"** Quoted in Marsha Francis Cassidy,
What Women Watched: Daytime Television in the 1950s (Austin, TX:
Univ. of Texas, 2005), 85.

165 **"Why on *earth*"** Art Linkletter, *Confessions of a Happy Man* (New York:
Random House, 1960), 191. After one painful misadventure exploring a
handbag as "red as a stop sign" that contained a large rat trap, Linkletter
admitted that he too "would resent having my handbag explored by some
clown like me."

165 **"with their purses"** Ibid.

165 **"exhibit the same"** "Women Cram Handbags Full of Many Odd Things,"
Life, Jan. 15, 1945, 90.

166 **for any emergency** Dan Beard of the Boy Scouts reported on his wife's claim that she could get by in the wilderness in a pinch with only the hairpin discovered in her purse. He brushed this off as so much posturing, part of a survivalist mythos spread by women to rationalize their loads. Dan Beard, "The Scout and his Equipment," *Boy's Life*, Feb. 1934, 35.

166 **"home away from home"** Franklin Adams, "Handbagitis," *Atlantic Monthly* 172, no. 6 (Dec. 1943): 15–17.

166 **cast the first "pebble"** Ibid.

166 **"handbag confidant"** Ibid. Worrying aloud that he had contributed "Another of Those Diatribes Against Women," Adams noted that women would not need such large handbags if they had decent pockets.

166 **"compulsive worrier"** "Secrets in a Woman's Handbag," *Los Angeles Times*, Dec. 1, 1957.

166 **umbilical cord** Daniel Harris, "Accessory in Crisis," *Salmagundi* (Spring 1997): 123.

166 **a kind of amnesia** Ibid., 126.

166 **collecting is involuntary** Ibid., 127.

166 **"crutch . . . pruderies and fears"** Ibid., 123, 130.

167 **"a very sensible adjustment"** "Secrets in a Woman's Handbag," *Los Angeles Times*. Dr. Elsa Robinson, professor of psychology at New York University, did not reflect further on any of the ramifications of her comment—why were women under pressure to appear well-groomed?

167 **private ablutions in public** Franklin Adams wondered what it meant that women could perform these rituals so freely, that women take all the "business of make-up" and, without any discretion, get to "work." He admitted that this caused in him the perverse desire to do the same, "to take out from his pocket a shaving kit, dip the brush in the tumbler, and shave at the table." Adams, "Handbagitis," 15.

167 **"a boy without a knife"** Beard, "Scout," 34–35.

167 **"tiny black pills, like seeds . . . things"** Katherine Mansfield, "The Escape," in *Bliss, and Other Stories* (New York: Alfred A. Knopf, 1920), 273.

167 **"Adolescent fears"** Glenna Whitely, "Purse-onally, A Handbag is a Necessity," *Chicago Tribune*, May 8, 1985, 11.

167 **"In shipwreck and storm"** Shirley Lord, "The Private World of the Pocketbook," *Vogue*, Dec. 1, 1973, 186.

168 **really "incredible"** Whitely, "Purse-onally," 11.

168 **"most would agree . . . purse"** Ibid.

168 **"My whole life"** Quoted in Susan Reimer, "Carried Away," *Baltimore Sun*, Sept. 17, 2000.

168 **is an extension of a woman's identity** Valerie Steele and Laird Borrelli, *Bags: A Lexicon of Style* (London: Scriptum Editions, 2005), 35–37.

168 **"daily doings and dreamings"** Howells, *Boy's Town*, 2. The curiosity about purses, especially, seems alive and well: when she was senator of New York state, Hillary Clinton was asked by the young girls participating in "Bring Your Daughters to Work Day" what she carried in her handbag. The official royal photographers to the British monarchy promised insights into the most reserved of monarchs in their 2007 book *What's in the Queen's Handbag and Other Royal Secrets*. Neither Bill Clinton nor Prince Philip have been asked what they carry in their pockets, at least as reported by the press.

169 **auctioning off the contents** "Madonna Auctions Contents of Handbag at AIDS Benefit," AP, May 26, 2008.

170 **"was able to"** Candice Chan, "Pockets and Purses Give Up Their Secrets," *New York Times*, Mar. 15, 2010.

171 **"souped-up" plastic cell phone case** Lisa Miller, "Men Know It's Better to Carry Nothing," *The Cut*, July 17, 2019, https://www.thecut.com/2019/07/if-men-carried-purses-would-they-clean-up-messes.html. Women "lug around the tool kits of servitude," Miller writes, sounding like American suffragists of the early twentieth century.

171 **"the good stories"** Vincent M. Mallozzi, "How They Proposed," *New York Times*, Jan. 21, 2021.

Chapter 6: Pocket Play

173 **"men have pockets"** Paul Johnson, "The Power of a Pocket: Why It Matters Who Wears the Trousers," *Spectator*, June 4, 2011. Dior's comment survives by way of the British writer Paul Johnson, who recalled Dior making it during a long-ago conversation. Johnson revealed nothing more about their encounter, and so it is unclear whether Dior acknowledged his own interest in lively pocket forms.

173 **"unmistakably Dior"** "Fashion: Plotted in Paris," *Vogue*, Apr. 15, 1949, 99.

173 **"whisked out beyond"** Ibid.

173 **"kangaroo pockets . . . calla-lily pockets"** "Fashion: The News in Paris," *Vogue*, Mar. 15, 1949, 74.

173 **pretty handkerchief** Useful pockets did not interest Dior. No one remarked on the fact that Dior's Bar day suit of 1947, which introduced Dior's luxuriously feminine "New Look" to the world, did not include not a single pocket. Compare the 1947 suit held at the Costume Institute (unpocketed) with the one held at the Victoria and Albert Museum (made in 1955 and pocketed).

174 **aesthetic propositions and ideas** Fred Davis, *Fashion Culture and Identity* (Chicago: Chicago Univ. Press, 1990), chap. 1, "Do Clothes Speak?" The meaning of clothing is limited to interpreting the visual and tactile attributes of cloth; cues about a garment's relative formality, reserve, youthfulness, or sexiness rely on the associations we have with how cloth is manipulated. Other than hoodies and graphic tees, which announce some affiliation or adage, clothing tends not to be adorned with symbolic language. This is one reason ornament can take on outsize roles.

174 **"no sooner put into use"** Ann Hollander, *Sex and Suits: The Evolution of Modern Dress* (New York: Alfred A Knopf, 1994), 15.

174 **"Pockets, pockets everywhere"** "Les Modes créées à Paris," *Harper's Bazaar*, Mar. 1915, 34.

174 **Erté's illustrations** Stella Blum, *Designs by Erté: Fashion Drawings and Illustrations from "Harper's Bazaar"* (New York: Dover Publications, 1976), preface and v–vi. Erté designed garments that were produced exclusively for export to B. Altman and Henri Bendel in New York during the nineteen teens, making him a "couturier for export only." Between 1915 and 1926 he contributed fashion designs to *Harper's* that were assembled into full-page spreads by the *Harper's* editorial team. Some of his fashion designs appear never to have been executed; his output was limited and very little of his work survives. He is remembered instead for his illustrations, especially his covers for *Harper's* (which continued until 1936), costume designs, and stage set designs.

175 **"a *new* decorative element"** "Vogue Points: Decorative Little Guideposts to Point the Traveler on the Right Road to Smart Spring Fashions," *Vogue*, Feb. 1, 1916, 36.

176 **"like beacon lights"** "Les Modes créées," 34.

176 **"Novel pockets"** *Women's Wear Daily*, Mar. 23, 1920, 22.

176 **"disliked intensely"** Quoted in Blum, *Designs by Erté*, xi.

176 **"doubly decorative"** "Vogue Points," 36.

177 **"frivol away"** "Fashion May Desert the Riviera but Erté Is Stimulated by Monte Carlo's Summer Skies," *Harper's Bazaar*, Aug. 1920, 49.

177 **to paint men's faces** Ibid. Erté contributed his own letters from Monte Carlo that included his observations on fashion and the scene. At times Erté referred to himself in the third person, but this letter is meant to suggest an author other than Erté.

177 **"pretty garden frocks"** Quoted in Blum, *Designs by Erté*, 42.

178 **clothing as her medium** Elsa Schiaparelli, *Shocking Life* (New York: Dutton, 1954), 59. Schiaparelli wrote that "dress designing, incidentally, is to me not a profession but an art." Toward the end of her career, she wondered: "Had I not by pure chance become a maker of dresses, what could I have become? A sculptor?" (249).

178 **"make the fantastic real"** Quoted in Ghislaine Wood, ed., *Surreal Things: Surrealism and Design* (London: V & A Publications, 2007), 15.

178 **"apparent craziness"** Schiaparelli, *Shocking Life*, 67.

178 **"fun and gags"** Ibid.

178 **"Dalí was a constant caller"** Ibid., 114.

178 **"We devised together"** Ibid.

179 **"anthropomorphic cabinet"** Dalí's drawing is titled *The City of Drawers: Study for Anthropomorphic Cabinet, 1936*.

179 **Freud identified** Sigmund Freud, *The Interpretation of Dreams*, trans. A. A. Brill (New York: Modern Library, [1899] 1920), 72. "Little cases, boxes, caskets, closets, and stoves correspond to the female part," Freud wrote, as well as "hollow objects (chests, boxes, pouches, &c.)."

179 **nothing if not salacious** Richard Martin, *Fashion and Surrealism* (New York: Rizzoli, 1987), 109. Martin argues that Dalí was fraught with anxiety over entry into the body of a woman, and that the series of drawers in his 1936 *Venus de Milo with Drawers* offered possible access. Dalí spoke of "kinds of allegories" related to the drawers and the need to smell the "innumerable narcissistic odors emanating from each one" (120).

180 **"the most incredible things"** Schiaparelli, *Shocking Life*, 115.

180 **"Not one [button]"** Ibid.

180 **shaped to resemble** Ibid.

180 **Did Schiaparelli tame** Martin, *Fashion and Surrealism*, 120

180 **have so "monotonously" attributed** Gaston Bachelard, *The Poetics of Space* (New York: Orion Press, 1964), 84.

180 **"hybrid objects"** Ibid., 78.

180 **"space that is not"** Ibid., 82.

181 **"frighten . . . preferable to mislead him"** Bachelard, *Poetics of Space*, 82.

181 **"cunning carpenter"** Janet Flanner, "Profiles: Comet," *New Yorker*, June 18, 1932, 23.

181 **"bright, impossible, impudent"** Schiaparelli, *Shocking Life*, 114. Schiaparelli's pink was a bit more vibrant that the paler pink associated with Sèvres, known as "Pompadour pink" for the manufactory's principal investor and promoter, Madame de Pompadour, mistress to Louis VX. It is possible that Schiaparelli was tipping her hat to other women who have employed the decorative in various power plays and ploys. In a joint venture with the king, Pompadour rescued a failing private porcelain venture to create Sèvres, establishing it as a showcase of French manufacture to rival Germany's Meissen factory. Pompadour's interest and support came about because she was looking for projects to cement her influence with the king once their sexual partnership ended.

182 **"like beacon lights"** "Les Modes créées," 34.

182 **"Who is left"** Robyn Gibson, "Schiaparelli, Surrealism and the Desk Suit," *Dress: The Journal of the Costume Society of America* 30, no. 1 (2003): 52.

182 **strategically showing some cleavage** When Dior included breast pockets, for example, he "stood them away from the bosom" to "make a sexy new décolletage," as *Harper's Bazaar* reported in 1949. "Paris: The Day-Length Dinner Dress," *Harper's Bazaar*, Apr. 1949, 111.

183 **"a dignity that was invulnerable"** Caroline Evans and Minna Thornton, *Women and Fashion: A New Look* (London: Quartet, 1989), 125.

183 **"the nearest thing"** Gianfranco Ferre, "Fashion: Impeccable, Untouchable; Karl Lagerfeld's Version of Dress-for-Success," *Vogue*, Jan. 1, 1985, 209.

183 **She likened tailoring** "Chanel Designs Again," *Vogue*, Feb. 15, 1954, 83.

183 **A dress must "function"** Ibid.

183 **"Place the pockets"** Ibid.

183 **"Never a button"** Ibid.

183 **"a key, a lighter, whatever"** Ibid.

183 **"leave [women] a fake"** Sally Dee, "Shortages: You Can Dodge Them," *Evening Star*, Apr. 4, 1943, 21.

184 **"the Paris-equivalent"** "The Trompe-L'Oeil Resort Dress," *Vogue*, Dec. 1, 1952, 154.

184 **"all absolute frauds"** Ibid.

184 **"there only by the grace"** Ibid.

184 **to show up women's predicament in a patriarchy** Evans and Thornton, *Women and Fashion*, 143. Schiaparelli's first break-out hit was her 1927 hand knitted sweater with trompe l'oeil bow around the neck, and as we've seen, Schiaparelli included trompe l'oeil pockets along with real ones in her bureau drawer suit. Illusory decoration (a fake bow), however, is not the same as illusory function.

184 **endorsing fraudulent pockets** An example is a 1959 bathing suit whose pockets helped elongate one's waist. In the caption, *Vogue* halfheartedly warned potential wearers that the pockets were "really fakes—put down those sea shells." "Fashion: 1959 Beach Changes; The Scene Brightens," *Vogue*, Jan. 1, 1959, 109.

186 **"horrifying . . . bow ties"** "Point of View: Style that Works," *Vogue*, Aug. 1, 1989, 267.

186 **"a Chanel" tarted up** See, for example, Jane Kramer, "The Chanel Obsession," *Vogue*, Sept. 1, 1991, 512–19, 608, 610.

186 **"dignified sense of humor"** "Point Of View," 267.

186 **"be more important than"** "Chanel Designs Again," 83.

187 **"I want my clothes"** Philadelphia Museum of Art, "Patrick Kelly: Runway of Love," Apr. 27, 2014–Dec. 7, 2014, https://www.philamuseum.org/exhibitions/799.html.

187 **"real prices"** Quoted in Dilys E. Blum "Patrick Kelly and Paris Fashion," in *Patrick Kelly: Runway of Love* (San Francisco: Fine Arts Museums of San Francisco; New Haven, CT: Yale Univ. Press, 2021), 24.

189 **"A fundamentally conservative affair"** "Pocket Picking," *Esquire*, Jan. 1, 1955, 82.

189 **"one of the few"** Ibid.

189 **"rugged masculinity"** Ibid.

190 **"transition between"** Ibid.

190 **"Made expressly for miners"** Levi Strauss and Co. advertisement, ca. 1890, reprinted in Emma McClendon, *Denim: Fashion's Frontier* (New Haven, CT: Yale Univ. Press, in association with FIT, New York), 12.

191 **"native to"** James Agee, *Let Us Now Praise Famous Men: Three Tennent Families* (Boston: Houghton Mifflin, 1969), 265.

191 **"the complexed seams . . . blueprint"** Ibid., 266.

191 **"complex and slanted structure"** Ibid., 265.

191 **"completing a satisfactory day's work"** Quoted in John Mollo, *Military Fashion: A Comparative History of the Uniforms of the Great Armies from the 17th Century to the First World War* (New York: Putnam, 1972), 207–8. Lord Wolseley, commander-in-chief of the British army, was a proponent of efficiency and described his complaints in an 1889 letter.

191 **a new model** Nick Foulkes, *Mogambo: The Safari Jacket* (Milan: Skira, 2011), 16.

191 **officers sought risk and adventure** Ibid., 9. One thinks of the safari jacket as originating in East Africa with someone like Ernest Hemmingway, but Foulkes demonstrates that it originated earlier, in India. "It was in India that the image of the big game hunter began to be formed and it was here that the safari jacket began to evolve," writes Foulkes.

192 **hunting suits** Some historians suggest that the Norfolk hunting suit was the model for modern military uniforms; the Norfolk hunting suit, however, did not typically have outer breast pockets.

193 **"the discovery that men"** William F. Ross and Charles F. Romans, *The Quartermaster Corps: Operations in the War Against Germany* (Washington, DC: Office of the Chief of Military History, Dept. of the Army, 1965), 195.

193 **"neat and snappy"** Ibid., 559. Eisenhower worried that the uniforms looked "a bit tough," and given "the natural proclivities of the American soldier," it would not take long for soldiers so attired to "quickly create a general impression of a disorderly mob" (559).

194 **"not just a fad"** "American Informal," *Apparel Arts*, Dec. 1949, 61–69.

194 **"natural casualness"** Ibid.

194 **"at the opera"** Ibid.

194 **Outerwear is "everywhere"** "Outerwear Is Everywhere," *GQ*, Sept. 1955, 98–99.

194 **"sporting stitching"** Ibid.

194 **"style significance"** Ibid.

194 **"ever hopeful"** Ibid.

194 **"clothes should be suitable . . . office"** "How to Dress in the Worst of Taste," *GQ*, Feb. 1964, 61.

194 **on a "tightrope"** "Casual Fridays without Tears," *GQ*, July 1995, 75.

195 **anti-colonial revolt** Foulkes, *Mogambo*, 24.

195 **"peaceful outings"** "Suited for the Non-Occasion," GQ, Feb. 1972, 104–5.

195 **"assertive touches"** Ibid.

195 **ready for every "non-occasion"** Ibid.

195 **Western regional wear** "Casual Check on California," *Apparel Arts*, June 1949, 66.

196 **"devoid of gimmicks"** "Jeaneology: A Fitting Tribute to Fashion's Hot Pants," *GQ*, Apr. 1977, 110.

196 **"styling with an extra zip"** Ibid.

197 **Pinky and Dianne** McClendon, *Denim*, 106.

197 **transposing pocket types** Women's wear does this, too. See, for example, kangaroo hoodie pockets on evening dresses.

198 **"suitable for the occasion"** "How to Dress," 61.

198 **"urban-survival uniform"** "The Splashy Seventies," *GQ*, Oct. 1980, 210.

198 **Young punk rockers** According to Jay Lee writing for *Esquire*, an important part of the rediscovery of cargoes' cool occurred when Che Guevara was photographed in cargoes pitching at a baseball game in 1958. Two distinct countercultures, punk and hip-hop, followed. Cargo pants were then co-opted by mainstream brands like Abercrombie and Fitch and Old Navy. Jay Lee, "Amazing Stories: The Intrepid Histories of Three Style Icons. Part 2: Cargo Pants," *Esquire*, Spring 2010.

198 **"Fashion pocket treatments"** "Pants," *GQ*, Feb. 1973, 97.

199 **"enough pockets, sealed with Velcro"** Peter Carlsen, "Clotheslines," *GQ*, Oct. 1980, 15.

199 **"You may be facing more traffic jams"** "What's Hot!," *GQ*, Sept. 1977, 172.

199 **Cargo pants were rediscovered in the 1990s** James Sherwood, "The Nineties Utility Movement: Prime Suspect in the Death of Designer Fashion," in *Uniform: Order and Disorder*, ed. Francesco Bonami, Maria Luisa Frisa, Stefano Tonchi (Milan: Charta, 2000), 176.

199 **"taking their cue from urban street style"** Jennifer Jackson, "Vogue's View: Working Class," *Vogue*, May 1, 1994, 119.

199 **"Everyone wants to look active"** "Moderate Report: Utility Chic; A Quick Interpretation," *Women's Wear Daily*, Nov. 25, 1998, 25.

200 **"ultimate athletes"** "Fabric for Fighters: Life-saving Research for Military Uniform Designs," *Made to Measure Magazine*, Aug. 8, 2012, https://www.madetomeasuremag.com/fabric-for-fighters-life-saving-research -helps-latest-military-uniform-designs.

200 **"Why wouldn't the general public"** Ibid.

200 **Civilian designers reflected on the craft** "Military clothing is like denim, the best-designed clothes in the world," remarked Anna Sui in a 1995 interview. "You can't get any better. It's functional, weather proof; everything is thought out in it, and that's what attracts us to fatigues." Quoted in Amy Spindler, "Design Review: From Lethal Cause to Artistic One," *New York Times*, Sept. 15, 1995, C23.

200 **tested at Camp Lee** Shelby Stanton, U.S. Army Uniforms of World War II (Mechanicsburg, PA: Stackpole Books, 1991), 110.

201 **Canadian Artic Patrol gear or Danish Airforce trousers** By the 1980s, Peter Carlsen of *GQ* complained that "much of the genuine surplus gear . . . is long gone," yet various brands continued to tout garments as authentic surplus. Peter Carlsen, "Express Male," *GQ*, May 1981, 108.

201 **"red devils with baggy pants"** Frank van Lunteren, *Spearhead of the Fifth Army* (Philadelphia: Casemate, 2016), 245.

201 **"inappropriate on the Versace runway"** Sherwood, "Nineties Utility," 177.

201 **"Combat pants"** Ibid.

201 **Women have historically adopted military looks** Who is to say, as Sherwood seemed to, who has the right to adapt such defensive garb? The public street has historically been a more dangerous place for women, and it does not seem fair to condemn women—even wealthy, privileged ones—for their efforts to appear threatening.

202 **"the new street-chic style"** "Urban Uniform," *Harper's Bazaar*, Nov. 2002, 210.

202 **"distinguished uniform"** "Military Issue," *Vogue*, Mar. 1, 2010, 447.

203 **"rugged to refined"** "Urban Uniform," 214.

203 **the decade's concerns** Richard Martin and Harold Koda, *Swords into Ploughshares* (New York: Metropolitan Museum of Art, 1995). The exhibition, *Swords Into Ploughshares: Military Dress and the Civilian Wardrobe*, examined the impact of military attire on fashion; it ran from September 7 to November 26, 1995. Martin quotes Menkes in his introduction.

203 **"Is fashion playing dangerous"** Suzy Menkes, "Fashion's Unsettling Reflection: Designers Focus on 1940s," *International Herald Tribune*, May 9, 1995.

203 **"that jean like silhouette"** "The No-Bro Car Go—," *GQ*, May 2011, 128.

203 **"Don't stuff"** Ibid.

204 **"heritage utility feature . . . statement"** "In the Pocket," *Women's Wear Daily*, Nov. 16, 2016, 22.

204 **an "eco-futurist" outlook** "Fashion: Marine Serre, Glenn Martens Look To Fashion's Future," *Women's Wear Daily*, July 6, 2020, 14.

204 **"black-ops bike couriers"** Chris Gayomali, "Errolson Hugh Sees the Future," *GQ*, May 2019, 86.

205 **"Gore-Tex gaiters"** Russell Smith, *Men's Style: The Thinking Man's Guide to Dress* (New York: Thomas Dunne Books, 2007), 232–33.

206 **"transcend their function"** "In the Pocket," 22.

206 **"fun and gags"** Schiaparelli, *Shocking Life*, 67.

206 **Miuccia Prada's transparent raincoat** Prada's transparent raincoat acknowledges the tradition of trompe l'oeil, like of the Hermès screen-printed dresses of 1952 that in painterly strokes outlined cuff, collar, buttons, and pockets (see figure 9 in this chapter).

Chapter 7: Pocket Utopias

209 **In their mimicry** Elyssa Dimant, *Minimalism and Fashion: Reduction in the Post-modern Era* (New York: Collins Design, 2010), 11.

210 **underlined this "relatedness"** "The World of Now," *Harper's Bazaar*, Feb. 1960, 77.

210 **"ordered perfection . . . galactic beauty"** Ibid.

210 **"perfect context . . . functional design"** Ibid.

210 **"bareness . . . weight and coverage"** Ibid.

211 *Just Imagine* For a discussion of the film, see James Chapman and Nicholas J. Cull, *Projecting Tomorrow: Science Fiction and Popular Cinema* (London: I. B. Tauris; New York, NY: Palgrave Macmillan, 2013). Costume design credited to Alice O'Neil and Dolly Tree. Because of the studio system, very little is known about the individual contributions of specific individuals to 1930s films.

211 **"New York gone futuristic"** Quoted in Howard Mandlebaum and Eric Myers, *Screen Deco: A Celebration of High Style in Hollywood* (Santa Monica: Hennessy and Ingalls, [1985] 2000), 169.

211 **As the hero zips** In a major subplot, a time traveler from 1930 attempts to adjust to the clothes of the future. In one scene, Single-O, an unreformed lush from the Prohibition Era, staggers down the street quite drunk, searching for the pills that have come to replace alcohol. He reflexively reaches for his pockets and, patting himself down vigorously in an extended bit of physical comedy, cannot find them. Single-O is tied to the needs and concerns of the

past—his discovery that food and drink come in pill form elicits the mournful refrain: "it's not like the good old days." Significantly it is Single-O, the only character with insight into two time periods, who feels the lack of pockets—*Just Imagine* suggests that the citizens of the future do not miss them.

211 **"invented" the future** R. D. Haynes, *H. G. Wells: Discoverer of the Future* (London: Macmillan, 1980), 2. As a young man, Wells worked as a draper's assistant; although the working conditions made the experience among the low points of his life, Wells's interest in the importance of cloth and clothing is evident in the attention he paid to dress throughout his written work. Also evident in Wells's prescriptions are the deprivations of his lower-middle-class upbringing and his sympathy for people striving to achieve a respectable appearance.

211 **"re-equipment of everyday life"** H. G. Wells, *A Modern Utopia*, ed. Gregory Claeys and Patrick Parrinder (London: Penguin Books, [1905] 2005), 13.

211 **contribution to futurist dress** "Fashion," in *The Greenwood Encyclopedia of Science Fiction and Fantasy*, vol. 1, ed. Gary Westfahl (Westport, CT: Greenwood Press, 2005), 284.

212 **"fussed over the costumes . . . accurately"** Christopher Frayling, *Things to Come* (London: BFI Publishing, 1995), 36.

213 **it should be "unobtrusive"** H. G. Wells, "Rules of Thumb for Things to Come," *New York Times*, Apr. 12, 1936, X4.

213 **"let yourselves go"** Ibid.

213 **"being inventive . . . silly"** Ibid.

213 **"audacity and risk"** Giacomo Balla, "The Antineutral Suit: Futurist Manifesto," Sept. 11, 1914, reprinted in Emily Braun, "Futurist Fashion: Three Manifestos," *Art Journal* (Spring 1995): 39.

213 **"innumerable pockets . . . impedimenta"** Quoted in Don Glassman, "H. G. Wells, Film-maker, Considers the Future," *New York Times*, Sept. 22, 1935, X5.

213 **"buckles and gadgets"** Ibid.

213 **"walls, fences, locks . . . reservation"** H. G. Wells, "Wells Sees Man Better Off in '88," *New York Times*, Jan. 16, 1938, 41.

213 **"we will have freer"** Ibid.

214 **"men and women of the future"** Wells, "Rules of Thumb," X4.

214 **"with pockets full of coins"** H. G. Wells, *Men Like Gods* (New York: Macmillan, 1923), 279.

214 **"portable radio telephones"** Wells, "Rules of Thumb," X4.

215 **would not be "obtrusive"** Ibid.

215 **"dignified . . . armored gladiator"** Ibid.

215 **"rigged up like a telephone pole"** Wells, "Rules of Thumb," X4.

215 **went "short"** H. G. Wells, *The Shape of Things to Come* (New York: Macmillan, 1933), 402.

215 **"is the abolition"** Ibid., 403.

215 **"he [would] find"** Ibid.

217 **"naked spacefarer"** Michael Chabon, "Secret Skin: An Essay in Unitard Theory," *New Yorker*, Mar. 10, 2008, reprinted in Andrew Bolton, *Super Heroes: Fashion and Fantasy* (New Haven, CT: Yale Univ. Press, 2008).

217 **New York's 1939 World's Fair** Jeffrey Meikle, *Twentieth Century Limited: Industrial Design in America, 1925–1939* (Philadelphia: Temple Univ. Press, 1979), 197.

217 **"the shape of things"** Ibid.

217 **"streamlined versions"** "Industrial Designers Dress Woman of the Future," *Life*, Jan. 30, 1939, 34.

217 **"stratospheric plane"** "Donald Deskey Foresees a Great Emancipation," *Vogue*, Feb. 1, 1939, 137.

217 **"a little drapery"** Ibid. The idea itself was not original: separates were an idea that sportswear designers were then exploring.

218 **"permanent . . . automatic lock"** Ibid.

218 **"completely emancipated"** Ibid.

218 **"being a woman"** Ibid.

218 **"comprehensive design"** Wells, *Modern Utopia*, 159.

218 **Simple and "unobtrusive"** Wells, "Rules of Thumb," X4.

218 **"we [will] wear less clothing"** Wells, "Wells Sees Man Better Off," 41.

218 **asceticism and restraint** Less obviously futurist in aura, 1990s minimalist fashions were widely understood to be a recession-era response to 1980s couture excesses: "in the early Nineties, people wanted only simple clothing to cancel everything out," Miuccia Prada told *Vogue*. Quoted in James Sherwood, "The Nineties Utility Movement: Prime Suspect in the Death of Designer Fashion," in *Uniform: Order and Disorder*, ed. Francesco Bonami, Maria Luisa Frisa, Stefano Tonchi (Milan: Charta, 2001), 177.

218 **"nothing else"** "Minimalist No More: Jil Sander," *Harper's Bazaar*, Mar. 1993, 307.

218 **"What you see . . . glitzy stuff"** Ibid.

219 **"like Christmas trees"** Ibid.

219 **"bigger bag!"** Madeline Fass, "5 Trends Every Minimalist Should Try This Spring," *Vogue*, Mar. 5, 2020.

220 **experimental cloth** Susan Elizabeth Ryan, "Re-Visioning the Interface: Technological Fashion as Critical Media," *Leonardo* 42, no. 4 (Aug. 2009): 307.

220 **between portable and wearable tools** Susan Elizabeth Ryan, *Garments of Paradise: Wearable Discourse in the Digital Age* (Cambridge, MA: MIT Press, 2014), 20.

220 **"wearable computing"** Steve Mann with Hal Niedzviecki, *Cyborg: Digital Destiny and Human Possibility in the Age of the Wearable Computer* (Toronto: Doubleday Canada, 2001), 55.

220 **"don't want to be bogged down"** Quoted in Ryan, *Garments of Paradise*, 63.

221 **"omnipresence, omnipotence and omniscience"** Philips Design, *New Nomads: An Exploration of Wearable Electronics by Philips* (Rotterdam: 010 Publishers, 2000), 4.

221 **"What people really want . . . Star Trek"** Quoted in Ryan, *Garments of Paradise*, 63.

221 **"progressive integration"** Ibid.

221 **"nomadic workers"** Philips Design, *New Nomads*, 28.

221 **"digital suit for professionals"** Ibid., 28–29. How this all worked was rather hazy, and no energy source was evident. The devices listed on the keypad were phone, pager, dictation, and radio; they were treated as "hidden secrets embedded in the garment and invisible to others until such time as the wearer decides to use one of them" (28–29).

221 **called the Levi's ICD+** Joseph Gleasure, "An Expanded History of Levi's ICD+ and Philips," *Shell Zine*, July 20, 2020, https://shellzine.net/levis-icd/. ICD was an acronym for Industrial Clothing Division.

222 **"smart pockets"** Ibid. The "smart pockets" of the "Surround Sound Audio Jacket," for example, connected its digital audio player to the interface with a jack plug.

222 **Assessing the failure** Rose Sinclair, *Textiles and Fashion: Materials, Design, and Technology* (Amsterdam: Elsevier, 2014), 367–68.

222 **"enhanced body care and adornment"** Philips Design, *New Nomads*, 121. "We can develop clothes that incorporate materials that help to de-stress the wearer by inducing subtle, ongoing relaxation of the body; this is in contrast to, for example, a massage device, which is generally applied to tired muscles in a direct and periodic way . . . Biometric sensors monitor the degree of relaxation and adjust the level of sensory stimulation accordingly" (124–25).

222 **preposterous working and nonworking objects** Joanna Berzowska, for example, explains that her work "undermines our expectations about technology. These works are not meant to solve problems but pose questions about how design might operate." Quoted in Ryan, *Garments of Paradise*, 162.

223 **"sucking stones"** Samuel Beckett, *Molloy*, in *Samuel Becket, The Grove Centenary Edition*, vol. 2, *Novels*, ed. Paul Auster (New York: Grove Press, 2006), 68.

223 **"comparative peace of mind . . . a round"** Ibid., 68.

224 **"wrestling and wrangling"** Ibid., 65. Rather than "increasing the number of my pockets, or reducing the number of my stones," Molloy realizes he must sacrifice the idea of "trim." He undertakes the round with one pocket empty and the others loaded; he is now sure to arrive at an "impeccable succession, not one stone sucked twice, not one left unsucked." "Freed from all anxiety," the solution, however, is "inelegant" in that it leaves him lopsided, unequally dragged down with the weight of the stones. "Here then were two incompatible bodily needs, at loggerheads. Such things happen."

224 **i-Wear Project** I-Wear was a consortium that included a range of companies interested in financing, sharing expertise, and developing products in the field of wearables, or intelligent clothing, as it was also called (the *i* for *intelligent*). I-Wear was a part of Starlab, a blue sky versus agenda driven research initiative in the model of Bell Labs, MIT Media Lab, or Xerox Parc. Starlab went bankrupt suddenly, in 2001, and Philips later purchased the intellectual property rights to i-Wear.

225 **Autumn/Winter 2000–2001 collection, "Dissections"** Andrew Bolton, *Supermodern Wardrobe* (London: V & A Publications, 2002), 18.

225 **Commuter x Jacquard by Google Trucker Jacket** Ivan Poupyrev, "More Than Just a Jacket: Levi's Commuter Trucker Jacket Powered by Jacquard Technology," *Keyword* (blog), Sept. 25, 2007, https://blog.google/products/atap/more-just-jacket-levis-commuter-trucker-jacket-powered-jacquard-technology/.

226 **Joseph-Marie Jacquard** Manuel De Landa, *War in the Age of the Intelligent Machine* (New York: Zone Books, 1991), 159.

226 **"seamless blending of digital"** Cooper Hewitt, "Interaction Design: Ivan Poupyrev," National Design Awards, 2019, https://www.cooperhewitt.org/national-design-awards/2019-national-design-awards-winners/.

226 **"breakthrough interaction technologies"** Ibid.

226 **"gifted and talented jacket"** Rafftraff, "Great Jacket - Limited Functionality," product review, https://www.levi.com/US/en_US/apparel/clothing/tops/levis-commuter-x-jacquard-by-google-trucker-jacket/p/286600000 (accessed Jan. 16, 2022).

226 **"to make the activated space"** Rachel Arthur, "Project Jacquard: Google and Levi's Launch the First 'Smart' Jean Jacket For Urban Cyclists," *Forbes*, May 20, 2016.

226 **"like a magician's trick"** Ibid.

227 **"being on"** Sherry Turkle, *Alone Together: Why We Expect More from Technology and Less from Each Other* (New York: Basic Books, 2011), 17.

227 **"We live in a time"** Bridget Cogley, "The Arrivals Designs Aer Parka with Pocket That Blocks Mobile Phone Signal," *Dezeen*, Nov. 26, 2019, https://www.dezeen.com/2019/11/26/the-arrivals-aer-jacket-blocks-signal/.

227 **"We began conceptualizing"** Ibid.

228 **futurist Amy Webb** Steven Zeitchek, "Futurist Amy Webb Says Babymaking Could Get Crazy and the Smartphone Will Die," *Washington Post*, Jan. 10, 2022.

228 **"civilization demands"** J. C. Flugel, *Psychology of Clothes* (New York: International Univs. Press, [1930] 1966), 187. "The need for carrying about a number of small articles is one of the graver disadvantages of civilization," complained the psychoanalyst Flugel, somewhat dramatically, in his 1930 book. A man well read in utopian fictions, including those of H. G. Wells, he saw a coming nude future, although one comically marred by "some sort of sartorial harness" in which people would need to carry all those small articles, for which he could not see an alternative.

229 **"serve as protection"** Quoted in Rachel Tashjian, "Let's Never Go Back to the Runway," *GQ*, July 10, 2020.

229 **reflect back the evil eye** Linda Welters, "Introduction: Folk Dress, Supernatural Beliefs, and the Body," in *Folk Dress in Europe and Anatolia* (Oxford: Berg, 1999), 8.

229 **"so when you die here"** Dmitriy Khavin, Ainara Tiefenthäler, Christoph Koettl, and Brenna Smith, "Videos show Ukrainian Citizens Confronting Russian Troops," *New York Times*, Feb. 26, 2022.

230 **"some good"** Michael Marder, "Vegetable Redemption: A Ukrainian Woman and Russian Soldiers," *Philosophical Salon*, Feb. 26, 2022, https://thephilosophicalsalon.com/vegetal-redemption-a-ukrainian-woman -and-russian-soldiers/.

230 **"the requisite twirl"** Jim Sabo of Dresseswithpockets.com, personal communication, Apr. 5, 2022. Sabo noted that, faithful to his pocket mission, he lists even those sites that do not give him a commission.

231 **"My ultimate goal"** Ibid.

231 **"Here at T-9 we're big on pockets"** Spring 2022 Catalog, Title Nine.

231 **sketch of a back pocket** See, for example, the product details for Radian's "Deep Pocket Skinny Jeans," https://radianjeans.com/products/deep-pocket -women-s-skinny-jeans-light-blue-mid-rise?variant=31629321732145 (accessed Apr. 26, 2022).

233 **"other selves"** Julian Hawthorne, "Pochiastry," *Christian Union* 32, no. 12 (1885): 6.

233 **"rough seems . . . edifice"** Thomas Carlyle, *Sartor Resartus*, ed. Rodger L. Tarr (Berkeley: Univ. of California Press, 2000), 50.

Illustration Sources and Credits

The author and publisher gratefully acknowledge the artists, designers, photographers, companies, publications, libraries, museums, and individuals listed below for supplying the necessary materials and permission to reproduce their work. Every effort has been made to trace copyright holders and obtain their permissions for the use of copyrighted material. The author apologizes for any errors or omissions and would be grateful if notified of any corrections.

Frontispiece: Pocket detail on a man's silk velvet court coat, embroidered with silver thread, purl and spangles, and glass pastes, 1780. Accession # 1611&A-1900. © Victoria and Albert Museum, London.

Introduction

Figure 1: *K* page from Sally Sketch, *An Alphabetical Arrangement of Animals for Young Naturalists* (1821). Courtesy of Osborne Collection of early children's books, Toronto Public Library.

Figure 2: H. A. Rey's illustration of Katy and Freddy in conversation with the aproned workman in Emmy Payne's *Katy No Pocket* (Boston: Houghton Mifflin Company, 1944). De Grummond Children's Literature Collection, The University of Southern Mississippi, Courtesy Estate of H. A. Rey.

Figure 3: Tullio Pericoli, *Ritratto di Robinson*, 1984, watercolor and ink on paper. Courtesy Tullio Pericoli.

Figure 4: Bernard Rudofsky, "24 Pockets," *Are Clothes Modern? An Essay on Contemporary Apparel* (Chicago: Paul Theobald, 1947). © 2022 Artists Rights Society (ARS), New York / Bildrecht, Vienna.

Chapter 1: Pocket Origins

Figure 1: Front cover of the Clemens family copy of *The Chronicle of the Cid*. The Mark Twain House & Museum, Hartford Connecticut.

Figure 2: Illustration in a 1414 edition of Giovanni Boccaccio's *The Decameron*. Paris, Bibliothéque Nationale de France.

Figure 3: One of a group of garments discovered in a peat bog from Norse Greenland and carbon-dated to between 1180–1530. Photo Peter Danstrøm, Nationalmuseet, Denmark.

Figure 4: Sculpture of Joan, the daughter of King Edward III, Westminster Abbey, 1377. © Dean and Chapter of Westminster.

Figure 5: Master E. S., *The Knight and the Lady with Helmet and Lance*, German, mid fifteenth century. New York: The Metropolitan Museum of Art, Harris Brisbane Dick Fund, 1922.

Figure 6: Contemporary international pictograms. Photo: Erik Gould.

Figure 7: "The Married Man's Complaint: Who Took a Shrew Instead of a Saint," ca. 1550s. The Bodleian Libraries, University of Oxford, Douce Ballads 2(150a), Ballad Round Number V29054.

Figure 8: Janet Arnold's drawing of the trunk hose worn by Svante Sture in 1567. Courtesy estate of Janet Arnold.

Figure 9: Ballad woodblock illustration, "The Plow-mans Prophesie," ca. 1550s. The Bodleian Libraries, University of Oxford, 40 Rawl. 566(120). Ballad Round Number V32041.

Figure 10: Vittore Carpaccio, *Young Knight in a Landscape*, 1510. Museo Nacional Thyssen-Bornemisza / Scala / Art Resource, NY.

Figure 11: Attributed to Maerten de Vos, *The Vanity of Women: Ruffs*, ca. 1600 (Detail). New York: The Metropolitan Museum of Art. Purchase, Irene Lewisohn Trust Gift, 2001.

Figure 12: Attributed to Maerten de Vos, *The Vanity of Women: Masks and Bustles* ca. 1600 (Detail). New York: The Metropolitan Museum of Art. Purchase, Irene Lewisohn Trust Gift, 2001.

Figure 13: Cornelis Ketel, portrait of Sir Martin Frobisher (1535?–1594), 1577. The Bodleian Libraries, University of Oxford, Bodleian Library LP 50.

Figure 14: England and Wales. Sovereign, *A Proclamation against the use of Pocket-Dags* (Imprinted at London: By Robert Barker, Printer to the Kings most Excellent Maiestie, 1613), RB 53282, The Huntington Library, San Marino, California.

Figure 15: Frans Hogenberg, *The Assassination of William the Silent*, 1584. Rijksmuseum, Amsterdam.

Figure 16: Pieter Bruegel, *The Misanthropist*, 1568. Courtesy of the Ministry of Culture, Museo E Real Bosco di Capodimonte, Naples.

Figure 17: Steven van der Meulen, Robert Dudley, Earl of Leicester, c 1564; oil on panel; Waddesdon (Rothschild Family). On loan since 1996; acc. no. 14.1996. Photo: Waddesdon Image Library, The Public Catalogue Foundation, Art UK.

Figure 18: © DIOR, Dior x Sacai collection, Spring 2022. Photo: Brett Lloyd / Total World.

Chapter 2: Pocket Proliferation

Figure 1: Illustration in *The Adventures of Captain Gulliver, in a Voyage to the Islands of Lilliput and Brobdingnag* (London: F. Newbery, 1776), Ch.770/46, British Library / GRANGER.

Figure 2: Anonymous, *The English Antic, or The Habit of an English Gentleman*, 1646. British Library / GRANGER.

Figure 3: Ballad illustration, "Cupid's Kindness to Constant Coridon, or, Fair Silvia Wounded with a Dart," 1675. The Bodleian Libraries, University of Oxford, UK, Douce Ballads 2(150a). Ballad Round Number, V8253.

Figure 4: Nicholas de Nicolai, "Aga Capitaine, general des Jannissaires," from *Costume Engravings Made during Travels in the East*, 1587. Rosenwald Collection, Library of Congress, Manuscript Division.

Figure 5: Illustrated page of Churyo Morishima's 1787 *Komo Zatsuwa* (*Red Hair Miscellany*). © The Trustees of the British Museum.

Figure 6: Court suit, France, ca. 1810, National Gallery of Victoria, Melbourne, Australia.

Figure 7: Pompeo Girolamo Batoni, *Portrait of a man in a Green Suit*, 1760s, oil on canvas, 39 1/8 × 29 1/8 in., Dallas Museum of Art, gift of Leon A. Harris, Jr. 1954.

Figure 8: Pocket detail on man's superfine wool suit coat, 1760–1770. Dutch. © Victoria & Albert Museum, London.

Figure 9: Drawing Design for Embroidery, Gentleman's Waistcoat Pocket; Designed by Fabrique de Saint Ruf; France; brush and gouache, watercolor, and graphite on cream laid paper; 20.6 × 32 cm (8 1/8 × 12 5/8 in.); Cooper Hewitt, Gift of Eleanor and Sarah Hewitt; 1925-2-507.

Figure 10: Joseph Noyes's jacket and detail, RHiX17 1689A and B. Courtesy the Rhode Island Historical Society.

Figure 11: Marcellus Laroon, "Old Cloaks, Suits or Coats" from *The Cryes of the City of London*, 1687, retouched 1755, engraving, © Museum of London.

Figure 12: Illustration in George Bruce & Co., *A Specimen of Printing Types and Ornaments Cast by Geo. Bruce & Co.* (New York, 1833). Courtesy, American Antiquarian Society.

Figure 13: Pocket tool kits. The Colonial Williamsburg Foundation. Museum Purchase.

Figure 14: Jefferson's Ivory Pocket Notebooks © Thomas Jefferson Foundation at Monticello. Photo: Edward Owen.

Figure 15: Rare Book Division, The New York Public Library. "Nine of Spades: Pocket Cases." New York Public Library Digital Collections. Accessed June 1, 2022. https://digitalcollections.nypl.org/items/510d47dd-cdea-a3d9-e040-e00a18064a99.

Figure 16: Anon. "The Reforming Constable," ca. 1750. © The Trustees of the British Museum.

Figure 17: Joseph Trammel, handmade tin carrying box for Freedom Papers made to be carried in a pocket, 1852. Collection of the Smithsonian National Museum of African American History and Culture, Gift of Elaine E. Thompson, in memory of Joseph Trammell, on behalf of his direct descendants.

Figure 18: Tie on pocket, eighteenth century. Wool embroidery, linen foundation, cotton backing; H x W: 36.8 x 22.9 cm (14½ x 9 in.); 1957-157-6; Cooper Hewitt.

Figure 19: "Tight Lacing, or Fashion before Ease" by Bowles and Carver after John Collet, London, England, ca. 1770–1775. © The Trustees of the British Museum.

Figure 20: Thomas Sanders, British, active 1767–1773. After Tim Bobbin (John Collier), English, 1708–1786. *Untitled*, plate 19 from Tim Bobbin [pseudonym of John Collier], *Human Passions Delineated (1773)*, 1773. Engraving. Fine Arts Museums of San Francisco, Achenbach Foundation for Graphic Arts, 1963.30.22613.

Figure 21: Simon Verelst, portrait of Mary Modena when Duchess of York, ca. 1675. Royal Collection Trust / © Her Majesty Queen Elizabeth II 2022.

Figure 22: John Collet, *An Actress At Her Toilet, or Miss Brazen Just Breecht*, 1779. Courtesy of The Lewis Walpole Library, Yale University.

Figure 23: "A Boy's First Trousers," *Peterson's Magazine*, 1860. Author's collection.

Chapter 3: Pocket Attitudes

Figure 1: Jean Dieu de Saint-Jean, *Ho'me de qualité en habit de garni d'agréments*, 1683. Paris Musées.

Figure 2: William Hogarth, *A Harlot's Progress*, Plate 1, 1732. Metropolitan Museum of Art, New York, Gift of Sarah Lazarus, 1891.

Figure 3: Thomas Hudson, *Portrait of William Shirley*, 1750. National Portrait Gallery, Smithsonian Institution, Washington, DC.

Figure 4: J. Elwood, *Print Shop*, 1790. © The Trustees of the British Museum.

Figure 5: *How D'Ye Like Me*, 19 November 1772. Printed by Carrington Bowles. © The Trustees of the British Museum.

Figure 6: "Full falls" breeches. Courtesy Historic Northampton, Northampton, Massachusetts.

Figure 7: *The Beauties of Bagnigge Wells*, 1778. © Museum of London.

Figure 8: Philibert-Louis Debucourt, "Conversation misterieuse," Plate 50 in *Modes et Manières du Jour*, 1808. New York, Metropolitan Museum of Art, Watson Library Special Collections / Irene Lewisohn Costume Reference Library, 233.4 D35.

Figure 9: A fashionable fop [Graphic] / Williams fect., 1816. Courtesy of The Lewis Walpole Library, Yale University.

Figure 10: Title page illustration from Frank Fergurson's *The Young man's Guide to Knowledge and Virtue* (Boston: Published by G.W. Cottrell & Co.; New York: T. W. Strong, 1853). Courtesy, American Antiquarian Society.

Figure 11: George Caleb Bingham, American (1811–1879). *Village Character*, 1847. Black India ink, wash, and pencil on rag paper, 20¾ x 16 x ⅞ in. (52.705 x 40.64 x 2.2225 cm). The Nelson-Atkins Museum of Art, Kansas City, Missouri. Lent by the People of Missouri, 8-1977/22. Photo © The Nelson Gallery Foundation.

Figure 12: "The Loafer," from *Prisoner's Friend*, May 15, 1847. Courtesy, American Antiquarian Society.

Figure 13: Frontispiece portrait of Walt Whitman, *Leaves of Grass*, 1855. Engraved by Samuel Hollyer after a daguerreotype by Gabriel Harrison. National Portrait Gallery, Smithsonian Institution.

Figure 14: Portrait of Ralph Waldo Emerson, by Elliott & Fry, published by Bickers & Son. Woodburytype on album page mount, 1873, published 1886 NPG Ax27806. © National Portrait Gallery, London.

Figure 15: "A 'Bowery Boy,' Sketched from the Life," in *Frank Leslie's Illustrated Newspaper*, July 18, 1857. Courtesy, American Antiquarian Society.

Figure 16: *Anapauomenos* (*Leaning Satyr*). Roman copy of a Greek original of the fourth century BC, usually attributed to Praxiteles. Galleria delle Statue / Museo Pio Clementino / Vatican Museums © Vanni Archive / Art Resource, NY.

Figure 17: L. Prang & Co., Eastman Johnson, and John Greenleaf Whittier. *Whittier's Barefooted Boy*. United States, ca. 1868. Boston: Chromolithographed and published by L. Prang & Co., No. 159 Washington St. Photograph. https://www.loc.gov/item/2003664015/.

Figure 18: "Fellows," three women in pants, cabinet card, White River Junction, VT, ca. 1890. Courtesy Catherine Smith.

Figure 19: Jonathan Bonner, American, b. 1947. Bill Gallery, associated artist/ maker, American. Ric Murray, associated artist/maker. *Front Pockets*, 1999. Bound album with forty-two tipped-in gelatin silver prints. Album: 19.3 x 31 x 2.2 cm (7⅝ x 12³⁄₁₆ x ⅞ inches). Gift from the Collection of Dr. and Mrs. Joseph A. Chazan 2006.126.1. Courtesy Jonathan Bonner. Photo courtesy of the RISD Museum, Providence, RI.

Figure 20: W. E. B. Du Bois, Exposition Universalle International of 1900. W. E. B. Du Bois Papers, Robert S. Cox Special Collections and University Archives Research Center, UMass Amherst Libraries.

Chapter 4: Pocket Sexism

Figure 1: Ammi Phillips, portrait of Harriet Campbell, ca. 1815. Courtesy Clark Art Institute.

Figure 2: G. M. Woodward, *Fashionable Convenience!!*, ca. 1789. Courtesy of The Lewis Walpole Library, Yale University.

Figure 3: John Cawse, "Parisian Ladies in Their Winter Dress for 1800." Library of Congress, Prints and Photographs Division.

Figure 4: Fashion Plate, "Les Modes Parisiennes," *Peterson's Magazine*, Nov., 1885. The Metropolitan Museum of Art, Thomas J. Watson Library, Gift of Leo Van Witsen, 2011 (b17509853).

Figure 5: "World's Use of Pockets," *New York Times*, August 28, 1899.

Figure 6: Frontispiece illustration by Arthur Rackham for the 1940 edition of Kenneth Grahame's *The Wind in the Willows*. Photo: Fleet Library, RISD Special Collections. Estate of Arthur Rackham / © Bridgeman Images.

Figure 7: Alice Duer Miller, "Why We Oppose Pockets for Women," *Are Women People? A Book of Rhymes for Suffrage Times*, 1915. Library of Congress, Rare Books and Special Collections.

Figure 8: Playbill for Charles H. Hoyt's *A Contented Woman: A Sketch of the Fair Sex in Politics*, 1898. Library of Congress, Prints and Photographs Division.

Figure 9: Kodak advertisement, "Pocket Photography," appearing in *Munsey's Magazine*, 1899. John W. Hartman Center for Sales, Advertising and Marketing History, David M. Rubenstein Rare Book and Manuscript Library, Duke University.

Figure 10: Kodak advertisement, "Take a Kodak with You," appearing in *Ladies Home Journal*, 1901. John W. Hartman Center for Sales, Advertising and Marketing History, David M. Rubenstein Rare Book and Manuscript Library, Duke University.

Figure 11: "Summer Fashions," *Harper's Bazaar*, June 1895.

Figure 12: WAAC recruitment poster, 1942. Schlesinger Library, Harvard Radcliffe Institute.

Figure 13: Claire McCardell sketch, "Pop over," 1942. Brooklyn Museum Libraries. Special Collections. © Estate of Claire McCardell.

Figure 14: Bonnie Cashin, purse-pocket skirt. The Metropolitan Museum of Art, Gift of Bonnie Cashin, 1982 (1982.40.3). © The Metropolitan Museum of Art. Art Resource, NY.

Figure 15: Adlers publicity material for Bonnie Cashin, 1952. Courtesy Estate of Bonnie Cashin.

Figure 16: "The Day Shift," Designed by Bonnie Cashin; Illustrated by Andy Warhol. Published in *Harper's Bazaar*, Feb. 1958. © 2022 The Andy Warhol Foundation for the Visual Arts, Inc. / Licensed by Artists Rights Society (ARS), New York.

Figure 17: "Women's Pockets are Inferior," Jan Diehm and Amber Thomas, *The Pudding*, August 2018, https://pudding.cool/2018/08/pockets/. Courtesy Jan Diehm and Amber Thomas.

Figure 18: Delilah S. Dawson (@DelilahSDawson), pocket tweet, June 20, 2018. Courtesy Delilah S. Dawson.

Figure 19: Pocket bounty in women's workwear brand Argent, 2019. Courtesy Argent.

Chapter 5: Pocket Inventories

Figure 1: Ralph Morse, "One Year's Dungaree Debris," *Life*, April 8, 1957. Life Picture Collections / Shutterstock.

Figure 2: "Contents of a Boy's Pocket," *Every Saturday*, August 1870. Courtesy, American Antiquarian Society.

Figure 3: Grace Albee, "Contents of a Small Boy's Pocket," 1937. Wood engraving; 13.0 x 11.8 cm (5⅛ x 4⅝ inches) (plate); Gift of Mrs. J. J. Bodell in memory of Joseph J. Bodell 52.140; Museum of Art, Rhode Island School of Design, Providence; Courtesy Estate of Grace Albee.

Figure 4: The Miriam and Ira D. Wallach Division of Art, Prints and Photographs: Picture Collection, The New York Public Library. "Lucy Locket, Lost Her Pocket," The New York Public Library Digital Collections. https://digitalcollections.nypl .org/items/68dc0359-781a-7a41-e040-e00a1806442f.

Figure 5: William Beechey, *Portrait of Sir Francis Ford's Children Giving a Coin to a Beggar Boy*, exhibited 1793. Photo: Tate.

Figure 6: *Black Soldier Seated with Pistol in Hand, Watch Chain in Pocket*. Between 1860 and 1870. Gladstone Collection of African American Photographs, Library of Congress, Prints and Photographs Division. Retrieved from the Library of Congress, https://www.loc.gov/item/2002719396/.

Figure 7: Abraham Lincoln's glasses, one of the objects found in his pockets on the night of his assassination, n.d. Alfred Whital Stern Collection of Lincolniana, Library of Congress, Rare Book and Special Collections Division. Retrieved from the Library of Congress, https://www.loc.gov/item/scsm001049/.

Figure 8: Still image from Disney's 1964 film adaptation of *Mary Poppins*. ©
1964 Disney.

Figure 9: Herbert Gehr (with Doctor H. Volmer-Pix, top), Contents of a woman's
handbag, 1939. Courtesy Estate of Herbert Gehr.

Figure 10: Herbert Gehr, Fashion photograph, woman and red handbag, 1939.
Courtesy Estate of Herbert Gehr.

Figure 11: François Robert, "21 Sweet'N Lows," *Contents* (2010). Courtesy
François Robert.

Figure 12: François Robert, "Ten Chicklets," *Contents* (2010). Courtesy François
Robert.

Chapter 6: Pocket Play

Figure 1: "Fashion: The News in Paris," *Vogue*, March 15, 1949. Arik Nepo /
Vogue © Condé Nast.

Figure 2: Illustration by Erté for "Les Modes créées à Paris," published in *Harper's
Bazaar*, March 1915. © 2022 Chalk & Vermilion / Artists Rights Society (ARS)
New York.

Figure 3: Illustration by Erté for "Fashion may desert the Riviera but Erté is stimulated by Monte Carlo's summer skies," published in *Harper's Bazaar*, August
1920. © 2022 Chalk & Vermilion / Artists Rights Society (ARS) New York.

Figure 4: Fashion Sketch from Bergdorf Goodman illustrating Elsa Schiaparelli's
bureau-drawer suit no. 235, 1936. The Metropolitan Museum of Art, New
York, Costume Institute, LY4051-2.

Figure 5: Salvador Dalí, *Venus de Milo with Drawers*, 1936. Photo: Art Institute
Chicago. © 2022 Salvador Dalí, Fundació Gala-Salvador Dalí, Artists Rights
Society (ARS), New York.

Figure 6: Elsa Schiaparelli. Evening Coat, winter 1938–39. Designed by Elsa
Schiaparelli and Embroidered by Lesage, Paris. Black wool with pink silk, gold
embroidery, sequins, and porcelain flowers. Philadelphia Museum of Art. Gift
of Mme Elsa Schiaparelli, 1969.

Figure 7: Gabrielle (Coco) Chanel, Suit, 1959. © The Museum at FIT.

Figure 8: "The T'rompe-L'Oeil Resort Dress," pictured in *Vogue*, December 1,
1952. © Norman Parkinson / Iconic Images.

Figure 9: Franco Moschino suit pictured in "Suitable Plaids," *Vogue*, August 1,
1989. Walter Chin, Vogue © Condé Nast.

Figure 10: Patrick Kelly, suit from *Mona's Bet* group, Spring/Summer 1989.
Courtesy of the Texas Fashion Collection, College of Visual Arts and Design,
University of North Texas.

Figure 11: Invitation to Patrick Kelly's Spring/Summer 1989 show. The Philadelphia
Museum of Art. Courtesy of Bjoorn G. Amelan.

Figure 12: Portrait of Frank Tengle near Moundville, Hale County, Alabama by Walker Evans, from James Agee's *Let Us Now Praise Famous Men*, 1936. Library of Congress, Division of Prints and Photographs.

Figure 13: World War I enlisted soldier's tailored woolen tunic with cigarette holder discovered in pocket, 1914–18. National Museum of African American History and Culture.

Figure 14: 79th Infantry Division soldiers Pfc. Arthur Henry Muth, Sgt. Carmine Robert Sileo, and Sgt. Kelly C. Lasalle after an October 1944 battle. US Army Signal Corps.

Figure 15: Safari suits in "Suited for the Non-Occasion," *GQ*, February 1972. Photo: Courtesy Earl Steinbicker.

Figure 16: Back-jean pockets in "Jeaneology: A Fitting Tribute to Fashions Hot Pants," *GQ*, April 1977. Photo: Courtesy John Peden.

Figure 17: Pinky and Dianne man's jacket, Repurposed Denim, 1973. © The Museum at FIT.

Figure 18: Jean Paul Gaultier, Suit coat with pockets, 1990. © The Museum at FIT.

Figure 19: Cargo pockets tested in Camp Lee Virginia from November 1942 until July 1943. US Army Quartermaster Board T 149 Final Report (Appendix Exhibits), National Archives.

Figure 20: Erin Wasson, New York, published in *Harper's Bazaar*, Nov. 2002, © Peter Lindbergh, courtesy Peter Lindbergh Foundation, Paris.

Figure 21: Roz Chast, "Introducing . . . New Grandma® Cargo Pants," *New Yorker*, July 12 and 19, 2021. Roz Chast / The New Yorker Collection / The Cartoon Bank.

Figure 22: Virgil Abloh for Louis Vuitton men's wear, Fall 2020. IMAXtree by Launchmetrics.

Figure 23: Marine Serre, Spring 2019 Ready-to-Wear. Courtesy Marine Serre.

Figure 24: Miuccia Prada, Autumn–Winter 2002–3, Raincoat. Photo © David Sims.

Chapter 7: Pocket Utopias

Figure 1: Simone d'Aillencourt, dress by Trigere, Cape Canaveral, Florida, November 13, 1959. Photograph by Richard Avedon. © The Richard Avedon Foundation.

Figure 2: John Armstrong, "Three Costume Designs," pencil on cream paper for *Things to Come* (1936), dir. William Cameron Menzies, Costume Designer John Armstrong. Courtesy British Cinema and Television Research Group Archive. © John Armstrong / Bridgeman.

Figure 3: Frank R. Paul, cover illustration of a "Flying Man," *Amazing Stories*, August 1928. Courtesy Frank R. Paul Estate.

Figure 4: Studio portrait of Raymond Massey as John Cabal in *Things to Come* (1936). British Cinema and Television Research Group Archive.

Figure 5: "Donald Deskey Foresees a Great Emancipation," *Vogue* (World's Fair edition), February 1, 1939. Photo by Anton Bruehl. © Vogue, Condé Nast.

Figure 6: A minimalist dress by CO Collections, Spring–Summer 2020. Courtesy CO Collections.

Figure 7: Joanna Berzowska, "Sticky" from *Captain Electric and Battery Boy*, 2007–2010. Photo: Guillaume Pelletier. Courtesy Joanna Berzowska.

Figure 8: Joanna Berzowska's luminescent pocket pebbles in the hip pocket of "Sticky" from *Captain Electric and Battery Boy*, 2007-2010. Photo: Guillaume Pelletier. Courtesy Joanna Berzowska.

Figure 9: Walter Van Beirendonck, Spring-Summer, 2021. Courtesy Walter Van Beirendonck.

Figure 10: Sharon Levy, "Oh, my God—it's got pockets!," *New Yorker*, January 20, 2020. Sharon Levy / The New Yorker Collection / The Cartoon Bank.

Acknowledgments

D ays after proposing this project as a dissertation I tried to get out of it, cognizant of the charge that pockets are too small to carry anything of real significance. I spent the time imagining, with some accuracy as it turns out, the raised eyebrows that were to follow. *You mean, you are writing about pockets, like this one in my pants?* Huh. Susan Mizruchi at Boston University not only encouraged me to continue but rolled her eyes demonstratively when she heard my alternative suggestions—a rare bit of reverse psychology during a mentorship that was unfailingly supportive.

In returning to pockets years later, I encountered many other cheer-leaders whose interest got the ball rolling. Podcasters Piers Gelly and Avery Trufelman asked insightful questions; I am inspired by their spirited curiosity and storytelling prowess. My agent, Susan Ginsburg, saw potential for a book. She offered always wise counsel and, with Catherine Bradshaw, taught me the ropes. I am grateful to Amy Gash at Algonquin Books for her confidence in this project and for her keen advice in shaping its arc. I truly enjoyed our conversations, even when we had to grapple with real conundrums. I thank the whole team at

Algonquin for stewarding this book through production and for their care in making it beautiful.

Much of the writing occurred during that first isolating pandemic year, when time felt amorphous and the being alone-with-people camaraderie of cafes and libraries was not an option. The experience was made much less lonely, however, with the help of an unexpected writing partner, my father Robert Carlson, who gallantly took on an unfamiliar field—and decidedly unlawyerly writing style—with assurance. He is a canny, sometimes ruthless editor and although he always hedged his comments as mere suggestion, I knew when I received some version of the "we need to talk" text that something I had attempted had really missed the mark. He is practically allergic to jargon, and if any remains, it is my fault alone. Thanks, Dad. That was such fun.

Other readers include my sisters: Julia S. Carlson, attuned to the nuance of words, slowed me down and made me better, as she has, it is fair to say, since the age of five. Janet Carlson, alert to rhythm, demonstrated the importance of a well-placed pivot. Colleague Jen Liese helpfully commented on an early book pitch. Pascale Rihouet read the first two chapters and offered great ideas, insisting, for example, that there must be a print depicting the first assassination by handgun. Gabriel Cervantes pinch-hit at a late stage, after we geekily marveled at the story of a pickpocket who lacks his own pockets in Defoe's *Colonel Jack*. He provided astute conceptual perspective.

Research was supported by generous grants and fellowships from the American Antiquarian Society; the Costume Society of America; the Humanities Foundation at Boston University; the Metropolitan Museum of Art; and the Winterthur Museum, Garden & Library. Several institutions allowed me to rifle, with gloved hands, the pockets of the garments in their care, including the Costume Institute, Historic Deerfield, the Museum at FIT, the RISD Museum, Peabody Essex Museum, and Historic Northampton. A special thank you to Dana Signe K. Munroe at the Rhode Island Historical Society for her reflections on Joseph Noyes's waistcoat. Research assistants Kyra Gabrielle Buenviaje and Sophia Ellis indefatigably chased down leads in the databases. Kyra Gabrielle Buenviaje in addition shared perceptive fashion insights. Marc Calhoun and Emily Coxe handily resolved a number of research puzzles. Bethany Johns and Doug Scott generously schooled me in questions of graphic design. Kristie Peterson helped decode the labyrinth world of image licensing and tenaciously tracked down some mysteries.

Friends, family, and colleagues pitched in with pocket references, and many more good-naturedly put up with just one more pocket story I tried out on them. Charlotte Biltekoff discovered a 1907 feminist polemic; Matthew Bird identified (and located patents for) all the objects a boy might hold in his pocket in 1937; Nancy Ekholm Burkert recounted her observations drawing Emily Dickinson's pocket; Stuart Burrows alerted me to Molloy's pocket accounting; Alison Carlson made a valiant pitch for Ötzi's bag; Anna Carlson forwarded a suffragist pocket; Julia Carlson noticed Sterne's pocket pantomime; John Dunnigan observed that furniture, too, made space for pocket caches; Tim Fulford sent Robert Southey's endearing reflections on his son's coming of age via pocketed trousers; Evelyn Fischer and Hannah Garrison kept it coming with memes and social media artifacts; Henry Hawk suggested a contemporary men's wear bag that perfectly echoed one depicted in a sixteenth-century portrait; Jessica Sewell introduced me to the resourceful Katy kangaroo; and Katherine Stebbins pointed out Jefferson's reliance on pocket-size tools. Students in RISD's Apparel Department have shared their inventive pocketing over the years, teaching me about all the thought that goes into including them.

For giving me a sense that objects, too, have stories to tell, I thank my mother, Nancy Whittaker Carlson. Whether taking me to view the latest costume exhibit or to peruse what was on offer at Bob Knopper's Dignified Junk and Bottle Shop, she pointed out nuances in material and form, turning those visits into adventures. (I still depend on your discerning eye, Mom!) Big hugs to Kieran and Eliza for listening to all those digressive pocket highlights and for the enthusiasm with which they greeted every discovery. And I thank Charlie for everything—you know, from the bottom of my pockets.

Index